SEARCHING
FOR ZION

Also by Emily Raboteau

The Professor's Daughter

SEARCHING

FOR ZION

EMILY RABOTEAU

Atlantic Monthly Press
New York

This is a work of creative nonfiction in which real events were molded into a narrative. There are no invented or composite characters, though the names of certain sources were changed to protect their anonymity. Conversations were tape-recorded, taken down by hand, or reconstructed from the author's memory immediately after they transpired. In places, time was compressed or reframed in service to the story. It's possible that alternative perspectives on some aspects of this account could be equally true.

Portions of this book first appeared in *Transition, Best African American Essays, The Best American Nonrequired Reading, The Oxford American, The Believer, The Guardian,* and *Guernica.*

The author and publishers gratefully acknowledge permission to reprint the following copyright material:

Extract from *Jerusalem and I* by Hala Sakakini Copyright © 1987. Permission granted by Sakakini Cultural Center, (مركز خليل السكاكيني الثقافي) 4 Raja Street, Ramallah, West Bank, Israel.

Excerpt from *No Woman No Cry: My Life With Bob Marley* by Rita Marley (with Hettie Jones) Copyright © 2005. Permission granted by Hyperion Books, an imprint of Buena Vista Books, Inc. 114 Fifth Avenue, New York, NY 10011

"Til I'm Laid to Rest," Words and Music by Mark Myrie, Paul Crossdale, Donald Dennis, Bobby Dixon and Melbourne Miller. Copyright © 1995 Universal—Songs of Polygram International, Inc., Germain Music Inc., Gargamel Music, Dub Plate Music Publishing Ltd. and Craid Publishing. All Rights for Germain Music and Gargamel Music Controlled and Administered by Universal Polygram International, Inc. All Rights for Dub Plate Music Publishing Ltd. in the United States and Canada Controlled and Administered by Universal—Polygram International Publishing, Inc. on behalf of Gunsmoke Music Publishers. All Rights Reserved. Used by Permission Reprinted by Permission of Hal Leonard Corporation.

"Rivers of Babylon," Words and Music by Brent Dowe, James A. McNaughton, George Reyam and Frank Farian. Copyright © 1978 Universal—Polygram International Publishing, Inc., All Gallico Music Corp. and Far Musikverlag. All Rights Reserved. Used by Permission. Reprinted by Permission of Hal Leonard Corporation.

"Slavery Days," Written by Winston Rodney and Phillip Fullwood. Copyright © 1975 Blue Mountain Music Ltd. Copyright renewed. All rights reserved. Used by permission.

"Payday," Words and Music by Joseph Constantine Hill. Copyright © 1999. Permission granted by Tafari Music, Inc. (ASCAP).

FIRST EDITION

Printed in the United States of America
Published simultaneously in Canada

ISBN 978-0-8021-2003-8

Atlantic Monthly Press
an imprint of Grove/Atlantic, Inc.
841 Broadway
New York, NY 10003
Distributed by Publishers Group West

www.groveatlantic.com

13 14 15 16   10 9 8 7 6 5 4 3 2 1

For my mother, Katherine Murtaugh, with gratitude

"You don't have a home until you leave it . . ."
—James Baldwin, *Giovanni's Room*

CONTENTS

PART I: ISRAEL

WE'RE GOING TO JERUSALEM

1

Do You Know Where Canaan Is?

THE SECURITY PERSONNEL of El Al Airlines descended on me like a flock of vultures. There were five of them, in uniform, blockading Newark International Airport's check-in counter. Two women, three men. They looked old enough to have finished their obligatory service in the Israel Defense Forces but not old enough to have finished college, which meant they were slightly younger than I. I was prepared for the initial question, "What are you?," which I've been asked my entire life, and, though it chafed me, I knew the canned answer that would satisfy: "I look the way I do because my mother is white and my father is black." This time the usual reply wasn't good enough. This time the interrogation was tribal. They questioned me rapidly, taking turns.

"What do you mean, black? Where are you from?"

"New Jersey."

"Why are you going to Israel?"

"To visit a friend."

"What is your friend?"

"She's a Cancer."

"She has cancer?"

"No, no. She's healthy."

"She's Jewish?"

"Yes."

"How do you know her?"

"We grew up together."

"Do you speak Hebrew?"

"*Shalom*," I began. "*Barukh atah Adonai . . .*" I couldn't remember the rest of the blessing, so I finished with a word I remembered for its perfect onomatopoetic rendering of the sound of liquid being poured from the narrow neck of a vessel: "*Bakbuk.*"

It means "bottle." I must have sounded like a babbling idiot.

"That's all I know," I said. I felt ridiculous, but also pissed off at them for making me feel that way. I was twenty-three. I was a kid. I was an angry kid and so were they.

"Where is your father from?"

"Mississippi."

"No." By now they were exasperated. "Where are your *people* from?"

"The United States."

"Before that. Your ancestors. Where did they come from?"

"My mother's people are from Ireland."

They looked doubtful. "What kind of name is this?" They pointed at my opened passport.

I felt cornered and all I had to defend myself with was my big mouth. It was so obviously not a time for joking. "A surname," I joked.

"How do you say it?"

"Don't ask me. It's French." There was a village in Haiti called Raboteau. That much I knew. Raboteau may once have been a sugar plantation, named for its French owner, one of whose slaves may have been my ancestor. It's also possible I descended from the master himself. Or from both—master and slave.

"You're French?" they pressed.

"No, I *told* you. I'm American."

"This!" They stabbed at my middle name, *Ishem.* "What is the meaning of this name?"

"I don't know," I answered, honestly. I was named after my father's great-aunt, Emily Ishem, who died of cancer long before I was born. I had little idea where the name came from, just a vague sense that like many slave names, it was European. My father couldn't name anyone from our family tree before his great-grandmother,

4

Mary Lloyd, a slave from New Orleans. Preceding her was a terrible blank. After Mary Lloyd came Edward Ishem, the son she named after his white father, a merchant marine who threatened to take the boy back with him to Europe. To save him from that fate, Mary shepherded her son to the Bay of St. Louis where it empties into the Mississippi Sound. There he grew up and married a Creole woman called, deliciously, Philomena Laneaux. They gave birth to my grandmother, Mabel Sincere, and her favorite sister, Emily *Ishem*, for whom I am named.

"It sounds Arabic," one of them remarked.

"Thank you," I said.

"Do you speak Arabic?"

"I know better than to try."

"What do you mean?"

"No, I don't speak Arabic."

"What are your origins?"

I felt caught in a loop of the Abbott and Costello routine, "Who's on first?" There was no place for me inside their rhetoric. I didn't have the right vocabulary. I didn't have the right pedigree. My mixed race had made me a perpetual unanswered question. The Atlantic slave trade had made me a mongrel and a threat.

"Ms. Raboteau! Do you want to get on that plane?"

I was beginning to wonder.

"Do you?"

"Yes."

"Answer the question then! What are your origins?"

What else was I supposed to say?

"A sperm and an egg," I snapped.

That's when they grabbed my luggage, whisked me to the basement, stripped off my clothes, and probed every inch of my body for explosives, inside and out. When they didn't find any, they focused on my tattoo, a Japanese character. According to the tattoo artist who inked it, the symbol meant "different, precious, unique."

I was completely naked, and the room was cold. My nipples were hard. I tried to cover myself with my hands. I remember feeling incredibly thirsty. One of them flicked my left shoulder with a latex glove. "What does it mean?" he asked. This was the first time I'd been racially profiled, not that the experience would have been any less humiliating had it been my five hundredth. "It means 'Fuck You,'" I wanted to say, not merely because they'd stripped me of my dignity, but because they'd shoved my face into my own rootlessness. I have never felt more black in my life than I did when I was mistaken for an Arab.

殊

Why was I so angry? As a consequence of growing up half white in a nation divided along racial lines, I had never felt at home in the United States. Being half black, I identified with James Baldwin's line in *The Fire Next Time* about black GIs returning from war only to discover the democracy they'd risked their lives to defend abroad continued to elude them at home: "Home! The very word begins to have a despairing and diabolical ring." Though my successful father, Princeton University's Henry W. Putnam Professor of Religion, was an exception to the rule that black people had fewer opportunities, and though I had advantages up the wazoo, I remained so disillusioned about American equality that much of my young adulthood was spent in a blanket of low-burning rage.

I inherited my sense of displacement from my father. It had something to do with the legacy of our slave past. Our ancestors did not come to this country freely, but by force—the general Kunta Kinte rap of the uprooted. But it had even more to do with the particular circumstances of my grandfather's death. He was murdered in the state of Mississippi in 1943. Afterward, my grandmother, Mabel, fled north with her children, in search, like so many blacks who left the South, of the Promised Land. It was as if my father, whose father had been ripped from him, had been exiled. My father's feelings of homelessness, which I took on like a gene for being left handed,

6

were therefore historical and personal. And truthfully, because he left my family when I was sixteen, my estrangement had also to do with the loss of him. My family was broken, and outside of its context, I didn't belong. The El Al security staff had turned up the flame beneath these feelings. At twenty-three I hadn't seen much of the world. I hadn't yet traveled beyond the borders in my own head.

But now I was boarding a plane to visit my best friend from childhood, Tamar Cohen. With Tamar, I had a home. We loved each other with the fierce infatuation of preadolescent girls—a love that found its form in bike rides along the towpath, notes written in lemon juice, and pantomimed tea parties at the bottoms of swimming pools. The years we spent growing up in the privileged, picturesque, and predominantly white town of Princeton, New Jersey, where both of our fathers were professors of religious history, were marked by a sense of being different. Tamar's otherness was cultural: her summers were spent in Israel, her Saturdays at synagogue, and, up until the seventh grade, she attended a Jewish day school. I was black. Well, I was blackish in a land where one is expected to be one thing or the other. That was enough to set me apart. I didn't fit. I looked different from the white kids, different from the black. My otherness was cultural too. I played with black dolls, listened to black music, and, thanks to my parents if not my school, learned black history.

Being "different" allowed Tamar and me to hold everyone else in slight disdain, especially if they happened to play field hockey or football. We were a unified front against conformity. We stood next to each other in the soprano section of the Princeton High School Choir like two petite soldiers in our matching navy-blue robes, sharing a folder of sheet music with a synchronicity of spirit that could trick a listener into believing that we possessed a single voice. When I received my confirmation in Christ at the Catholic church, I borrowed Tamar's bat mitzvah dress.

We were bookish girls, intense and watchful. We spent afternoons sprawled out on my living room rug doing algebra homework while listening to my dad's old Bob Marley records—*Soul Rebels*,

7

Catch a Fire, and our favorite, *Exodus.* Our Friday nights were spent eating Shabbat dinner at her house around the corner on Murray Place. I felt proud being able to recite the Hebrew blessing with her family after the sun went down and the candles were lit: "*Barukh atah Adonai, Eloheinu melech ha'olam . . .*" Blessed are You, Lord, our God, sovereign of the universe . . . I didn't actually comprehend the words at the time, but I believed the solemn ritual made me part of something ancient and large.

Perhaps stemming from that belief, much to my father's chagrin, I started to keep kosher, daintily picking the shrimp and crab legs out of his Mississippi jambalaya until all that remained on my plate was a muck of soupy rice. It was her father's turn to be upset when we turned eighteen and got matching tattoos on our left shoulder blades. The Torah forbids tattooing (Leviticus 19:28). Tamar's might someday disqualify her from burial in a Jewish cemetery but we were determined that, no matter where in the world we might end up, no matter how much time might pass, even when we were old and ugly and gray, we would always be able to recognize each other.

Tamar's father was an expert in medieval Jewish history, while mine specialized in antebellum African American Christianity. Both men made careers of retrieving and reconstructing the rich histories of ingloriously interrupted peoples. Tamar and I knew at a relatively young age what the word *diaspora* meant—though to this day that word makes me visualize a diaspore, the white Afro-puff of a dandelion being blown by my lips into a series of wishes across our old backyard: to be known, to be loved, to belong.

Our fathers were quietly angry men, and Tamar and I were sensitive to their anger and its roots. I was acutely aware of that grandfather I had lost to a racially motivated hate crime under Jim Crow, though my father didn't discuss the murder with me. He didn't need to give words to my grandfather's absence any more than Tamar's father had to give words to the Holocaust. We were raised on diets of pride, not victimhood. Still, there were powerful ghosts in both our houses.

★   ★   ★

A few years after the Crown Heights Riot, my father brought Tamar and me to an exhibit at the Jewish Museum in New York. In collaboration with the NAACP, it linked Jewish and African American experience. Our trip must have fallen during Passover because I can remember nibbling on matzo and leaving a trail of unleavened crumbs. Klezmer music played in a room showcasing a silver candlestick bent by a bullet in a Russian pogrom. The next room displayed photographs of lynched black men. In each of those men's tortured faces I saw my grandfather, and I found myself on the verge of tears, more from outrage than from sadness. "Go Down Moses (Let My People Go!)" issued from the speakers:

When Israel was in Egypt's land,
Let My people go!
Oppressed so hard they could not stand,
Let My people go!

Go down, Moses,
Way down in Egypt's land;
Tell old Pharaoh
To let My people go!

"I like this music better than klezmer," Tamar said. I trained my ears on the lyrics I knew so well. They soothed me, just as they are meant to.

"This is a liberation song," my father explained. "Do you girls know where Canaan is?"

"Israel," Tamar answered.

"In a sense. But that's not the place this song is about. Look." He pointed to a picture of Frederick Douglass with an attached quotation that read: "We meant to reach the North, and the North was our Canaan."

My father told us that afternoon how pivotal the Old Testament story of Exodus and the Promised Land was for African slaves in America, whose initial embrace of Christian tradition was born

9

out of kinship they felt with the Hebrew slaves. They found hope
in the scriptures about Moses, the trials of the Israelites, and their
journey from bondage into Canaan. "I'll meet you in de mornin',
when you reach de promised land: on de oder side of Jordan, for
I'm boun' for de promised land . . ."

"Maybe that's why you like this music, Tamar," my father finished. "When we sang freedom songs about the ancient Israelites,
we linked ourselves to you. Our people have much in common."

Tamar and I nodded in agreement. We were connected by histories of oppression, but more than that, we both had *soul*. In addition
to appreciating the right music, having soul meant that when you
witnessed a poster for the auction of a thirty-year-old slave woman
named Mary or a yellow star pinned to the little brown coat of a
nameless child, what you felt was not *guilt* but rather the itch to
smash your fist into somebody's face. Tamar was my soul sister. I
didn't see her as white any more than I did my own white mother,
who was, simply, my mother. So it didn't confuse or surprise me
when Tamar suddenly turned to me in choir practice one rainy
morning in April 1992, when the Los Angeles Riots were burning
on the other coast, to proclaim, *"I'm not white."*

We had been rehearsing the Spanish cellist and conductor Pablo
Casals's sacred motet, *Nigra Sum*, whose Latin text is taken from
the Song of Songs and reads:

Nigra sum sed formosa filiæ Jherusalem
  I am black but comely, daughters of Jerusalem,

Ideo dilexit me rex
  Therefore have I pleased the Lord

Et introduxit me in cubiculum suum.
  And he hath brought me into his chamber.

I thought I understood why she made her proclamation at that
moment in choir practice. "*Nigra sum sed formosa*" brought tears
to my father's eyes when we sang it a few weeks later at the

spring concert. It was deep and rotund, darkly contralto, heavy-bottomed, bluesy. It was a song you wanted to be about yourself.

Tamar and I parted ways for college. While I was busy reading Hurston, Ellison, and Wright and working with inner-city youth in a program modeled after the Black Panthers, she was busy writing a thesis on Jewish history and practicing her Hebrew with foreign students from Israel. Either we followed stricter identity codes or the codes became stricter as we grew. Neither of us became joiners, per se. She didn't attend Hillel Society, nor did I hang out at the Afro-American Center. But her new best friend was an Israeli named Sari, and mine, a half Nigerian called Nkechi. We called each other less and less. Shortly after we graduated, she moved to Israel and became a citizen under the Law of Return—*aliyah*—which is the right all Jews have to settle there with a visa, providing they aren't perceived a danger to the state. The millennium passed. We hadn't spoken in months when she phoned at the start of the second intifada to ask me to visit.

Her voice surprised me. It had a desperate timbre. I decided to go.

After I made it through the degrading security check and the longest flight I'd ever taken, I fell in love with Jerusalem. I'd expected to land in a desert place, hostile and khaki and hard as a tank, because that's what I'd seen on TV and because El Al's staff had been so aggressive at the airport. The armed patrolmen on every corner fit my mind's picture, but the beauty of Jerusalem did not. I wasn't prepared for it to look so much like San Francisco. Tamar led me through that ancient city of soft hills and olive trees, bulbous rooftops and rock-jumbled valleys. Its limestone buildings blushed in the sunset and the air over Mount Zion was as delicate as gauze. I followed her down endless narrow lanes where Arab kids rode donkeys and kicked rubber balls. We no longer shared the same references and private jokes, but we still remembered songs from the repertoire of our high school's choir. We sang these as we walked.

Jerusalem contained more different visions of heaven than any other city; everyone brought his or her own dream of paradise. It was dizzying to walk simultaneously where, supposedly, Muhammad had ascended to heaven to meet with God, Jesus had been crucified and resurrected, and Solomon had built the First Temple—and also where, any minute, a bomb might go off.

I'm in Zion, I thought. This is it. I'm actually here.

"Watch out," Tamar warned me in the Garden of Gethsemane. She said there was such a thing as Jerusalem syndrome, also known as *fièvre Jerusalemmiene* and Jerusalem squabble poison—a psychosis known to push some tourists into a state of dangerous rapture. If I wasn't mindful, I might catch it. She must have sensed my arousal. When we entered the mouth of Lion's Gate and walked along the Via Dolorosa, when I smelled the peach tobacco smoke from a narghile pipe, when I saw the red wool of the Bedouin rugs on display in the Old City, when I heard the calls to prayer from a hundred mosques at dusk, my heart swelled round like the Dome of the Rock, and I halfway understood why men would fight rock over stick, hand over fist, bomb over gun, in order to call this place their home.

Tamar told me there was no real word in the Hebrew language for "home." The masculine term for "house," *bayit*, came closest but, to her ear, was not equivalent. A house was limited by walls. A home was not. She was against the separation barrier that many Israelis had started lobbying for. Alarmed by the climbing number of suicide bombings in Jerusalem, the barrier's supporters hoped a wall along and inside the West Bank would protect Israeli civilians against further attacks. Its construction would begin two years from now, a concrete scar on the landscape we traversed, growing as tall in some places as twenty-five feet and consisting of security checkpoints, sniper towers, trenches, and barbed wire. "They're calling it a security fence," Tamar said, but she worried it would become an "apartheid wall," reducing the scant freedoms of the Palestinians on the other side.

Expatriating to such a violent realm must have been a difficult decision for Tamar, politically, spiritually, personally. The new dark circles under her pretty brown eyes made her look older. But at the time, all I understood was that she'd taken the opportunity to make this place her own. As complicated and confusing as that choice must have been, I felt enormously jealous of her ability to make it, and more than a little rejected that she had.

While I continued to feel unsettled, Tamar now had a divine Promised Land, a place to belong, and a people who embraced her. At least, that's how it looked to me. Here she was in Zion. It was a real place: a providential, politically sanctioned place, with roots and dirt she could hold in her hand. For all the majesty of Jerusalem and the warmth of my friend, the soldiers on the street made it hard to forget my confrontation with El Al's security. They hadn't believed America could be my home and had made it plain Israel was no house of hospitality. So where was my home?

I remembered my father's talk with us all those years ago about the location of Canaan Land. For Jews, it was here. For black slaves, it had been the North. Frederick Douglass had said so. But my father hadn't revealed what happened when they reached the North and didn't find it. Maybe Malcolm X summed it up best a hundred years after emancipation in his "The Ballot or the Bullet" speech: "If you black, you were born in jail, in the North as well as the South ... Long as you south of the Canadian border, you're south."

Jerusalem wasn't the imagined heaven that America's black slaves had to look forward to in the afterlife once they had reached the North, realized its shortcomings, rubbed their eyes, and asked each other, "Where de milk an' honey at? An' de streets all paved wit gold?" While Black Zion was a wish, Israel was real. Jerusalem seemed to me a place where the *air* was gold—a photographer's wet dream. I swear, the light had an imperial quality against my skin. It was a place I could drool over and visit, where my price of admission was a steep dressing-down, but where Tamar could live as a citizen with a physical address. Her beautiful old Arab house featured tile floors, arched doorways, and room for a piano. It stood in a dusty alley in the German Colony off Emek Refaim, a street name meaning "valley of the ghosts."

One of the ghosts was a woman named Hala Sakakini. She once lived a few doors down at number 10 but left her home to escape the Arab-Israeli War. That was in 1948, the year the State of Israel was proclaimed. Over seven hundred thousand Palestinian refugees fled at that time. Their houses were quickly expropriated by Holocaust survivors and Jewish immigrants from Arab lands. Many Palestinians, including Hala Sakakini, expected to return. They refer to their exodus as the *Nakba*, or "cataclysm" (much as Afrocentrists refer to the centuries of African suffering through slavery and colonialism as the *Maafa*, a Swahili word for "disaster," and as Jews refer to the Holocaust as the *Shoah*, Hebrew for "catastrophe.") In her memoir, *Jerusalem and I*, there is a photo of Hala in her living room, shortly before the *Nakba*. She sits in an armchair in front of a large ornate radio in the light of a gooseneck floor lamp, unsmiling, with a hard set to her jaw. She describes revisiting her occupied home after the exodus:

> We knocked on the door. Two ladies appeared . . . We tried to explain: "this is our house. We used to live here before 1948 . . ." The elderly lady was apparently moved but she immediately began telling us that she too had lost a house in Poland, as though we personally or the Arabs in general were to blame for that. We saw it was no use arguing with her. We went through all the house room by room—our parents' bedroom, our bedroom, Aunt Melia's bedroom, the sitting room and the library . . . the dining room, the kitchen . . . everything was so different. It was no more home . . . we stood there as in a daze looking across the street and the square at our neighbours' houses . . . It is people that make up a neighbourhood and when they are gone it will never be the same again. We left . . . with a sense of emptiness, with a feeling of deep disappointment and frustration.

I wondered who used to live in Tamar's house. Where was that displaced person now? I failed to ask Tamar if she wondered about this too. It was easier, in my envy, to think she had usurped her address. My umbrage with El Al had turned in haste to the State of Israel. My anger at Israel was premature and tinged by the loss of my friend to a state I feared would corrupt her. What kind of Zion was this, superimposed on top of another nation? What kind of screwed-up Canaan has an intifada? How could this madhouse deserve Tamar more than I?

I was pondering these questions when Tamar's boyfriend, Yonatan, set *Lady Sings the Blues* on the turntable, told me he loved Billie Holiday with all his might, and asked me in earnest if I thought he understood her as well as I did. "Of course you don't," I scoffed, because my broken, darling Billie was singing "God Bless the Child" in her ripped-satin voice, and what could he possibly be thinking? He could have his Canaan Land, but Lady Day belonged to me.

Once upon a time, Tamar had been my tribe, but a shadow wall had crept up between us. I couldn't shake the uneasy feeling that, in spite of her leftist stance, which was about as far left as she could stand without falling off the edge, she was complicit in an unjust occupation. Zion was a tinderbox of contradictions that left me confused. It didn't matter to me then that the State of Israel was declared, in large part, in reparation for the Holocaust, or that some of its people were being attacked. Palestine was under its colonial thumb. It didn't matter that Tamar didn't live in a settlement, or that she participated in peace protests and rallies, or that she rolled her eyes at the slogans in her neighbors' windows (GOLAN HEIGHTS IS OURS!). They were still her neighbors, and she'd chosen to leave me and live among them. It didn't matter that she wasn't the one who had shined a flashlight between my legs to look for a bomb. I couldn't shake the feeling that her choice to be Israeli had turned my best friend white.

We were floating. Our twin tattoos were on display, but there were no living fish in the Dead Sea to look up at our naked backs and notice. It was nighttime at the nadir, literally the lowest point on the planet. Home was halfway around the world, and we were adrift in the still water, its salt lifting us up like hands. The lights of Jordan twinkled on the distant shore, and above us stirred a soup of stars thick enough to mix with a spoon.

"It's so good to see you again," she whispered.

"You too. I'm glad I came here," I answered, "but I miss black people."

I was surprised to hear myself say it, but it was true. With the exception of Maine, I'd never traveled to a place without black people.

"There are black people here, silly," Tamar said. "You're not the only one."

"Where are they?"

"All over."

"Really?"

"Sure. The Falashas."

"Who?"

"Beta Israel. The Ethiopian Jews. And there's a bunch of black Americans squatting in the desert—the Black Hebrews. I think they're from Chicago."

"What are they doing here?"

"Why don't you ask them? They're not far. Israel's only the size of New Jersey." She splashed me. "If you really want to see 'your people' that badly, we can find them."

"I'd like to, but I'm leaving in two days."

Tamar sighed. "I wish you didn't have to go."

There is such a thing as a black Jew. I rotated the thought in my mind. I'd always considered the two groups to be mutually exclusive. A light wind rippled the water. I shivered. I closed my eyes and perceived the imperceptible tilt of the earth on its axis. The pigeonholes I knew were collapsing. It was a delightful feeling, much like one I'd had at fifteen when my father brought my younger brother and me along on a research trip to London. There we sat across from two nattily dressed black men in worsted wool jackets on a tube in the Underground.

"I'm positively knackered," said one to the other. My brother and I stared at each other in amazement to hear a black person speaking in a British accent. You could be black in a wider world than we knew, where we were never quite black enough or entirely too black. You could be black in surprising ways. "I'm positively *knackered*," we repeated giddily for weeks on end. To this day I confuse that word's meaning—exhausted—with what it made my brother and me feel on the Underground—thrilled. I felt that way again learning about the black Jews from Tamar. I went home, where I thought of them often together with an increasing desire that was somehow mixed up with the kinship I'd once felt for my best friend.

Six months after I returned from Israel, I witnessed the Twin Towers collapse from my rooftop in Brooklyn. A crop of American flags sprung up in the days that followed. Along with the tragic signs for the missing, the stars and stripes were everywhere. Connected by loss, New Yorkers made eye contact for the first time. Their eyes were more open, the irises enlarged. You could tumble through those portholes directly into the sadness of people's hearts. Such vulnerability was as rare in the city as a seat on the subway at rush hour. I remember strangers hugging one another in Washington Square near New York University, where I'd just begun to attend graduate school. But I also remember the increasing din of patriotism, how the talk turned swiftly to "us" and "them," and that other naked emotion you could read in people's eyes—fear.

"Go home!" a drunk man shouted at me one night in mid-September as I ascended the stairs of the Pacific Avenue subway station. I might have told him that's exactly where I *was* going if he hadn't first lobbed a bottle at my head. It struck behind my left ear with astonishing force before smashing on the street. The Masjid

Al-Farooq, one of the oldest Islamic centers in the city, was just down the block from the station, and a few more blocks from my apartment on Fourth Avenue next to a Kentucky Fried Chicken. The mosque, whose calls to prayer accented my days as much as the smell of fry oil, had become a target of scrutiny since 9/11.

It was a beer bottle. Like a character in a cartoon, I saw stars when it hit me. After the initial shock of pain, I remained disoriented, confused. What was this guy thinking? With a little distance from the incident with the teenagers at El Al, I'd figured out what was behind their aggression. It had a lot to do with me getting lippy. But I hadn't said jack squat to this clown. I wasn't even wearing a headscarf.

He roared, "We don't want you here!" or something similarly original, as I scuttled home, gripping my scalp. There is a sickle-shaped scar there now, in what is supposed to be an erogenous zone, where the hair refuses to grow. I should have gotten stitches. Instead, I shampooed out the blood while consoling myself with esprit de l'escalier. What was the best zinger to pitch back at a fellow with such strong aim?

—You've made it plain you're a Michelob man.

—If you thought that was half empty, I can tell you it was half full.

—Thanks, I just bought this trench coat and was looking for the perfect accessory. Who knew it was a head wound?

My father responded by writing an Op-Ed to the *New York Times*, which they did not publish. It is dated September 21, 2001, and opens with the details of what happened to me, except that in his report, the projectile is a can of soda rather than a bottle of beer, and it only grazed my head rather than cutting it. I'd softened the story for my father at the time, so it would hurt him less. I didn't want him to feel helpless to protect his child. But also, the stakes were so low. What right did I have, with my light-skinned privileges, to make a stink when far worse indignities had befallen others and him? What did it matter that I felt unwelcome here when my literature professor, a novelist from Kenya, had actually been exiled from his country for criticizing its politics? When my own grandfather had been shot dead in Mississippi for defending a black woman to a white man? I had risked nothing. We were not on the same continuum.

Yet, when I discussed that night with my father, I didn't diminish what had hurt me most. Though there were people out on the streets of downtown Brooklyn, no one came to my aid. My father lamented this in his letter before describing me to the reader: "My daughter is African American. I am black and her mother white. Her ancestry includes Africans, Native Americans, Germans, Irish, and French. She is light-skinned, dark-haired, and dark-eyed. She could and has been identified as Hispanic, Indian, and now, apparently, Arab." He asserted first and foremost that I was African American. I'd always felt that I was, or a subset of that, since African Americans were a mixed race anyway, but didn't my scramble of features cancel each other out? I was an invisible woman. Mine was the profile of a mutt, a Rorschach, a ghost.

Correctly, my father's letter goes on to say that this was a minor incident "compared to the murder of a Sikh in Dallas, or the almost fatal beating of a Muslim woman pulled from her car in Los Angeles, or the shooting of [Guinean immigrant] Amadou Diallo in New York." But amid mounting accounts of violence and harassment against Muslims, my father questioned those who condemned such hateful acts as "un-American." He pointed to our nation's thorny history: the enslavement and segregation of African Americans, the conquest and displacement of Native Americans, the relocation and internment of Japanese Americans, and so on. Wasn't such ugliness a part of America's character, as sure as the nose on its face?

This wasn't the kind of message people wanted to hear at the time, and maybe that's why the *Times* chose not to run the piece. Yet it meant the world to me that my father wrote it. I read it as a love letter and also as an illustration of the distress that I grew up learning at his knee:

> I watch as we wave flags, and celebrate the heroism of the rescue workers, and sing "America the Beautiful." Rightfully so, we have

experienced a terrible tragedy and our people have come together to help each other in ways that are moving and beautiful. And yet, I think that is not the full reality. We have to acknowledge that there is a face of America that is not beautiful, but is horribly ugly in its hatred, its self-righteousness, its bigotry, its racism, and its xenophobia. This too is a face of America, a face that has been exposed to some of its citizens for a very long time . . .

Around the time my father wrote this letter, Tamar came back to the States to celebrate Rosh Hashanah with her family. I was relieved to see her again, though there was little to say. We walked across the Brooklyn Bridge and found ourselves stepping in quiet ash at the foot of a twisted twenty-foot waffle of metal at Ground Zero. I gagged on the lingering smell of burnt wire and flesh. Sickened and stunned, I spouted the cliché we all said then: "It feels like a movie." Tamar looked at me sideways. "You know," she said, "in much of the world, this kind of thing goes on all the time."

She was right, of course. She lived with the daily consequences of her nation's bullying; lived with the ruptures, the bombs, the protests and uprisings. She had to confront this strife and examine her place within it. Now I had to do the same.

My face was American, no matter what others saw. I was from this place. I began to see how globally hated my country's government was, and, by extension, its citizens. It didn't matter that my friends and I hated George W. Bush's government too, or that we didn't support it. The more I looked, the more I wanted to look away. While our war on terror advanced against the wishes of the United Nations, I worked three jobs, scraped together my money, and left the country whenever I saved up enough to afford it. When I was mistaken for an Arab a third time, by a young Moroccan laborer in Andalusia, Spain, I didn't correct him. Instead, I climbed into his boat and sailed home with him to Tangiers, where his mother cooked us an apricot tagine. In Brazil, I began writing a novel about a girl who hated to be asked what she was. I learned to speak Portuguese.

Every time I fell in love with a city where I could easily blend in, I imagined what it would take to stay there for good. Then I would run out of money and have to come home. More and more, I hated to return. In my travels, I learned what people really thought of us—Americans were greedy, domineering, self-righteous, and dumb. Too easily, I agreed with these stereotypes. If someone asked me where I was from, I answered "New York" rather than "the U.S.A."

When Hurricane Katrina hit the Gulf of Mexico in 2005, the fallout confirmed my worst feelings about our government. It would take ten months for federal money to be approved for housing reconstruction. "George Bush doesn't care about black people," said the rapper Kanye West at a concert for hurricane relief on live TV, and it was hard not to agree as I sat in front of the TV screen in a state of near paralysis. I scanned the black bodies abandoned in the Superdome and marooned on rooftops for the faces of my relatives, who lived in Bay St. Louis, Mississippi, a beach town fifty miles from New Orleans that lay underneath fifteen feet of water. My grief didn't protect my cousins from the deluge. My bitterness about the infrastructure that had failed them didn't bring them to dry land. It took months for us to locate them in their great dispersal. This was another diaspora. But what did my sense of loss matter to my homeless Mississippi aunties as I posed in yoga class or walked my dog?

I published my novel and was made a professor, like my father. I moved to Harlem to be closer to my job. My apartment was on the fifth floor of a walk-up on 148th Street, a few blocks from the brownstone where Ralph Ellison lived when he wrote *Invisible Man*. Around the corner, at the intersection of 146th Street and St. Nicholas Avenue, a boarded-up shell of a building from the 1890s with a two-thirds round facade rose like a castle tower. It had lost its windows, its front stoop, and its original entrance to salvage. Someone had affixed a curious sign to its incongruous steel door. My friend and neighbor, Sharifa, who had a knack for spying such messages, brought the decaled letters to my attention.

PROMISED LAND, it said.

Looking upon it, I remembered again what my father had said to me and Tamar about the story of Exodus. How the slaves had dreamed of a Promised Land. What happened to the dream when they didn't find it, even after emancipation and reconstruction, even after generations? Zion became an abstraction, a picture of heaven, a pie in the sky. Or the unlikely dream of going back to Africa. Or some other fuzzy synonym for freedom. Or this very place, Harlem, the destination for so many of the six million blacks who left the feudal caste system of the American South during the great migration. *Promise Land.* I wondered about the sign's tense. Was it meant to convey that the land that had been promised had yet to be delivered?

There were other, less mysterious signs, like the invective I read on a banner strung between two windows on 134th Street: PROS-PECTORS GO HOME! Harlem was the black city within the city, receptacle of dreams. But now the community was visibly shifting. It didn't matter that I belonged halfway to the race being squeezed out of Manhattan's final frontier of affordable real estate. As much as I hated to watch the sad, slow effects of gentrification spill over the stately brownstones of Sugar Hill and Strivers' Row, home of Madam C. J. Walker and Langston Hughes and all those wild jazzmen I loved so much, I couldn't pretend, with my Ivy League degree, that I wasn't a member of the gentry. I myself was not dis-inherited. Recognizing this, I began to feel my terrible whiteness, and I was ashamed.

Avoiding my reflection in storefront windows, I meandered through Harlem and beyond: north to the Cloisters at Fort Tryon Park, east to the movable Macombs Dam Bridge and into the Bronx, west over the George Washington Bridge across the dirty Hudson, south down the long finger of Manhattan. On one of these rambles, in the shadow of the elevated subway tracks off 125th Street, I came across a short stretch of the alleyway called Old Broadway. And there, in the middle of the alley, stood a small sweet shul with a dirty facade and bulletproof stained glass windows. Here was Harlem's last remaining synagogue, a remnant from the neighborhood's former days of Yiddish theaters and crowded Jewish tenements. When the darker "undesirables" began pouring in, Harlem's upwardly mobile Jews flew to the nearby neighborhoods of Washington Heights and the Upper West Side, or farther off to the outer boroughs. In the case of East Harlem, the flood of incoming Puerto Ricans and outgoing Jews was called the New Spanish Inquisition. When blacks started flocking in droves from Georgia and the Carolinas to Harlem in the 1920s, the number of Jews dropped from nearly two hundred thousand to just five thousand. By the Depression's end, there were barely any Jews left in Harlem at all. Yet this synagogue remained. I stopped in front of it. Why did I feel I'd been there before? It was Friday evening and the sun was setting. I was suddenly starving for Shabbat dinner at Tamar's old house on Murray Place. Tentatively, I pushed open the heavy wooden door.

"Welcome!" cried an old black man with a velvet *kippah* on his head. "Good Shabbos." He adjusted the *tallis* on his shoulders and took my hands in his. "This is wonderful," he smiled. He had the whitest teeth. "Another wandering Jew has found her way home." Either as a result of his kindness or as a result of his mistake, I was afraid I might begin to weep.

2

The Land of Oz

MEANWHILE, ISRAEL WAS at war again. Somehow six years had gone by since my visit to Tamar. Back in Jerusalem, she had settled down with an Argentine Jew who shared her last name and together they had a daughter, Nina. I returned to Israel in the summer of 2006 in order to visit them and also to find those black Jews. I'd never forgotten what Tamar told me, floating in the Dead Sea. There were black people in Israel. Did those people think they were home? Did Tamar? And might there be a place in Zion for me?

On the flight, I finished the patchwork quilt I was sewing for Nina, who had just celebrated her first birthday. I labored over this quilt. It was hand-stitched in strips, chromatically schemed like a rainbow. The last step was to finish the border, now fastened by forty little pins, ten on each side. I worried that security would mistake the pins for tiny explosive devices. They didn't confiscate the baby's quilt. They didn't strip-search me in the basement. Instead, they brought me behind a heavy black curtain, rifled through my luggage, and stole my iPod.

Without my collection of reggae music, I grew restless on the long flight to Tel Aviv. The jumbo aircraft was nearly empty. Maybe the five or six of us on board were foolhardy to make the journey. Israel was in its sixth day of fighting with Lebanon, exchanging escalating fire with extremist Shiite militia, Hezbollah. It was a grossly lopsided exchange—Beirut was being steadily, mercilessly destroyed.

"The boss has gone crazy," said my seatmate, an old woman with cat-eye glasses and hair dyed a menopausal shade of red. "But it's good we're going. Israel, she needs us."

Later, Tamar explained the common Israeli expression. It meant the state's method of responding was disproportionate to the attacks. The state was "the boss" going crazy on Beirut. But Beirut was biting back and northern Israel was not a safe place either. My mother had begged me to postpone my trip. In my hunt for aliens I was flying headlong into a war zone.

When I arrived in Tel Aviv, the first thing I did was go looking for black people at a reggae club on Harakevet Street. THE RASTA was painted in block letters on a pan-African green, gold, and red sign above a chain-locked doorway. A stocky Russian Jew in a leather jacket guarded the entrance.

"You don't want to go in there," he warned me.

A fighter plane roared above us. And then another.

"Yes I do."

"No." He crossed his arms.

"Isn't there a show tonight?" I looked at my watch. A band called Tony Ray and Amjah was supposed to play at ten. It was now rounding midnight.

"It's not for you. Karaoke is next door."

"But I came for this."

"You won't like it. Believe me. They get drunk and fight like animals. It's messy."

"Look," I said. "I came all the way from New York for this."

"It's not safe."

"I'm flattered that you think I'm a child, but I'm pushing thirty."

"It's too dangerous."

"Are you going to let me in or not?"

The guard sighed, got down from his stool, unlocked the door with a great show of annoyance, and called for the club owner, none other than Tony Ray himself. Ray was a tall man in his early fifties. He had a head of graying beaded dreadlocks, a gold tooth, and an easy manner.

"Don't pay that bald-head guard no mind. You're just early, little daughter. We on colored-people time," he said, leading me to the bar and pouring me a liberal shot of cheap rum. Behind the bar hung an embossed picture of Haile Selassie, a small felt banner of the Lion of Judah, and a poster of Bob Marley. On the shelf with all the liquor bottles sat a glow-in-the-dark plastic alien smoking ganja.

As we talked, I learned Tony Ray was from Jamaica, by way of England. As a Rastafarian, Tony Ray believes that he is ancestrally tied to Ethiopia; that his captive forebears originated from that homeland. Jamaica's slaves were taken from Africa's west coast—from Benin and Ghana in the seventeenth century and, later, from northern Angola, eastern Nigeria, and the Congo region. Tony Ray, like most Rastas, likely has no ancestral ties to Ethiopia at all. But, like most Rastas, he believes the Messiah has come and gone in the form of Ethiopia's last emperor—formerly known as Ras Tafari—Haile Selassie, who claimed to descend directly from King Solomon and the Queen of Sheba, and that Ethiopia is the Promised Land.

"How'd you wind up here instead of Addis Ababa?" I asked him. The choice seemed out of step with Rasta's "Back to Africa" repatriation platform.

He explained that he'd come for a three-month tour with his band as a young man, "and I tell you, I no like it one bit. Israeli folk are rude and out of order. You see me?"

I nodded.

"Then I return to London, where they act so civilized, but underneath their smile them want kick them boot inside I'n'I mouth. I start fi miss Israel. My gut was craving figs! So I come back, and now it's thirty years gone past. I'n'I is a natty Nazarite now. Is my place this." He spanked the bar with a wet rag for emphasis and began wiping it down.

The door swung open and a young man sauntered in with an electric bass. "Jamaican-boy!" he cried.

"Etiopian-bwoy!" Tony Ray answered, embracing him. "You ready to make music, my brethren?"

By three in the morning, in my beer-soaked haze, I thought I may as well have been in Addis Ababa. I was positively knackered. The Rasta was packed shoulder to shoulder with Ethiopians, stirring it up to the reggae of Tony Ray, backed by the Amjah on trombone, bass, drums, and krar. Hardly anyone in the crowd spoke English, but they all knew the lyrics of the Bob Marley covers—"Redemption Song," "Buffalo Soldier," "Stir It Up," "Jamming." So we danced and sang: "Iron, Lion, Zion," until somebody opened the door, allowing a trapezoidal wedge of July sunlight to land on the edge of the dance floor, and I realized with a shock that it was morning. The guard snored on his stool in the entryway, slumped like a teddy bear. Out on the sidewalk of Harakevet Street, it took me a full minute to remember where I was. I blinked. The fighter jets droned overhead.

Since the first place in Israel I went looking for black people offered me little more than a contact high, I asked Tamar's friend Yitzhak for another experience. He invited me to an absorption center in the northern port city of Haifa, roughly thirty miles from the Lebanese border.

"What exactly is an *absorption center*?" I asked Yitzhak on the taxi drive from Tel Aviv up the coastal highway. Our driver was an impressively muscular man in his fifties. Because his name was Oz, I felt we were heading toward a magical realm rather than ground zero of Israel's latest war. I would rather have put my question to Yitzhak's friend and bandmate Abate, who had actually lived in an absorption center when he made aliyah from Ethiopia in 1999, but Abate's English was limited. He sat in the front seat, cradling the beat-up case of his soprano saxophone. I watched his face in the rearview mirror. He had a pencil-thin mustache, a slightly receding hairline, and preternaturally large eyes—Louis Armstrong eyes—through which he looked out at the passing road signs in studied silence.

Abate's integration into Israel was a painful one. While he'd enjoyed a successful jazz career in Addis Ababa, toured through Europe and the Eastern bloc, and even played at Kim Il Sung's birthday in North Korea, he wasn't known as a musician in Israel, didn't speak Hebrew, and had to work several menial jobs to support his family. One was washing dishes in a restaurant; another was at a chemical factory. He worked nights as a security guard. A grant from the Ethiopian Jewry Heritage organization eventually enabled him to quit all but the night job, leaving him enough time to practice his sax in the day, but the chemicals and dishwater had damaged his hands. He had to wait a long, long time for his fingers to heal.

Tamar had introduced me to Yitzhak, a serious, bespectacled composer in his thirties who described his sound as "third-stream jazz." Yitzhak had two things on his lap in the backseat of the taxicab that day: an electric keyboard and a rolled-up marriage license that had just been rejected by the chief Rabbinate Council on the grounds that it didn't conform to their standards.

"What did you say?" he asked me. He seemed distracted by the traffic jam of vehicles heading in the opposite direction. Ours was the lone car on the highway traveling north.

"An *absorption center,*" I repeated. "What is it?"

Before Yitzhak could answer, his cell phone rang. It was his fiancée. I would have to wait until we got to the absorption center to discover what it was.

"Don't go to Haifa!" she screamed, loud enough for me to hear.

Yitzhak pacified her in Hebrew. I'm guessing he told her the same thing he'd told me in English, which was that, as an army reservist, it was his civic duty to go. It was the will of HaSokhnut, the Jewish Agency. This bureaucratic arm of the Israeli government facilitates immigrant absorption into Israel. Tamar later described it to me as "floundering" and "inept." The Jewish Agency had ordered Yitzhak to play music for the "Falashas." A USO sort of thing.

In the ancient South Semitic ecclesiastical language Ge'ez, the word *falasha* means "landless one" and, by association, "wanderer," "exile," "stranger." It is used to describe the Beta Israel, meaning "House of Israel," Ethiopian Jews whose tradition holds that they descend from the line of Moses himself—specifically from the lost tribe of Dan—though the origin of their Judaism remains contested by scholars, unlike the Lemba, a South African tribe of black Jews whose DNA has linked them to ancient Judea. Many scholars theorize that Ethiopian Jews converted from the Christian faith during the thirteenth and fourteenth centuries. Ethiopisant Ephraim Isaac, on the other hand, believes that Jewish presence in Ethiopia dates back to the period of the First Temple, hundreds of years before Christ. He points out that the Bible mentions Ethiopia more than fifty times, "but Poland, not once." One thing is certain: the Beta Israel have longed for Jerusalem for centuries. Maybe for millennia.

The Israeli chief Rabbinate recognized the status of Ethiopian Jewry in the mid-1970s and, in so doing, paved the way for a mass exodus under the Law of Return. Coming mostly from the mountainous northern Gondar region, where they made up only a small minority of Ethiopia's population and were denied the right to inherit land unless they converted to Christianity, their number in the State of Israel is now nearly 120,000. A third of these Ethiopians were born in Israel. This is thanks in large part to two massive, highly publicized "rescue" efforts, Operation Moses (1984) and Operation Solomon (1991), which airlifted the Beta Israel from Africa. *Falasha* is decreasingly used in Israel to describe Ethiopian Jews like Abate, because they themselves prefer that the term not be used. It has a pejorative tinge, like the Hebrew word *kushi* (darkie), but is not as strong a word as *nigger* in the United States.

As Yitzhak placated his fiancée, Oz directed my attention to a sprawl of modest white houses around Hadera. "Look at their ugly houses!" he spat. "They're not like us. They have ten, twelve children, and they don't take care of them. They're like cockroaches." He was speaking, of course, about a community of Palestinians. I wondered if Abate could understand Oz's speech and, if so, whether or not it made him as uncomfortable as it made me. I wondered if his allegiance was torn, if the return to the Promised Land, whose government had "saved" him from the "Dark Continent," was worth the decline of his musical career. I wanted to ask him if this was home.

"Are you American?" Oz asked me.

"I'm from New York," I said.

"Israel is the America of the Middle East!"

"Because of its modernity or its Manifest Destiny?" I asked coolly, having already dismissed him as a racist.

Sensing my critical tone, Oz answered my question with a question. "Do you have any children?" He was probably trying to find a point of connection, but I felt judged, as if he meant to imply only a childless woman could be so reckless as to drive into a mortar attack.

"No, I'm child-free." I hoped to end the conversation there but Oz tightened his greasy ponytail and started in.

"Me? I have four children. Two of them are mine, and two of them I adopted from my best buddy. He was killed when we were soldiers in Lebanon, so this war is nothing new to me. Maybe you heard about the missile that hit a car in Haifa yesterday? Don't worry, Miss. You can be comfortable in my cab because I know what to do. If we hear a siren I will park, and we will find a safe place."

Oz offered me a piece of hard candy, which I refused. Then he fisted his right hand to flex a muscle in his forearm, which was marred by an ugly keloid scar. "You see that? I got that in '82 from the same bullet that went into the center of my buddy's face."

I wanted to touch the scar but resisted the urge.

"These people are animals," he said. "They want to kill us."

"What a coincidence!" said Yitzhak, who had shut off his phone by this point. "Abate! Show them *your* scar."

Abate rolled up the long sleeve of his button-down shirt.

"He got that in an Ethiopian war."

The scar on Abate's left arm looked just like the one on Oz's right. The two of them clasped hands in the front seat in a gesture of solidarity. I'd seen this symbol before, a white hand holding a black one. In my lexicon, it was supposed to mean *Peace*.

Yitzhak gave me a loaded look over the top of his spectacles. "You see?" he asked. "We have a lot in common."

Abate lowered his sleeve.

"We have a lot to learn from the Ethiopians in this country," Yitzhak continued. "We have a lot of chutzpah in our personality. It makes us prickly. But the Ethiopians are a gentle people."

I'd heard the Beta Israel characterized as gentle before. They tended to be talked about in two contradictory yet equally patronizing ways by Alpha Israel: either in terms of docility—*humble, peaceful, quiet, soft*—or with regard to their inability to hold their liquor—*drunk, messy, sloppy, loud*.

"I wasn't interested in playing music with Abate at first," Yitzhak revealed. "I don't like world music, but I've learned a lot from him. He's an amazing musician. Do you want to hear a song he wrote for the Ethiopian radio station? Put on that CD, Abate . . . That's Abate singing. You'll hear him sing later today too. It's in Amharic. Hey, Abate, what do the words mean?"

Abate carefully translated the lyrics into Hebrew. Oz laughed and slapped his thigh. Then he corrected Abate's pronunciation.

Yitzhak translated into English for my benefit: "Abate is singing, 'The fool who tries to crush the State of Israel will himself be crushed.'"

These were the last words I recorded before we arrived. I shut my notebook, no longer knowing what to think.

Haifa was a ghost town. The beach was empty. The streets were empty. The stores were closed. The absorption center was an ugly four-story complex with a Star of David and the Lion of Judah painted on the wall next to the front door. Almost all immigrants from Ethiopia move through way stations like this on their path to Israeli citizenship.

This one housed three hundred Beta Israelites, some of whom had immigrated as recently as two weeks before, others of whom had already lived there for as long as eight months. The rooms were overcrowded, crammed with bunk beds and fold-up cots. In the kitchen, foil-wrapped trays of food were rationed out to the head of each household, shriveled vegetables and globs of macaroni and cheese. There was no *berbere* spice of Ethiopian cooking in the kitchen. There were not enough bathrooms in the building. Classrooms furnished with child-size desks were used to give both adults and children lessons in dietary laws, Hebrew, and hygiene. A picture of Theodor Herzl, the founding father of Zionism, hung on the wall.

In such rooms, the Beta Israelites are "assimilated" before being shunted to the ghettos of Netanya, Rehovot, and Ashdod. Instead of job-skills training and exposure to the mores of Western society, they are given Orthodox lessons in how to pray. While some of the Beta Israel express gratitude for this instruction, others find it humiliating. They can't be granted full Jewish status or marry religiously unless they undergo formal conversion by immersion in a *mikveh*, the ritual bath. Many of the Kessim, Jewish priests who led the spiritual community back in Ethiopia, don't want their brand of Judaism converted to mainline Israeli Chief Rabbinate standards. The Kessim's status in the community has dropped precipitously as a consequence of the conversion efforts made in classrooms like these. This is where they begin to lose institutional power.

In a concrete lot behind the absorption center, two female Israeli soldiers corralled dozens of Ethiopian kids into a moonbounce, one of those air-inflated nylon pleasure houses you might find at a carnival. A third soldier with a rifle strapped to his chest was busy spinning cotton candy onto cardboard wands. The kids looked dirty, like they hadn't had a bath in a good long while.

I wondered if they would grow up and join the "lost generation." Israeli schools make few allowances for cultural difference. As a result, some twenty thousand Ethiopian teenagers have fallen behind, grown disaffected, and dropped out, with no plans to join the army or go to college. This generation identifies less with Ethiopian or Israeli culture than with the black pride, oppositional politics, and message of self-reliance found in the music of rap artists like Tupac Shakur and in reggae clubs like The Rasta. This is a weird circularity. The Jamaican searches for Ethiopia. The Ethiopian searches for Israel, arrives, then searches for Jamaica. And I, the so-called African American, search for what, exactly?

"The Promised Land." It seems always out of reach, somewhere on the other side of the planet. Maybe Jamaica will turn into the Promised Land for those bouncing doe-eyed children someday. Maybe America will. Or maybe they'll look back to Ethiopia, the land of their fathers, just as I sometimes look back to the Deep South, where my ancestors lie. I wondered if this was what it meant to be black—to be gazing like Janus, forward and back.

In the meantime, the children were walking on the moon. Their parents looked afraid. A rocket had ripped into the building across the street the day before. This was the landscape of their new home. I suspected that today's concert and candy were meant to keep the Ethiopians quiet.

"You don't see this on the news," said Oz, "but you should. You see what we do for these people, because we are Jews? *This*"—he indicated the bright moonbounce—"is Israel."

Assuming he was right, I wondered what those children were doing there. Everyone else in the city with the means to leave had left. Why *wasn't* this in the news? Tamar had shown me an article in the *Haaretz Daily* newspaper about the pets that got left behind by the city's evacuees:

> More than 8,000 dogs and cats have been abandoned in the north by owners who have fled south. These include street cats who lost their food supply ... "Numerous abandoned dogs are roaming the streets in the Galilee ..." says veterinarian Gil Shavit of Yesod Hama'ala ... "There is no excuse to abandon a dog. This is a very sensitive creature that is adversely affected by being deserted."

Where was the article about the Ethiopians? Where does one even *find* a cotton candy machine in the middle of war? I thought of Katrina—the dispossessed being left behind in the face of disaster. Then I tried to put things in perspective. It seemed an Ethiopian Jew in Israel had more value than a dog, since the Ethiopian was being taught Hebrew and fed sweets. Still, a dog was worth far more than an Arab, whose value was only that of a cockroach.

Of course, it was ridiculous for me to identify Ethiopian Jews as my kinsmen just because their skin appeared to be black, and for me to think they were black just because they appeared to be second-class citizens. Several groups in Israel can lay claim to "blackness" as characterized by marginalization, disenfranchisement, and second-class citizenship.

When Sephardic Jews began immigrating to Israel in the 1950s from the Arab nations of North Africa and the Middle East, they met with poverty, low-paying jobs, life in the slums, and widespread discrimination by the European Ashkenazic Jews who preceded them. In 1970, an antiestablishment group of Sephardic youth organized to struggle for their civil rights. "We're gonna piss on the Wailing Wall," ran a line in a poem published in their magazine. They called themselves the Black Panthers. Later waves of *aliyot* brought Mizrahi and Russian Jews who met with a similar fate.

One of the employees at the Haifa absorption center told me, "We have never dealt well with immigrants. Maybe it's worse for the Falashas because they're black, but it's always been hard for immigrants here. We haven't learned from our mistakes." She shut her eyes and pinched the bridge of her nose between her forefingers, as if trying to relieve herself of a migraine. Then she said, "You have to realize how hard this is. Imagine if the United States had to absorb all of Mexico. Where would you put all those people?"

"These people don't like to be called Falashas," I said, somewhat possessively, still clinging to my association as if it mattered.

The Beta Israel don't think of themselves as black—at least they didn't while they were in Africa. They thought of themselves as *queyy*—red or brown, a harmonious shade that God finally got right after botching his palette on white and black people. What's more, they distinguished themselves racially from their black African slaves. Like non-Jewish Ethiopians, Beta Israel is separated into a master caste, the *chewa*, and a slave caste, the *barya*. This hierarchical relationship has not been dismantled through the process of immigration because the *chewa* have kept quiet about their slaves in Israel. The *chewa* justify slave ownership by maintaining that the *barya* have different bones and descend from the cursed line of Ham. The same biblical tale was racially interpreted to support the Atlantic slave trade. In Genesis, when Ham sinned against his father, Noah, by looking upon his nakedness, Noah condemned Ham's son to servitude. A warped logic dictated that if the sons of Ham were a different race, then it was in keeping with scripture to treat them as slaves. It was a slap in the face for the *chewa* to arrive in Israel along with their chattel and be referred to as *kushis*, or blacks.

As for their participation in the Israel Defense Forces, the Beta Israel soldiers are known for being fearless, for fighting as though they have something to prove—which they probably do. They often volunteer for the most dangerous posts, like border patrol, where their duty is to frisk and humiliate Arabs—the baddest niggers of the holy land.

Before I could peel my notion of blackness off of Beta Israel and paste it onto Palestine, Yitzhak whisked me away from the moonbounce by the elbow and tried to redeem himself.

He didn't agree with everything Oz said in the cab. He didn't think all Arabs were inhuman. He even went to protest the building of the separation wall. He marched on their side because it was too much like apartheid for his taste. When Israeli soldiers came to stop the protest, one of them pointed an M16 at his chest. This soldier was Ethiopian. Yitzhak realized this man could kill him. That he might die that day. As his heart drummed against his sternum, he asked himself what he would be dying for, which side he was on. "Do you know what the Palestinian standing next to me said? 'Look at that filthy *kushi* who wants to shoot us. I can't believe it's come to this. My homeland is being run by monkeys.'" Yitzhak was terrified the Arab would yell "Go back to Africa!" and the soldier would open fire. "It gets so confusing here sometimes," he finished.

"No shit," I said.

A siren wailed and the whole lot of us—children, soldiers, masters, slaves, black, white, and *queyy*—flew down into the basement. The basement was set up for the concert with folding chairs. The soldiers walked around the dank periphery, spraying bottles of perfume, presumably to mask the fetid odor of sweat. Something cracked outside. It sounded like the scratch of a needle on a record followed by a low boom. "Was that a *ketubah* rocket?" I asked.

"No," said Yitzhak, laughing at my poor Hebrew. He held up his marriage license like a baton. "*This* is a *ketubah. That* was a *Katyusha,*" he joked. I didn't think it was funny, but just when a drumroll would have spiked the punch line, a second explosion sounded. I had to crap suddenly, but there was nowhere to go. Instead, I helped Yitzhak set up his keyboard while Abate warmed up the crowd with a song. I wondered what he was telling them. I wondered what I was doing there. And then they began to play the blues.

Let me be precise. It was unbearably hot. The women sat on the left. They wore colorful head wraps and Jewish-star necklaces, seemingly at odds with the Coptic crosses tattooed on their foreheads, though these are less a symbol of Christianity than a phylactery protective charm against evil. The men sat on the right. They wore *kippahs*. The children sat on the floor, holding hands. The room reeked of perfume. Everyone was very still. Everyone was watching Abate. He had his saxophone strapped around his neck. When he closed his eyes and opened his mouth, the basement widened into a vast space. He sang in Amharic, backed by Yitzhak on stride piano, and when his voice grew jagged, he wet the reed of his horn and transformed the line of the Ethiopian song into flights of improvised jazz. Then Abate circled back to the plaintive root of his own voice.

The two-man band played in a minor pentatonic scale, one mode of which is called *tezeta*. The word means "nostalgia." I looked at the delicate faces of the women, some of whom were nursing babies.

Recognizing Abate's song, some of them began to smile. Tezeta is the form in which the Jews in Ethiopia express their longing for Jerusalem, but that's not what Abate was singing about. This song expressed his longing for *Ethiopia*. It was the blues—a tone that goes straight to the heart, the sound of the Negro spirituals, the sound of "Amazing Grace." It didn't matter that I didn't understand the words. Everyone in that basement understood the song. It was a sorrow song about homesickness, and it soothed us in our fear. I realized then that I had done Billie Holiday a great disservice when I told Yonatan that he couldn't comprehend her depth.

3

Tezeta

TEZETA WAS ALSO the name of the woman I talked to at the Israel Association for Ethiopian Jews. The IAEJ office was inside a Jerusalem shopping mall and decorated with children's artwork that portrayed the dramatic exodus of the Beta Israel from Africa in sequential order, like the Stations of the Cross. The best of these was a tempera painting of a fat blue propeller plane with white stars on its wings. The airplane flew above several brown-faced figures in a yellow desert landscape. All but one of these figures held the Torah in their upraised hands. The one who didn't belong stood in the lower right-hand corner holding a red umbrella, as if she knew in her knees it was going to rain.

"Why are you interested in us?" Tezeta asked with suspicion. She was a fiercely determined and articulate woman in her late twenties, with a wild, natural hairdo, kohl-rimmed eyes, and a direct stare. She had recently quit her job as anchorwoman on the Ethiopian cable access channel in favor of championing basic civil rights for Beta Israel. Her organization is primarily sponsored by American Jews, as are the majority of Ethiopian causes in Israel. Jews in America financially support Ethiopians through acts of charitable giving more than they do any other Israeli immigrant groups. I wondered if these acts were motivated, in part, by guilt over race relations in America and fear that such relations might take hold in Zion. Tezeta herself had an American sponsor for a while. This benefactor sent her five hundred *shekels* a month but abruptly withdrew funding, according to Tezeta, when she went backpacking through Europe and forgot to send him the personal letters he'd come to expect about how grateful she was for his money.

A postcard of Martin Luther King Jr. was tacked to the wall by Tezeta's desk. I pointed at his picture. "I'm interested in you because his dream is important to me," I said.

And then, because I was still thinking about the meaning of her name and the transformative power of Abate's music, I asked Tezeta what she thought of Idan Raichel. Raichel is a white Israeli musician whose eponymous debut album, *The Idan Raichel Project*, went triple platinum when it was released in 2002 and won him "Artist of the Year," "Album of the Year," and "Song of the Year." His success owed much to the Ethiopian folk music sampled in his songs. Idan Raichel has toured the United States during Black History Month and has been described as the Israeli Bob Marley. Since he doesn't play reggae, I can only assume he's called this on account of his waist-length dreadlocks. He is lauded for introducing Israel both to Amharic music and to the diversity of Beta Israel.

"I know Idan Raichel," said Tezeta. "You want to talk to him?"

"I'm more interested in talking to one of the Ethiopians he exploited by neglecting to pay them for his success," I said.

Tezeta laughed and leaned toward me conspiratorially. "My best friend sings in one of the hit songs—'Bo'i.' She's really mad. He doesn't give her any money, and do you know how much money he has from her voice? His pockets are fat from our music. Ever since Idan Raichel made it big, I want to run and see what kind of car he drives because I can remember when he drove a jalopy."

"Maybe he's a necessary evil," I suggested. I told her about how much Abate's music moved me. Then I told her about The Rasta, how its door had been guarded, effectively segregating the club. "Maybe it takes someone like Idan Raichel to get Israel to open its ears to what you have to offer. Maybe he's a cultural bridge."

"I don't think so," she said. "Ethiopian music can only make it in Israel if it has white in the middle. If you take away the white, they don't want it. I know Abate. He is saying something deep. For Israeli listeners, they will be amazed to hear him play the sax.

He will give them something rich they don't know. But they are deaf and blind to him. We all hear Idan Raichel on the radio. He sounds like cheap popcorn. He doesn't have anything new to give to an Ethiopian."

I tried to extend the implied metaphor about unfair trade to her own experience by asking Tezeta what she'd given Israel and what Israel had given her in return, but she was reluctant to talk about her service in the army and dismissive about her journey from Ethiopia during Operation Solomon fifteen years before.

"I'm supposed to be grateful to Israel for saving me," was all she said.

This is the image the world has, that a fleet of planes swooped down like a flock of angels, scooped up the endangered black Jews in the nick of time, and delivered them from starvation into Israel's bosom. It's true that Operation Solomon rescued the Beta Israel from violence in Addis Ababa during a civil war, but their journey to Jerusalem began long before that. At the start of their journey, they weren't at risk, they weren't starving, and they weren't particularly impoverished. Jerusalem was a magnet, and the force of its pull was stronger than the force of Ethiopia's push. What prompted tens of thousands of the Beta Israel to abandon their relatively safe and comfortable lives to migrate to the point where those planes would pick them up? Opportunism was a factor, but more than that, the pull was their longing for Zion.

I pointed again at Dr. King's picture. "He said he went to the mountaintop and saw the Promised Land. I'm guessing this isn't it?"

Tezeta snorted. "I'm not a Zionist. Zionism was a bad idea. Israel wants to be a melting pot for all the world's Jews to make them one thing. She is very sexy. She has what every strong nation wants—a stable economy and an atom bomb. But we don't have any tolerance."

"Are you saying multiculturalism can't exist here?"

"I am saying this does not exist in Israel."

"And absorption is the price of Zionism? Everybody must conform?"

SEARCHING FOR ZION

"Yes. You are right. Maybe we embrace Ethiopian music when a white man brings it on a plate, but they cannot see them as a full human. They want them to be white."

I pointed out Tezeta's pronoun confusion. She alternated between *we, they, us, them, ours,* and *theirs* to talk about both Israelis and Ethiopians, and I didn't think it was because English was her third language. Which did she feel she was—Israeli or Ethiopian?

"I don't know. I have my feet in two lands. I don't know what I am."

"Tell me about it," I said. "Tezeta, are you black?"

"There are a lot of blacks here. The Mizrahi is black, the Bedouin is black, the Yemenite is black, the Moroccan is black, and the Ethiopian is the most black because we came to Israel last. The next to come will be more black than us. It doesn't matter the color of their skin."

"Are the Palestinians black?"

"No. They are not playing in the game. We don't absorb them."

The next day, Tezeta and her boyfriend, Tsuri, brought Tamar and me to Mount Herzl National Memorial Park. Tamar described the park as "the heart of the Zionist commemoration machine." The Holocaust memorial complex, Yad Vashem, is there, as are the military cemetery, the burial sites of Golda Meir and Yitzhak Rabin, and the construction site of a brand-new memorial whose design Tsuri consulted on. It was being erected to commemorate the thousands of Beta Israel who died trying to reach Israel. Tsuri showed me the architectural design for the memorial, which included four round, thatch-roofed huts. Having more facility with Hebrew than Tezeta did with English, Tamar served as translator: "He says those are what their houses looked like in Gondar."

Tsuri pointed to a part of the construction site where a worker manned a backhoe kicking up yellow dust. Tamar tried to keep up with his torrent of words. "He says the huts will go there in a diamond. One, two, three, four . . . The idea was for each house

41

to have text on the walls, a monologue about the exodus by four different Ethiopian characters . . . a mother, a child, a father who leads the family, and a holy man. He wanted visitors to be able to go inside their houses and read their stories."

Tsuri seemed angry.

"What's he saying?" I asked. Tamar struggled to keep up with his tirade. "He's saying that the Jewish Agency didn't approve the design."

"Why not?"

"He says they were afraid the Falashas would go in there to drink and do drugs . . . They're allowed to have the structures, but they have to be closed."

"So nobody can go inside," I clarified.

"That's right," Tamar translated. "No doors. You can only see the huts from the outside."

"But that's ridiculous," I said. "If the story remains hidden, then this is a memorial with no memory."

"I *told* you," Tezeta interrupted, gesticulating wildly. "They do not want what is in our heart. They only want what is in *her* heart." She meant Tamar.

I felt a stab of protection for my old friend. I knew her measure from our teenage years, when she'd thumped out "Golliwogg's Cakewalk" on the upright piano in her parents' dining room, raced down Linden Lane on her red-and-white Schwinn, and baked lemon squares to make other people happy. She'd become an adult away from me—a secular non-Zionist, a librarian and editor, and a mother. I'd been too harsh, in my younger days, to judge her for migrating here. Tamar was doing what she could to make Israel a saner place, much more than I was doing for America. For one thing, she had enrolled her daughter, Nina, in a socially conscious day care with Palestinian kids and teachers where she would learn to speak Arabic. This may have been a little act, but it was an attempt to bridge a big divide. She was that small ax Bob Marley sang about, not some stick figure. I wasn't so sure the State of Israel wanted what was in Tamar's heart. Yet she seemed nonplussed by Tezeta's criticism and I admired her, as I often did, for her quiet strength.

"For us they only want to pat themselves on their backs," Tezeta continued. "Do you think they asked Tsuri to work for this memorial?"

She turned to her boyfriend and spoke at him with ardor. It took me a moment to realize her torrent of words was in Amharic. Amharic is a softer-sounding language than Hebrew, but she was speaking it hard.

Tsuri sighed and tucked the blueprints into his bag. Then he said something brief and looked with resignation at the backhoe. "He says they didn't ask him," Tamar translated. "He heard they were building the memorial, and he fought to be included on the steering committee."

"He is the only Ethiopian making this. They think they know better than us how to show our exodus," Tezeta hissed.

On our way through the cypress trees down the mountain, Tamar admitted that when she'd come to Israel for summer camp in her youth, she'd felt the land belonged to her, and she to it. "The counselors instilled a sense of ownership in us," she said. "I thought the 'Falashas' were foreigners, but I didn't think of myself as a foreigner. It's ironic, isn't it? They were living here. I was only visiting."

"It is not ironic," said Tezeta. *Chutzpah.* That is the word for how she said this: "Israel does belong to you. Not to us."

"Do you guys think of this place as your homeland?" I asked the young couple.

Tsuri was tight-lipped. Tezeta was fed up. "I have told you! I'm not a Zionist! The Ethiopians dream of Zion as a place that our grandfathers dreamed. But they need to wake up from that dream and see how this Zion treats us. That dream is not real. The day we say our dream is just a dream is the day we will stand up for our rights. But the Ethiopians want to stay asleep. They say, 'I dreamed to be here. I am a Zionist and I belong to Zion.' Israel doesn't want them. She only wants them if they play the game by her rules, pray the way she tells us, think the way she tells us, be the Jew she wants. It was not my dream to be a citizen of Israel. If you want to listen to that kind of talk, you should go and see my boss."

Danny Admasu was a chain-smoking man in his early thirties who looked like he hadn't slept in months. He had been airlifted from Sudan during Operation Moses in 1984, an era I remember for Live Aid, Hands Across America, the hit song "We Are the World," and starving Ethiopians on the cover of *Time* magazine. Since he had been in Israel longer than Tezeta, Danny's English was more assured, almost poetic.

"I wrote this," he said, pulling a yellowed clipping from the *Jerusalem Post* off the bulletin board in his office. "It gives you an idea of my politics." The headline read: WHICH WAY FOR ETHIOPIAN ISRAELIS? The article focused on discrimination against the Beta Israel in the school system, the civil service, the private sector, and the housing market, as well as their lack of representation in government and all other centers of power.

"What about the Ethiopian on *The Ambassador*?" I teased, referring to the reality show that pitted fourteen young Israelis against each other in tasks designed to boost Israel's disintegrating world image. "And wasn't there an Ethiopian singer represented on *Israeli Idol*?"

"They didn't win," he said. "They were just window dressing to complete Israel's cultural menagerie."

"What about Addisu Messele?" I asked about the former lone Ethiopian-born member of the 120-person Knesset, Israel's House of Representatives. "Window dressing?"

"More or less."

"I bet your article got you in trouble," I ventured. "You called the Ministry of Absorption *a disgrace*. That's pretty bold."

"I am bold—I'm an Israeli. We know how to shout to get our point across. But you're right. The government doesn't like me because I'm speaking the truth. My goal is to change their idea that we're not worthy. They don't understand. They think Jewish means white."

He offered me a cigarette. I declined.

"They want you to think they love us because we're all Jews, but they don't think we have the same bones and blood."

"I heard about how they dumped all the Beta Israel blood out of the blood bank because they feared it was infected with AIDS."

"How did you hear about that?"

"I read about it."

"Are you American?"

"I'm from New York."

"Americans have a tendency to talk about the ethos of the community, and not of the individual. You think this war is between Israel and Lebanon, for example. You think about who is right and wrong, but you don't think about the experience of the soldier."

I considered how quickly I'd written Oz off on the ride to Haifa. He was a man who had seen his best friend's face blown away. Who would I have turned against had I witnessed the same thing done to Tamar?

"I will tell you my story," Danny offered. "Imagine you are me. You are a little Jewish boy in Gondar, where you shepherd goats. Every morning you drink fresh milk from the goats you tend. But the real food in your life as you grow up is the dream of Jerusalem. This dream is in everything you do—the way you pray, the blessing, all the Jewish ceremonies. In every sentence the word *Jerusalem* comes up."

He stopped to ash his cigarette.

"One day, your father says to you, 'We're going to Jerusalem.' Imagine your surprise. You didn't know it was a real place. You thought it was a dream as far away as the moon. Your father has sold your goats and everything else but the donkey to carry the food. You begin walking with everyone else from your village. You're doing what Moses did to get to Israel. Every father in the village is a Moses.

"They knew there would be sacrifice. Somebody was going to die along the way. They were willing to pay whatever it cost to get to Jerusalem. Looking back, it was crazy. The government regime did not allow emigration. They arrested us along the way and sent us back to the village. So we began again. We walked at night and hid in the day. My sister was arrested three times, and she bore a kid in jail."

"Wait, was she pregnant already?" I asked, on the edge of my seat. "Was she raped?"

"That is another story for another time and place," Danny deferred. "Imagine you are still on the road, walking from Ethiopia to Sudan. It takes two months. The weak ones didn't make it this far. You made it, but you have to stop walking because you ran out of food and water. You are so thirsty you would gladly drink your own urine, only you are too dehydrated to urinate. You live in a refugee camp, and it is hell. Sometimes the Red Cross brings medicine, but forty to sixty people die there every day from starvation and snakebites. Israel finally hears about you, but they don't think you're a Jew because you're *black*. You yourself didn't know there were *white* Jews. You have never seen a white person before.

"America is putting pressure on Israel to save you. A big safari truck comes to pick you up and drives you for three hours with your father to a big airplane. You have never seen an airplane, so you don't know it's strange that they ripped out the seats to fit more of you inside. On the airplane they feed you bananas. You eat so many you get sick. When you arrive in Israel your father is crying because he thinks he's in heaven. You made it. You know you are home.

"That is *my* story. The story the world knows is how Israel endangered herself to bring poor people from Africa. That's a lie. I started my way to this land that I knew from the stomach of my mother without their help. My father put me in danger for this dream. He made it come true. I don't need permission from anyone to prove I'm Jewish. Israel doesn't need to feed me lies to turn me into an Orthodox Jew. I was Jewish before I was born."

Danny lit another cigarette, leaned back, took a long drag, and exhaled a slow rhapsodic haze of smoke. He had finished the narrative of his amazing journey homeward at the exact spot where spiritual Zion butts heads with political Zion. The euphoria of his arrival must have worn away fast, perhaps beginning when he stepped off the plane onto the tarmac and, along with everyone else on board, was bestowed a Hebrew name. Or did he like to be called Daniel? I wondered what his name used to be, the one his father gave him. I wondered when exactly the word *home* began to take on a "diabolical ring" for him and his father, but I didn't ask Danny about the second half of his journey. I understood that along with his activism, the dream was what kept him alive. Like Tezeta, he was stuck between two lands, his dislocation in one due to the sacrifice of the other. It didn't matter that home was a myth he was still walking toward. Maybe it mattered that he was walking on the backs of Palestinians to get there, but I don't think Danny thought about that. It only mattered to him that he hadn't stopped walking.

We were quiet for a while. Then I asked, "Do you know who James Baldwin is?"

He didn't.

"You'd like him. He's a black American writer. He said, 'I criticize my home because I love it.' Or something like that." One paragraph in Danny's article, in particular, had made me think of Baldwin:

More than two decades have passed since the first significant wave of Jewish immigration from Ethiopia to the promised "Land of Milk and Honey" began. While coming on aliyah and being physically present in Israel fulfilled half of the dream, the intolerance towards their language, culture and color, which they have encountered in every aspect of life since their arrival in Israel, has buried the other half of Ethiopian Jewry's dream. Today we can speak more aptly in terms of the crushed dream.

"You speak as though you love it here," I said.

Danny was unequivocal. "I do love Jerusalem. I am speaking the truth."

4

Transitioning

I AM SPEAKING THE truth," said the priest at a Sabbath service in the multipurpose room at the Kingdom of Yah, home of the African Hebrew Israelites of Jerusalem. This was the other group of black Jews Tamar had mentioned six years ago. She would not have been easily welcomed, as a white woman, to their village in the desert, and so I'd gone alone. At the service, I wore a white head wrap and a loose black dress that came down to my sandaled feet. The room was lit by a dozen menorahs. I sat between my hosts, Crowned Dr. Khazriel, head of the School of the Prophets, and one of his many wives, Sister Aturah. She had lent me the dress because the knee-length skirt and tank top I showed up in were "immodest."

The priest was reading from the book of their prophet, Ben Ammi Ben-Israel, a former foundry worker from Chicago, born Ben Carter, whom the African Hebrew Israelites call Abba and believe to be the Messiah. He claims that in 1966 he had a forty-five-second vision from an angel who told him it was time for him and the rest of his lost tribe to return to Jerusalem. Their tradition holds that they were exiled from the Holy Land during the Roman invasion nearly two thousand years ago, migrated southward through the centuries down the Nile, and then westward to the coast of Africa where a great number of them were captured and shipped into slavery, a kind of modern Babylon, as a curse for sinning against God's law. They distinguish their progenitor from Judah, the Jewish father. Their father is Adam, the original man.

They differentiate their curse, referred to in Leviticus and Deuter-onomy as a great dispersal and a voyage into captivity by boat, from the eternal curse of Ham. While they believe Ham's curse cannot be redressed, the African Hebrew Israelites believe their curse *can* be, by living according to certain principles, including a vegan diet.

The idea of undoing a "curse" can be seductive for black Ameri-cans who have grown up in inner-city slums, who can reach only four hundred years into their history before bumping against a wall. Being a charismatic leader, Ben Ammi convinced thirty black followers of his angelic vision. First, they traveled to Liberia to cleanse themselves of their slave mentality. In 1969, they showed up in Israel and were told by the Chief Rabbinate that they were not Jews. But the African Hebrew Israelites saw themselves as the original Jews. They refused to convert, calling the Israelis "heathens" and publicly threatening to run them into the sea. The 1970s and 1980s were contentious years for the African Hebrew Israelites in Israel. They couldn't work there legally, having only temporary visas, and were often deported for alleged money-laundering and airline ticket fraud schemes.

The priest read some more scripture from Ben Ammi's holy book—*God, the Black Man, and Truth*—and then launched into a sermon, much of which I agreed with. Up to a point.

"You can't get to freedom on an airplane."

"Tell it!"

"An airplane won't take you there. Brothers and sisters, I'm here to tell you, freedom is a place in your *mind*."

"That's right!"

"Back there we were sick."

"I was dying!"

"Sickness, perversion, and death abound in the land of Great Captivity, but our greatest sickness there was of our *spirit*. We didn't choose to live there."

"No!"

"They took us in chains! That place of wickedness was not our home. Theirs was not our way. Why would you want what they teach you to crave? A big house with a *garage*? A house for your *car* when your brother was homeless? You wanted it because you were sick. You were thinking like them. Why would you poison your body with cigarettes, knowing they would kill you?"

"Because I was sick!"

"You were thinking like them. Why would you believe the earth moves around the sun? Does that make sense?"

"No!"

"No. The earth is the center of the universe. Jerusalem is the center of the earth. If the earth moved around the sun, then how could the sun rise and set every day? You didn't use your *mind*. You listened to their lies. You let them tell you Jesus was white, Adam was white. Jesus wasn't white. Neither was Adam. They were black men with wooly hair."

"That's right!"

"Why would you let your child play with a toy gun? If you let your child shoot water, he will grow up and think it's a game to shoot a bullet! Why would you allow him to shoot a brother over a pair of hundred-dollar sneakers or a vial of crack? Because you were sick. Our bodies weren't in shackles, but our minds were. They told us we were nothing, and we believed them, but we're not at the bottom of their boat no more. They told us we couldn't do it, but we did. We built the boat. We drive the boat."

"Amen!"

"They want you to believe we're a cult. Say the whole word!"

"Culture!"

At this point, I started to feel a little uneasy. I wasn't sure if it was the sermon or the head scarf—Sister Aturah had wrapped mine too tight, and I was afraid I might pass out.

"You don't go to Japan and say, 'That's a cult.' That's a *culture*. We're a *culture*. They say we're a weird sect. Say the whole word. We're a *section* of the Hebrew Israelite nation living in Dimona, Israel, Northeast Africa. If you conform to our vision, you will not be sick. You will not need a medicine chest. Diabetes—what's that? Cancer—what's that? Depression—what's that? Can I get a witness?"

"I haven't been sick since I came to the Kingdom nineteen years ago—not once!" someone shouted.

"The Torah speaks of people who lived nine hundred years, so why can't we? This is possible, people. Nine hundred years is a blink of Yah's eye and we are his *chosen* people. We don't have to die. Heaven is possible in the mind and body, and we are living proof. We don't use the word *death* around our children. Our children don't know the meaning of that word. We are making new people, with new minds, befitting of this new world."

"Hallelujah!"

After the service was over, Dr. Khazriel and Sister Aturah walked me through the Village of Peace to the guesthouse where I was staying. My room was decorated with generic Afrocentric prints, a seven-foot-tall wooden giraffe, and a poster of Ben Ammi's benevolent face. Aturah was quiet in her husband's presence. I learned that they'd been married only a few weeks before, and that none of his fourteen children were hers. I imagine that being middle-aged and childless was hard for her in a community that forbids birth control and puts a high premium on a woman's ability to bear children.

All of the women I met in the Village of Peace introduced themselves to me in terms of their motherhood, as in, "I'm Sister Zehorah, mother of eight." They told me that a man's wife is a piece of him just as Adam's rib is a piece of Adam, and that while Man keeps his hand in the hand of Yah, Woman keeps her hand in the hand of Man.

Aturah walked a few steps behind her new husband and me, her head bowed. I turned to ask her if the priest was using a metaphor when he spoke about immortality.

"Oh, no," she said.

"You don't believe in death?"

"We call it *transitioning*," she said softly.

I thought it would be gauche to ask where they put their dead people. "Do you celebrate funerals?" I asked.

Dr. Khazriel gave her a look.

"Everything we do promotes life and healing," she said. "What we put in our bodies, what we put into the earth, how we sing. We don't sing the blues anymore."

Dr. Khazriel had a slight lisp. He waved his cane at the crooked little tar-papered shacks that make up the Kingdom of Yah. "None of this was here when I came," he said, fingering his gray beard. Although he is not one of the founders of the kingdom, Dr. Khazriel arrived a few short years after its inception. He was seventeen years old when he came to join his aunt and the swelling number of other African Americans who'd settled in the Negev Desert near a nuclear reactor, where the State of Israel had allowed them to squat. At the time of my visit there were an estimated twenty-five hundred members living in Israel, where they had recently gained permanent residency status. Their population has grown thanks to polygamy and to widespread proselytizing efforts in "the provinces," which include Baltimore, Houston, Detroit, Atlanta, and New York. The African Hebrew Israelites make up the largest single community of African Americans living outside the United States and, Dr. Khazriel told me, "the only progressive one—a historic fact in itself. We built this nation with our own hands."

The sprawling shantytown didn't look like much to me, but then I considered their accomplishment. My hosts pointed out their school, their sewing center, their bakery, their gym, their library, their "House of Life" (there is no need for a hospital in a land without sickness)—all of this built from scratch in thirty-some-odd years. These people make their own clothes, grow most of their own food, and, most important, govern themselves.

Where the Beta Israel represent the bitterness, disorientation, and disillusionment of Zionism's dream deferred, members of the African Hebrew Israelite community believe, or are indoctrinated to believe, that they have fully arrived in Canaan. Because the Chief Rabbinate of Israel has never acknowledged them as Jews, they've never enjoyed any of the rights of citizenship that Israel has to offer. This rejection has forced them to fashion their own Zion. Because they've never been forced to assimilate to dominant Orthodox Judaism, they've managed to maintain and forge their own unique Judaic identity. Theirs is a fully operable, self-sustained nation-inside-a-nation with one interesting concession. About seventy African Hebrew Israelite youth had enlisted in the Israel Defense Forces.

I asked Dr. Khazriel if their participation in the IDF conflicted with the African Hebrew Israelites' governing practice of promoting life. "The priest said it was sick for a child to play with a toy gun, but some of your young people are handling real guns right now in Lebanon. What are they fighting for?"

"That's a good question, Sister Emily. I see you have a sharp mind. What you see surrounding you is our spiritual home but it's also a physical realm. We have to protect our village. We're a spiritual entity in a secular world with social realities. Those scuds and rockets are real. Outside of a war atmosphere, killing is not acceptable, but we live in a punishing atmosphere of war. We're not disconnected from greater Israel," Dr. Khazriel reasoned. "We live here, and so we have to show solidarity. But our involvement in the army is only transitional."

I told him I'd been witness to the hard transition Beta Israel was making into Zion. "It's truly a shame what's happening to them," he said, shaking his head. "They're African Hebrew Israelites too. We all descend from Judea, but when they returned home, they began to lose their original form."

We arrived at the guesthouse. "There used to be a baseball diamond scratched in the sand right here," Dr. Khazriel said. "The day I arrived, there was a pickup game going on. My aunt said, 'Boy, this is the kingdom of heaven, and these are the saints.' I said, 'If this is heaven, then where's Jesus?' She pointed at the pitcher and said, 'Right there.' Do you know who she was pointing at?"

"Abba?" I guessed.

"See that, Aturah? She's sharp as a sword." He laid his hand on my shoulder. "We could use a mind like yours in the Kingdom."

Abba, Ben Ammi Ben-Israel, stood in a resplendent, canary-yellow robe, in the center of a large painting hanging above the table in the conference room of the School of the Prophets where Dr. Khazriel instructed me further in his beliefs. Twelve other men figured in the painting, just like the apostles at the last supper. The other decorations of note in the classroom were a picture of Martin Luther King Jr. and a world map.

"Do you really believe Ben Ammi is the Messiah?" I asked.

Dr. Khazriel gestured at the painting. "Those men represent our governing body," he began. "Our government must remain in a prophetic mode. Many men have had visions—Frederick Douglass, Martin Delany, Father Divine, Garvey, King, Malcolm—and all of their visions failed. Why? Because all black visionaries in America become martyrs. The man who can electrify and unify a black movement is an automatic target. We had to authenticate Ben Ammi's vision by calling him the *Messiah*. That title gives him absolute authority."

"As the son of God?"

"As the anointed leader of the Kingdom of Yah. He's our ruler. We couldn't be free until we had our own nation. 'He who rules Jerusalem rules the world.'"

"Sounds like a crusade."

"It is. All men have focused on Jerusalem since the dawn of mankind. Do you know why?"

"Your priest said Jerusalem is the center of the universe."

"Good listening. Israel began with correct socialist aims, but you don't see too many kibbutzim anymore. Jerusalem has fallen under the control of profane and perverted European empires. Their dominion has brought the world to darkness. Euro-gentiles have corrupted earth-centered concepts more than any other people. They have distorted the institutions of liberalism and democracy. You'd have to be blind not to recognize this as a fallen world."

Dr. Khazriel pushed up the loose sleeves of his dashiki and counted out a list of recent calamities on his fingers: tsunami, Katrina, global warming, the present war with Lebanon . . . He fisted and unfisted his hands.

"We're at a time of transition. Those empowered to administrate the earth are about to have a rude awakening. Their time of rule is up." He pounded the table with his fists. "Our purpose is to restore Jerusalem, Africa, and the earth. The diaspora cannot save Africa, but Africa can save the diaspora."

"Save, how?"

"There's no spiritual impetus for the black diaspora to save Africa. With all its resources, scholars, and religious leaders, the black diaspora is out of focus. Sister Emily, let me ask you a question. Do you think of Africa as a prophetic or pathetic realm?"

"Um . . ."

"You can admit it."

"Well, I've never been there. I'd like to go," I said. Africa was a logical destination for a seeker like me, but it seemed too vast a territory, too mythic to enter, too distant to confront. I needed a stepping-stone to get me there.

"You're there right now! This is it. You're in Africa." Dr. Khazriel swiveled his chair and pointed a pen at little Israel on the world map, hanging off Egypt like an earlobe. "All that separates you from the mother continent is the Suez Canal. The Kingdom of Yah is the New Jerusalem. We're not built out of brick and mortar alone. We're building a new mind beyond the shackles we once knew. We've recovered from chattel slavery. We've saved ourselves from stress and harm, trauma and drama, from the dialysis machine, hypertension, and heart attack, from kidney failure, self-hatred, and jail. We've reversed all that impurity by restoring Hebraic concepts of interdependent community, love, and humanity. By doing that, we're restoring Africa, which will in turn restore the earth's populace. No brag, just fact."

Dr. Khazriel held out his hand. "This hand is humble. This hand reaching out to save the earth is black. People don't want to hold this hand. They are selective about salvation. Look at this mess." He brought out a copy of *The Economist* and slapped it on the table. Bill Gates was on the cover, holding a black baby. "What does that say?"

"Billanthropy."

"That man has thirty-four *billion* dollars. His impulse is greed, profit, big business, tax-deductible philanthropy. When is it enough? There is no possibility for contentment in the framework of capitalism. Do you know why they crucified *him*?"

Dr. Khazriel signaled the picture of Martin Luther King Jr., which was the same image as the one in Tezeta's office, only much bigger. "Because he was a Hebrew. Their edict was to stop the rise of the black Messiah."

"COINTELPRO?" I knew he was referring to the FBI's covert and often illegal Counter Intelligence Program designed to dismantle civil rights, black nationalist, and other social justice movements.

"Yes, Sister. They got rid of him, of our king, because he spoke the powerful phrase 'Promised Land.' That's a Hebrewism. It comes from Old Testament theology. Hebrewisms are the basis of all black protest social movements. Did you ever read about us in school? Had you ever heard of a black Jew?"

"No," I admitted.

Dr. Khazriel shook his head, sadly. "We've been omitted from the annals of history. But I want you to see that we're not a fringe. We're not a myth blown out of a vacuum. I want you to read this"—he held up the holy book—"as a history text. Begin with Genesis. *That's* our history."

Sister Aturah, in a purple robe and a matching head wrap, entered the room quietly to serve us watermelon. "This was grown on our farm," she whispered, setting it down. "It's very sweet."

"Thank you, Aturah," said Dr. Khazriel. "Do you have something you want to tell Sister Emily on her quest for truth?"

"Yes, I do."

"Tell it."

"This is an island of sanity. This is the place our soul was crying out for."

"Aturah might also have said that we see ourselves as the fulfill-ment of Dr. King's dream," Dr. Khazriel added. "Isn't that right?"

"Yes," she answered, looking at her feet.

I began picking out the little black seeds from the fruit. Pathetic and prophetic. To me their world was both. "So this is Canaan Land?" I asked Dr. Khazriel. The reason I didn't put my question to his wife was because I didn't think she was at liberty to say, "No."

"I was born into a Detroit ghetto," he answered, biting into a slice of the melon. He wiped the juice from his chin and grinned. "If I wasn't here, I would be dead."

On my last day before leaving Israel, Tamar and I walked baby Nina through a mob of displaced Israeli settlers dressed in orange. They had chosen this color to protest the prime minister's plan to disengage from Gaza. It was Tisha B'Av, the fast of the Ninth of Av, a holiday that observes the many tragedies that have stricken Jews throughout history including the destruction of the First and Second Temples and the expulsion of the Jews from Spain. These settlers were mourning the loss of their homes in Pales-tinian territory.

"I guess they see the disengagement as tantamount to the de-struction of the Temple," Tamar marveled. She hadn't foreseen the march, and soon we were tangled in it. There were thousands of protesters, shouting, singing, waving the Israeli flag, flooding us in a rage of orange.

"I can't believe these people," Tamar said, plowing her way through the crowd with the stroller. "Move!"

These were the hard-core Zionists who clung so ferociously to the concept of home that they risked strangling it. I could see why Tamar wanted to separate herself from them but I could also see what underlay their blind and dogged devotion. For them,

Zionism was the political movement that supported the modern
state of Israel as a homeland for Jews. Its imperative was so intense
precisely because of the Holocaust and the tragedies mourned on
this holy day, Tisha B'Av.

"MOVE, people!" Tamar pushed, determined to free us from
the crowd.

We escaped behind the walls of the Old City, wended through
the maze of its narrow, cobbled streets, bypassed all of its wares—the
blue and white Armenian ceramics, the backgammon sets inlaid
with mother-of-pearl, the beads, the baklava, the incense sticks, and
doumbek drums. We wound up outside St. Anne's Church, home
to the ruins of the curative Bethesda Pool where, according to the
Gospel of John, Jesus performed a miracle of faith.

"Do you want to be healed?" Jesus asked a man with useless legs.
The man said yes. "Then get up and walk!" Christ commanded,
and the man was lame no more.

"I want to show you something special," said Tamar, leading
me into the basilica. Except for two coiffed middle-aged women
sitting in the back pew with their hands folded, the church was
empty. Tamar unstrapped Nina from her stroller. "This church
has a fifteen-second echo," she whispered. Nina squealed and her
voice ballooned outward to fill the unadorned space, as high as the
vaulted ceilings. The baby widened her eyes in wonder.

"Excusez-moi. Êtes-vous américaines?" asked one of the women
in back, fingering the silk scarf at her throat.

"Sort of . . ." said Tamar.

Sort of . . .

Sort of . . . came the echo.

"Ah!" clapped the French woman, and her clap became a can-
non's boom. "Do you know how to sing?"

"Dites-leur de chanter 'Amazing Grace,'" her friend suggested. The
last word bloomed from her lipsticked mouth.

Grace.

Grace.

"J'aime cette chanson."

"We know it," Tamar smiled.

We know it; We know it; We know it . . .

We do. We walked up the aisle side by side, sat Nina in the first pew with her quilt, took our places at the altar just as we used to stand in our high school's choir, looked at each other, and began. We sang that mournful hymn composed by a white man who'd sailed the seas on slave ships, witnessed the shackled hold, felt compassion, and attempted to expiate the sin of his complicity through the act of composition.

We sang in two-part harmony. Our voices cast out like fishing lines into the void. They unraveled into water and swam back to us, doubling and quadrupling in volume, backward and forward, a current running in all directions, a passage, a map. This was our sweet sound. Wanting to be cradled in it, the baby scooted backward off the pew and crawled toward us in her sagging diaper across the marble floor.

We transposed from major to minor key. Nina stopped three feet from us and stood. In the end, this is Zion: the song about our wretchedness lifting up to save us, our voices leashing us together, the child walking toward us on unsteady legs. Two steps. Her first. She will fall down, but right now our song holds her up like hands, and this is a taste of Zion, right here, in the second before she does.

When we finished, we would leave this space. The French women would return to France. Tamar and Nina would return to their apartment in Jerusalem. I would go home to Harlem where, more often than not, the people I thought of as my kin looked upon me as an interloper. Maybe it was just the power of the moment, or all I'd heard from the Ethiopian Jews, the African Hebrew Israelites, and everyone in between, but now more than ever I wanted to feel connected to a place, a people. I didn't honestly know where that would be, but as we gathered our belongings and left the basilica, I already knew I'd travel the world to find out.

PART II: JAMAICA

BELIEF KILL AND BELIEF CURE

5

Home to Roost

To celebrate the close of the spring 2008 semester, my father met me for lunch at Miss Maude's Spoonbread Too restaurant near 138th Street on Lenox Avenue in Harlem. We were both relieved to be finished teaching for the school year. He was going through a rocky period in his marriage to my stepmother and had lost a great deal of weight; so much weight that he'd bought new clothes. Instead of one of the bright dashikis he typically wore, my father was dressed in a linen shirt. This confirmed a suspicion of mine that for the past few years he'd been sporting dashikis less as a political statement and more to hide the belly of late middle age. I was mad at him for his role in the unraveling of his second marriage, but rather than confronting difficult emotions, we were speaking in abstract terms about black nationalism.

Our conversation was sparked by a man selling bootleg recordings of Malcolm X speeches down Lenox Avenue, an appropriate venue to set up shop, since this street is also known as Malcolm X Boulevard. Actually, our conversation was sparked by one particular speech, which came crackling out of the man's janky boombox as fresh and searing as it must have sounded in 1963: "God's Judgment of White America," more popularly known as "The Chickens Come Home to Roost."

Over Miss Maude's barbecued ribs my father and I began talking about the Nation of Islam, cycled back to the Haitian Revolution, skipped across the Atlantic to Patrice Lumumba in the Congo, then stateside again to the Black Panthers and the more militant Black

Liberation Army, before, over sweet potato pie, lighting momentarily on the Republic of New Afrika, a movement to form an independent black majority country composed of five Southern states: South Carolina, Georgia, Alabama, Mississippi, and Louisiana.

"Some of these groups held black nationalism sacred," my father said. "Their vision called for the creation of a black nation-state. It was a radically different approach from that of the black church, which believed the ultimate Zion was heavenly, or within. But too often, it was based on a faulty premise."

"What do you mean?"

"Well, the modern nation-state is supposed to be synonymous with identity. When people ask us what we are, we're inclined to say we're American, or hyphenated Americans."

"Not me," I pointed out. "People don't believe me."

"That's because your face shows racial mythology to be a lie. It confuses people. The state"—my father held up his right hand—"is a political entity. The nation"—he held up his left hand—"is a cultural entity." He clasped his hands together. "But when these two entities coincide in countries with histories of slavery or other systems of racial hierarchy, identity gets confused with race. If you do not easily belong to a race, then you cannot easily be an American."

"That's what I've been trying to say," I groaned. "It's such a ridiculous cliché—the 'tragic mulatto' whining about not belonging. I don't want to be that person. That's not who I am."

"Then refuse the mythology."

"Easier said than done when everybody buys into it. It makes me want to live somewhere else."

"Where?"

"I don't know yet." I toyed with my pie. I was now thirty-two years old, twice the age I'd been when my parents divorced, yet I felt sixteen again, like my family was coming undone. I had grown to love my stepmother after years of resenting her. I loved her children too, my stepsister and stepbrother, and their children. I was afraid of losing them, and along with the traditions we'd created over the years, I was afraid of losing my father again. The heart is an emotional entity. The mind is a rational entity. But when these two organs coincide in bodies with histories of divorce, love gets confused with the desire to put the family back together again. To make what is broken, whole. "I'm thinking of going to Jamaica next month."

My father looked at me carefully. "It's a mistake to conflate nationalism and religious idealism, sweetie," he said softly.

Suddenly I was very angry, without understanding why. "What's that supposed to mean?" I snapped. I felt we were speaking in codes.

"You're searching for Zion. You feel personally injured that America isn't the Promised Land. That could be described as a black feeling. While it may be true that this nation was founded on the utopian ideals of religious freedom, it's just as true that it was founded as a result of a growing global economy that exploited the labor of slaves. Right?"

"Right."

"But the Promised Land, at least the one Martin Luther King spoke of, stands over and against nation-state idolatry. It subverts nationalism and borders and the kind of island mentality of pushing 'We're number one,' or 'Us vs. them.' King wasn't talking about a country when he talked about Zion," my father said as he called for the check.

I insisted on paying for our meal. It mattered to me that my father should see me as an adult rather than a child. "What was King talking about?" I asked.

My father smiled, wearily. "What kind of teacher would I be if I just *told* you the answer?"

"You're not my teacher. You're my dad," I thought but did not say. Of course, he was both.

That June, just after Barack Obama cinched the Democratic Party nomination, I flew to Jamaica. A trip to the Caribbean *and* a potential black president. I was happy at the time, in a bipolar kind of way. On the flipside of my good feeling lay a dark and restless unease.

The island looked like a little green lung from my plane window. Though it's the third-largest island in the Caribbean, Jamaica is only the size of New Jersey, where I grew up, the third-smallest state in the U.S.A. I wasn't going to the splashy resorts of Negril or Montego Bay. I was going to hardscrabble Kingston. With its precipitously high murder rates, it's not a city that attracts many tourists. But Kingston was the beating heart of reggae and I was on a quest to find out more about the Rasta faith. Reggae in general, and Bob Marley's music in particular, expressed a longing for home I felt in my core, and it did it in a way that made me want to dance.

Bob Marley emerged as a voice with the Wailers around 1970, some forty years after the faith, Rastafari, was born. Under his ambassadorship, reggae has become among the most popular music in the world. It's a multimillion-dollar industry with universal appeal, especially to young people who respond to its hard stand against oppression. I was one of those young people. Like so many dorm rooms, mine had been a smoke-filled cave pulsing with the sounds of Bob Marley and the Wailers, but also the Slickers, the Heptones, the Pioneers, the Paragons, Freddie McGregor, the Ethiopians, the Melodians, Desmond Dekker, Burning Spear, Culture, Jimmy Cliff, and the Gaylads, all of whom hailed from this mighty little island, this former colonial outpost that refused to be a backwater place.

"Holy Mount Zion," they sang over the off-beat, time and time again. Zion, sweet Zion—a train was taking them there, or a Black Star Liner, or a ride on a lion. It was a holy place, a place no sin could enter; there was no night in Zion. It was where they were from, Holy Mount Zion. Inside its gates, that's where they wanted to be. They were "moving to the Promised Land."

I knew this Zion was a holy place, a dwelling to roost, a country that was supposed to offer some kind of cure for the long disease of slavery. Maybe I'd find the Zion they sang about in Jamaica, in spite of my father's warning. I hadn't found it in Israel. But I knew next to nothing about the religion that underscores so much of what we hear in reggae, which is not only protest music but also sacred music.

My plan was to talk to the Rastas on their home turf. Funnily enough, the nightclub I danced at in Tel Aviv—The Rasta—moved me to visit reggae's homeland. Since my trip to Israel, black folks who'd been brave or troubled enough to strike out from "home" for the Promised Land had begun to inspire me. My travel described an almost stock quest for racial identity. It wasn't unlike the quests that had Ethiopian Jews and African Hebrew Israelites making their exoduses to Israel, and Rastas trying to get "home" to Africa. And it was quite like the quest that drove Barack Obama to write *Dreams from My Father: A Story of Race and Inheritance*.

Obama's first memoir charts his return to Kenya on the heels of the death of his absentee father. It finds him longing for, choosing, and constructing his blackness even as he examines his mixed heritage. His white mother, the parent who raised him, is virtually absent from the text. In my own work, I'm guilty of similar omissions. From my seat on the plane I gazed down at the first black nation I would ever visit, a stepping-stone to Africa, and wondered: Why, in both my professional and personal life, am I drawn toward my black side?

"You only ask questions like that because you almost look white. It's not an issue for your brothers," my mother once pointed out. She was a second-grade schoolteacher, gifted at simplifying math for smaller minds. My three brothers were darker-skinned than I, corkboard to my wooden spoon. Unlike them, I'm white enough to "pass," but perhaps as a vestige of the old "One Drop Rule" peculiar to our nation, in many circles I'm considered a light-skinned black woman.

That social and legal classification of individuals as black, so long as they had one drop of black blood, eluded my friend, the late Irish writer Nuala O'Faolain. When I confessed to Nuala that my mother, too, was Irish but that I myself had never been to Ireland, she exclaimed in her lilting brogue, "Never!? But why have you never gone home? Have you had a look at yourself of late, love? How in Jesus's name can you call yourself black?"

How could I explain the schizophrenic sense that half my ancestors had oppressed the other half and that I preferred to be on the right side of history? Time after time, I tried to ally myself with the people on the wrong side of the barrel of the gun. "You wouldn't get it," I stammered at Nuala, red-faced and defensive.

"Oh, I wouldn't, would I?" Nuala brayed, reminding me that Ireland was the first colony of the British Empire and had remained one for seven centuries. "And since it's only a New York minute in the stretch of history we Irish have been white ourselves, let's just call a spade a spade. No pun intended. Your father, the black—he left your ma, I take it? Aw, wipe the look of surprise off your mug before I drink you the rest of the way under the table. He's a father, isn't he? More often than not, at the end of the day, it's what the lot of them do. Call it blackness if you must, but it's the heels of your da you're chasing."

So here I was, flying into Kingston rather than Dublin. One thing became clear when I arrived: in Jamaica, I was a white woman. It didn't matter what I said to the contrary because in Jamaica, race is more purely a construct of skin tone. I stood out in Kingston's Trench Town, Coronation Market, and Emancipation Park. It was impossible to blend in. I was the easiest mark for miles. "Hey, white lady," jeered a Rastafarian selling homemade brooms on Orange Street. "How you like me country?"

I told him that the last time I was this much in the minority, I was a black person in Vermont.

This provoked the Dred to school me about our origins. We did not, he emphasized, come from the same tribe. I, as a Caucasian, descended from the line of Japeth, while brown men, I presumed like my brothers, descended from the line of Shem, whereas he, a Black, descended from the line of Ham. Later on I looked for evidence of this in the scriptures of Genesis he referenced. I was baffled by his exegesis. Then again, the Rasta was baffled by my claim that I, too, was black.

"Not every kind of Rasta will talk to white people," cautioned Charmaine, the ageless, dimple-cheeked woman who ran my hotel. When I closed my eyes, her Jamaican accent was cousin to Nuala's Irish brogue. "I don't even understand the Rastas and I'm from here," she admitted. "I do admire some of their practices, such as their diet and their drumming, and I do respect the ones who stand by their principles, but there are so many sects who don't. I can't keep all of them straight. Plus, how can they in good conscience adore Haile Selassie? Wasn't he a dictator who did abominable things? I tell you, that man was a wretched tyrant. At least it's clear why people adore Jesus. He was a magician. He multiplied a loaf of bread and made water into wine."

In spite of Charmaine's misgivings about Rastafari, no other faith has held such a sacred place in the mainstream of popular culture. Bob Marley is seen as a legendary pop hero, yet he is also considered by many Rastafarians to be a prophet of the movement. He once said: "I don't have prejudice against myself. My father was a white and my mother was black. Them call me half-caste or whatever. Me don't deh pon nobody's side. Me deh pon God's side, the one who create me and cause me to come from black and white." I loved that quote. It was, like Bob Marley's music, a kind of palliative cure for racial division. I appreciated the man's radical disregard for such categorizations and I wondered how much Rastafari had to do with his liberated attitude.

I thought the faith might offer me some kind of answer, some kind of clue toward finding home. I didn't think of myself as the "tragic mulatto," straight out of central casting. The role was an embarrassing cliché from a dusty, bygone era, but I struggled against it all the same. If Barack Obama could transcend it, why couldn't I? I belonged nowhere. I wasn't well. Was the sickness my own, my country's, or a combination of the two?

6

The Twelve Tribes

IT WAS NINE on a Saturday night in the Twelve Tribes of Israel headquarters at 83 Hope Road. Of the many sects of the Rasta faith, I'd chosen the Twelve Tribes to speak to because Bob Marley was a member. I sat along one edge of a lopsided card table under a mango tree at a reasoning session with three Rastas: Shadrach, Culture, and Reuben Savage. Above our heads whirled a slow lasso of marijuana smoke. It smelled skunky and sweet. About our feet a chicken pecked hopefully in the dirt. The evening's peepers chirped to locate one another in the dark. Off in the distance the foothills and spur ridges of the Blue Mountains rose softly, darkly from Kingston's squalid harbor.

Culture sat to my right. A dark-rum-colored man with heavy eyebrows in the shape of a V and sweatbands on his wrists, he sat slumped with his head of dreadlocks resting on the back of his folding chair. He was compact as a spark plug and suspicious of me.

"How do I'n'I know you not an agent set upon us to spy on our ways? I don't care if you CIA, John Public, informer, or FBI. You don't see no security gate on property here. No guard dog." Culture pulled at the front of his red mesh tank top as though overheated. "I don't care why you come, mon. I'n'I gave you entrance 'cause the works of the Almighty is free."

"Thanks for letting me in," I said. I asked the Rastas if it would be all right to use my notebook to write down their words. They said they didn't mind. As with Tezeta and Dr. Khazriel in Israel, their mistrust of my enterprise was overruled by their mandate to get the story right.

Due in part to its openness to non-black members and to the popularity of its most famous practitioner, Bob Marley, the Twelve Tribes of Israel has twenty-one headquarters (also called organs) spread across the globe in places as nearby as Trinidad and as far-flung as New Zealand. The Twelve Tribes is just one sect of the Rastafari faith, which has several different branches (also called houses or mansions, in reference to John 14:2, "In my Father's house are many mansions").

Of the Rasta mansions, the Twelve Tribes is the largest, most influential, and most widespread. It's also the newest, having been founded in 1968 by a former ice cream vendor named Vernon Carrington, known to his followers as Prophet Gad. Other sizable Rasta mansions include the Bobo Shanti, the Nyabinghi, and the Ethiopian World Federation, though there are many small splinter groups and individual Rastas often belong to more than one.

These groups don't all share the same beliefs and practices. Some require dreadlocks and believe that ganja is a telephone to God, but some don't. Some shun the Bible as a book of lies while others repeatedly read it cover to cover. Some embrace all races while others take a black-supremacist, militantly antiwhite stance. Many, but not all, adhere to a strict, salt-free, vegetarian, Ital (vital) diet. What, then, do the houses of Rastafari have in common? A defiant, anticolonialist mind-set, a spirit of protest, a reverence for former Ethiopian emperor Haile Selassie, and a notion that Africa is the spiritual home to which they are destined to return.

The HQ in Kingston is the chief administrative artery of the Twelve Tribes, a meeting place consisting of two or three acres of adjacent plots of land. Given my understanding of Rastafari as an unorganized religion, a faith with no church, no dogmatic hier-archy, and no official doctrine, I was surprised by how organized the headquarters was. At the entrance of the fenced-in compound hung a large banner of the Lion of Judah. On the concrete southern wall someone had lovingly painted the faces of Rasta mainstays Haile Selassie, Marcus Garvey, and Bob Marley in a triptych. You can't get away from these three faces in Jamaica; their eyes follow you everywhere. From the green heights of Port Antonio in the northeast to the white sands of Treasure Beach in the southwest, you find them watching. They follow you in the bar, the jerk shack, the fruit stand, the post office, the alleyway.

At the center of the property stood a few rows of little conjoined cottages where dues-paying visitors were welcome to stay as long as they had the proper identification—a type of Rasta passport signifying their membership and alternative citizenship to the Twelve Tribes of Israel. On the west side of the compound was an open-air kitchen selling paper plates loaded with mouthwatering fried fish, bammy, and callaloo. Two teenage boys kicked a soccer ball back and forth in the yard. Small groups of people were gathered here and there, eating, laughing, and skanking around to the Melodians' "Rivers of Babylon" (an interpolation of Psalm 137) spilling from a boom box leashed to the mango tree by its electric cord:

By the rivers of Babylon,
Where we sat down,
And there we wept
When we remembered Zion.
Oh, the wicked carried us away in captivity,
Required from us a song,
How can we sing King Alpha's song
Inna strange land?

"Why you come here?" Culture took a long drag from a spliff the width of a carrot and flared his nostrils to let loose the smoke.

"Rastafarianism interests me because—" I began.

"We not a –ism," Culture corrected. "Ism mean schism."

A commonly held Rasta belief is that English is a biased language, an agent of Babylon contrived to "downpress" black people. For example, the personal pronoun "me" is thought of as a subservient term. I'n'I is used instead to reflect the belief that God dwells in all of us. We cannot differentiate ourselves from God or each other. I'n'I expresses equality and inner divinity, sort of like the Sanskrit salutation *namaste*: I honor the divine spark in you that is also in me. I'n'I can mean "us," "him and her," or "you and them." Tainted words like "me" are thus dissected, reshaped, and recast with new meaning. Politics is politricks. Consciousness is I-sciousness. Sound and sense have equal emphasis, so homonyms abound. Wisdom can't be wise if it's dumb so it's wismon, mon. Word-sound is power. Innerstand? That's Dread Talk.

"I came here to learn more about your faith," I revised, self-conscious about my speech. "Most of what I know about Rastafari I learned from Bob Marley."

I have always loved the humanist idea that no one is superior to anyone else; that we all share one blood and one heart, as Marley sang. Bob Marley and the Wailers' last three albums, *Confrontation*, *Uprising*, and *Survival*, are particularly underscored (they might have said "overscored") by Rastafarian ideology, which can sound universal but is Pan-Africanist in spirit. The anthems "Redemption Song" and "Africa Unite" are unambiguous messages for blacks in the African diaspora to "emancipate" themselves from "mental slavery" and return to Africa, their native land.

"I'm interested in your longing for Africa as home and I came here to try to understand why you believe Zion is in Ethiopia," I finished. I didn't say anything about how out of place I'd always felt in the United States, with its racial obsessions. While Culture may not have related to me, I related to his sense of statelessness.

"We not about belief. We about knowledge. Rastafari is a way a life. We a *move*ment, not a *stay*ment," said Culture.

"What do you mean by 'a way of life'?" I asked, perplexed. I liked him for his wit but Culture was beginning to remind me of the Cheshire Cat.

"To innerstand that, you must be mystically incorporated," Culture replied. "Do you overstand what I'n'I mean when I talk about mystical incorporation?"

73

"No, I really don't," I admitted. Either this guy wasn't going to give me a straight answer or my question about Zion didn't have one. I needed a hit of his holy weed to help me dig beneath the boilerplate but I thought it improper to ask. Most Rastas take a line in Revelation to partake of the herb as an injunction to smoke marijuana. For all I knew, it was a sacrament for members only, like taking the Eucharist wafer in Holy Communion.

"One body! One love! What faith you belong to?" Culture asked. What had begun as my interview with him was fast turning into his interview of me.

"I'm a lapsed Catholic," I said, lamely, recalling how bored I felt back home with my family in the pews of St. Paul's Church; the weak handshakes of the other congregants when it came time to say, "Peace be with you"; how much livelier the worship was at First Baptist on the corner of John Street and Paul Robeson Place where we went once a year to celebrate Martin Luther King Day. I responded to the music: "Rock-a My Soul," "Wade in the Water," "Ev'ry Time I Feel the Spirit," and "Down by the Riverside," hymns wet with sorrow and electric with exultation. I felt God in those songs and I felt God when I listened to Bob Marley. We sure as hell didn't sing songs like that at St. Paul's.

I turned from Culture to Reuben, at my right, a thin earnest man whose face was open and kind. His gums were dark, almost purple, and his teeth were straight and white as the keys of a piano. He wore a dove-gray button-down shirt, a red-gold-and-green circular pendant, and, on his left hand, a thick silver ring engraved with the Star of David. These accessories were imbued with meaning. The pendant bore the colors of the Ethiopian flag; the ring signified allegiance to the Jewish tribe. I hoped to steer us back to the topic of Zion, but suddenly that seemed too abstract a voyage. Listening to Bob Marley sing was far more concrete than discussing the inspiration for his songs. "Do you think of Bob Marley as a prophet?" I asked Reuben anyway.

"Him a prophet and a minister. Music was given to every man, especially we the children of Zion. As it is written, we praise Jah in his sanctuary with trumpet, lute, and harp," Reuben said softly, alluding to Psalm 150. His voice was like flannel, almost a whisper. "Jah move through Bredda Bob fi make him preach Jah word."

"What I'n'I preach is a circumcision of the *heart*," Culture interjected, sharp as a piccolo. "A whole lot of people them think a church is a building. But the Bible does tell us where two or three gather in the name of the Lord, He is there."

"Cho, mon. Make I'n'I speak now," said the third Rasta, Shadrach. He had on a loud sweater that could have come out of Heathcliff Huxtable's closet on *The Cosby Show*. I couldn't understand how Shadrach could stand wearing acrylic in the middle of July. Maybe his circulation was poor. He was considerably older than the other two Rastas; old enough to remember waving the Union Jack as a boy in short pants on King Street when the queen rolled by in her topless motorcar, stiffly waving her gloved arm at the crowd on her yearly visit to Jamaica. He was also old enough to remember the first Grounation Day, a Rasta holiday that commemorates April 21, 1966, when Emperor Haile Selassie visited Jamaica and was met at Kingston's Palisadoes Airport, much to his surprise, by a crowd of one hundred thousand drum-banging Rastas who saw him as their god and king.

Shadrach's long white locks were tied back with a shoelace. He had a braided beard, tinted eyeglasses, a slight stutter that didn't affect his grandiloquence, and vitiligo on his fingertips, which were pink as an albino's. He pushed the sweater sleeves above his elbows and took a drag from the "chalice" of weed on the table before him. "A whole lot a people them mix up around religion. Them say fi them thing is right—Rasta, Muslim, Christian, Jew—but in all of them denomination you find good and bad. Belief kill and belief cure. No true?"

"True," I said, recalling my complicated conversations about Zionism in Jerusalem.

Shadrach took another hit. "I'n'I must put away our petty difference. We all come from one root. One blood. The truth is not about black nor white. The truth is not about writs nor rights.

The dawta here no seek indoctrination. Tell us, dawta, what you seeking?"

"Home," I said quietly.

"Then you must read the Bible and find truth for yourself," Reuben interjected. His Star of David ring caught the light as he spoke. "Read the book from beginning to end. Don't just pick and choose. Start at Genesis 1. Finish at Revelation 22."

Dr. Khazriel had instructed me to do the same thing in Israel, more or less—read the Bible as a history book. I was loosely familiar with the Bible from a childhood of classes in the Confraternity of Christian Doctrine and weekly attendance at Catholic mass. Yet I had never met a group of people as versed in the Bible as the Twelve Tribes members. They, and other Rastafarian mansions, preach that the stories of the Old Testament refer to black Africans who descended from the Jewish fathers, Abraham and Jacob. White Christians, they believe, altered this fact to keep Africans in a subordinate position.

"A chapter a day keep the devil away!" piped Culture.

"If you seek, you shall find," said Shadrach, extending a lit match to Reuben, who had just finished rolling his own joint.

"I tell you this, sistren," Reuben said. "The truth will be revealed to you if you seek it but not through the path you come by. The path not by genealogy, geography, or blood but by *spirit*."

I inhaled, knowing he was right as soon as he said it. At its root, my quest wasn't about identity. It was about faith.

"None but ourselves can free our minds." Reuben spoke with his hands. The hand holding the joint described ovals of smoke that disappeared in the air. "The place you looking for is a inborn place. Zion can only reveal itself unto you when you know who you are," he told me. "If you read the book, then you will see you are a true Jew."

A Jew?

Some people consider Rastafari a Third World millennial Jewish sect. Not only are the Rastas philo-Zionists, but their identifying dreadlocks are inspired by the same Nazarite vows that inspire the side locks of the Hasidim. Their Ital food is influenced by the same Old Testament laws as the kosher diet. And the lion, Judaism's symbol for the tribe of Judah, is Rastafari's ubiquitous symbol for Haile Selassie, who claimed to have descended from that tribe. But unlike the Jews, who await the coming of the Messiah, the Rastas believe the Messiah was incarnate in Christ, and reincarnated as the Ethiopian king. They see Haile Selassie as the second coming.

"Do you think of yourselves as Jewish?" I asked.

"We not Jew*ish*," Culture corrected my language yet again. "We Jews."

I wasn't surprised by his assertion. The African Hebrew Israelites had told me the same thing back in the Negev Desert, picking and choosing passages from the Bible to prove it, just as passages can be chosen from the Bible to prove anything. It was an attempt to locate the black diaspora in history, to tie their condition to the experiences of old, and to make a modern faith ancient. For the Rastas, as with all black denominations steeped in the Judeo-Christian tradition, Exodus is the most important book. If there was a Zion for Egypt's slaves in ancient times, there must be a Zion for the children of slaves in the modern era. If Jamaica was the Rastafarians' land of captivity, it followed that they were its Hebrew people.

"Okay," I thought now. "Fair enough." We may as well have been listening to Desmond Dekker's infectious ska hit, "The Israelites," which compares earning a living in Jamaica to slaving for the Pharaoh.

Who *doesn't* want to think of themselves as one of God's chosen people?

"Often we hear a complaint about Judaism: 'How can I find my unique expression in a system that is so bound by rules and structure?'" began Margaret Adams. She was delivering the Shabbat sermon at Shaare Shalom Synagogue on the corner of Duke and Charles Streets in downtown Kingston. I was there because I wanted to learn of the links between Rastafari and Judaism and also because I was as surprised to find Jews in Jamaica as I had been to find blacks in Israel.

Sephardic Jews began sailing to Jamaica in the sixteenth century during the Spanish Inquisition. There are an estimated two hundred Jews left on the island, most of them living in Kingston, though there were only a dozen in the synagogue on the day I visited. The floor was carpeted with sugar-white sand, and the pews shone with dark varnish. The cantor was a large black man with a voice like James Earl Jones. Next to me sat a black boy who didn't appear to have been bar mitzvahed yet because he wasn't wearing tefillin like the other men. In front of me sat a pear-shaped white woman accompanied by her mentally retarded daughter, a girl of about ten in an excellent bow tie sailor minidress. She had psoriasis scabs on her ankles and elbows. The girl was tone-deaf but sang the entire service, including parts she wasn't meant to, at an artlessly high ampage of joy. During the mourning prayer she hopped from her seat and embraced another congregant who had begun to cry.

"We have structured prayer because that gives us the framework to truly express ourselves," Margaret continued. She was a tall, thin white woman who looked like a librarian, and though it shouldn't have surprised me, given how long her ancestors had been in Jamaica, I was thrown by her Jamaican accent. "The words, precisely crafted by prophets, are the vessels that we fill with our own personal thoughts and feelings. Imagine the prayer book as the sheet music, our soul as the symphony, and each of us as the conductor. The music we make is beautiful and unique."

Margaret was speaking about *Parshas Naso*, that week's Torah portion, which the tiny congregation read in both Hebrew and English. I followed along as best I could from the moldy prayer book. In *Parshas Naso*, one by one, on twelve successive days, the prince of each of the Twelve Tribes brought his own set of offerings to celebrate the completion of a tabernacle built in the desert. It was a long chapter, with eighty-nine verses that began to numb the mind because each of the princes brought the exact same offering: a 130-shekel silver bowl, a seventy-shekel silver basin, a ten-shekel gold incense ladle, and a total of twenty-one animals. The Torah repeats the exact same description twelve times.

"This seems to contradict the basic principle that the Torah is never superfluous and does not contain even one extra letter," Margaret continued. "Why doesn't the Torah simply list the offerings brought by the first prince, and then say that the other tribes brought the exact same thing? Because despite bringing the same offerings, each of the princes actually brought his own offering for his own reason.

"God says: 'The offerings of the princes are as beloved to me as the song the Jewish people sang at the Red Sea.' Three million men, women, and children witnessed the miraculous splitting of the sea, as the verse says, 'This is my God and I will glorify Him.'

"But shouldn't the verse say, 'This is *our* collective God?' No. Millions of individuals saw the same thing, but each experienced it differently, as 'my personal God.' Hence, the Midrash draws the comparison: just as the Red Sea was a unique personal experience, so too each of the twelve princes brought a unique personal offering."

If Reuben from the Twelve Tribes was right that I was on a spiritual quest and Margaret was right that each of us has a personal God, then who was mine and how did I experience Him or Her? I'd felt it, a brush with the divine, when Tamar's daughter, Nina, took her first steps at St. Anne's Church in Jerusalem. And I felt it again here, just as briefly, when the girl with Down's syndrome gave me a hug after the service. She mashed her head against my chest with so much ardor I almost choked. Banded in her arms, I felt a flood of warmth. It had been some time since I'd been physically touched like that, without the expectation of something sexual in return. For three seconds I was completely content. Then the little girl let me go. She was no longer an angel. She was just a girl.

"Shalom," said her mother, in a Jamaican accent. "Sarah likes to welcome newcomers." She put her hand on her daughter's rectangular head.

"Shalom," I echoed.

"SHALOM!" shouted Sarah before running off to hug somebody else.

"I admire her lack of self-consciousness," I told her mother.

She nodded. "It's one of many great things about her. Who knows where it comes from? What about you? You look like a sabra. Are you from Israel?"

"No," I said. "I'm from New York." I looked up at the vaulted ceiling of the whitewashed synagogue. I envied how at home Sarah and her mother seemed in this space, how familiar its rituals seemed to them, how at ease they were with each other. "This is a beautiful building," I observed. "How long have you been coming here?"

"My family's been in Jamaica for three hundred and fifty-two years," Sarah's mother smiled. "So I guess you could say I've been coming here for a long time." I sensed this was a line she'd used many times before, that she was as accustomed to justifying her citizenship as I was to evading mine.

Back at the headquarters a few nights later, I discovered Culture, Reuben Savage, and Shadrach smoking ganja in the same positions at the lopsided card table under the mango tree where I'd left them, like pieces in a game of chess that hadn't been touched. That night they explained that their founder, Prophet Gad, linked each calendar month with the personality of one of Jacob's twelve sons. Therefore, Twelve Tribes members organize their beliefs around a symbolically rich alternate horoscope, beginning in April, with Jacob's son, Reuben.

Reuben Savage explained that the twelve tribes also correspond to different bodily functions. He recited these: "Reuben of the eyes, Simeon of the ears, Levi of the breath, Judah of the heart, Issachar of the hands, Zebulun of the belly, Dan of the backbone, Gad of the penis, Asher of the thighs, Napthali of the knees, Joseph of the calves, Benjamin of the feet." An exquisite corpse took shape in my mind, a Frankenstein of parts. Reuben went on, "Together these parts make up the one body of Our Lord and Savior Jesus Christ, who has been revealed to I'n'I in the divine personality of His Imperial Majesty Emperor Haile Selassie I."

"Lord of Lords!" Culture crowed. He set a challenging gaze upon me. "What you know about H.I.M.?"

"His Imperial Majesty?"

"Yeah, mon."

I knew a few things about Haile Selassie. I knew that he was heir to a dynasty that traced its origins to King Solomon and the Queen of Sheba. I knew that when he was crowned emperor of Ethiopia in 1930, many blacks in the Americas interpreted his coronation, which was highly publicized at the time, as a fulfillment of a prophecy of the rise of a black redeemer king. To Rastafarians, the emperor was much more than just a political leader. He was the Messiah, the conquering Lion of Judah, King of Kings and Lord of Lords. And Ethiopia, which they believed Haile Selassie had successfully defended against fascist invasion under Mussolini, was the Rastas' vision of the Promised Land.

On top of that, he was a supremely gifted speaker. He delivered one of the most powerful oratories of the twentieth century, popularized in the lyrics of Bob Marley's "War," at the United Nations General Assembly in 1963:

> That until the philosophy which holds one race superior and another inferior is finally and permanently discredited and abandoned; that until there are no longer first-class and second-class citizens of any nation; that until the color of a man's skin is of no more significance than the color of his eyes; that until the basic human rights are equally guaranteed to all without regard to race; that until that day, the dream of lasting peace and world citizenship and the rule of international morality will remain but a fleeting illusion ...

This much I had memorized easily, as most of it was set to the music.

"How you know all a that?" asked Culture.

"I read about it," I said. I also knew that Haile Selassie was a pint-sized demagogue under whose rule hundreds of thousands of poor Ethiopians starved to death, but I didn't mention that part. As they say in Jamaica, "When you go a donkey house, doh talk 'bout ears." Rasta theology centers on the divinity of Selassie as a living manifestation of Jah (Jahweh), the all-knowing and all-loving God. Denigrating H.I.M. in front of Culture, Reuben, and Shadrach would have been more than uncouth; it would have been sacrilegious, cause for the Rastas to clam up and kick me out.

"I'm here to get a better understanding."

Culture flinched at my word choice. To his ear, it smacked of subservience.

I corrected myself. "A better *overstanding?*"

All three Rastamen nodded, pleased.

I continued. "Do you really think of Haile Selassie as the Messiah?" I knew that Selassie didn't see himself that way, though he didn't do much to dispel the idea.

"Well, we identify Christ in His Majesty flesh," said Reuben, slowly. "We see His Majesty as a Godlike person and we glorify His Majesty continually. We regard Haile Selassie as our savior and our light. As you have read, so it was. His Majesty said our destiny is in our hands but we must never forget our backbone, never allow uniforms of neocolonialism whatever their guise may be, fi take hold a any of us. Ethiopia was never conquered by outside forces. Ethiopia was the only independent country on the continent of Africa. So I'n'I the Rasses see this as a holy place that stretch forth her hand to us."

Although I hadn't read the Bible cover to cover, I knew the scripture Reuben was alluding to. It was a central tenet of the black church: Psalms 68:31.

"We know that is a righteous piece of land," Culture said, "genesis of mankind, beginning of life. A handful of us seek fi go back a Ethiopia."

I wasn't sure if he was talking about a physical journey or a mental exercise. Rastas identify the situation of slavery and cultural denigration as "Babylon," a state of political, cultural, psychological, and spiritual domination that all blacks must resist. More broadly speaking, Babylon is any system that tries to oppress others. A primary goal of their faith is to remind blacks of their heritage so they can escape Babylon for prouder shores. For Africa or for the dream of Africa. For Ethiopia. For the eternal return. For home.

While in Jamaica I'd learned of a small town in Ethiopia, 150 miles south of Addis Ababa. Shashemene.

This is the story of that place, whose name sounds on the tongue like a wish: In 1948 Haile Selassie granted five hundred hectares of fertile farmland to descendants of African slaves in the West wishing to repatriate to the homeland. Though most of that land was nationalized in the 1970s after Haile Selassie was deposed, for the community of Rastafarians who settled and remained in Shashemene it represents the fulfillment of their beliefs—Zion made manifest.

"Are you trying to get to Shashemene?" I asked about the town to which several Rastafarians have emigrated.

"Yes, of course, I'n'I wan go home," Culture said.

Reuben explained, "Slavery might not happen to us, but we feel it in our heart and mind 'cause it happen to our forebears. Rastafari need to come together as one fi leave this here Babylon and repatriate to Africa. I'n'I from Jamaica. I'n'I born here, but Ethiopia is our home."

"What are you doing to try to get back?" I asked.

"Some of us petition the queen fi give us the backing to return," said Shadrach.

"What queen?" I asked, confused.

Shadrach snickered. "What queen you think? Elizabeth II."

"Whore a Babylon," muttered Culture.

I was surprised that the term made me cringe. "But what authority does *she* have?" I frowned. "I thought she stopped being your monarch in '62 when you became independent."

"The queen still head a Jamaica through a commonwealth we part of," Shadrach explained.

"But isn't the British Empire over and done with? She's not really still your queen, is she?"

"The queen is queen," said Shadrach, as definitively as he'd referred to Selassie as the King of Kings.

What bizarre parentage, I thought: the whore of Babylon and the Lion of Judah. It occurred to me I was sitting in the company of orphans. Maybe all quests are, in essence, the search for the parent who isn't there.

Elizabeth the Second, by the Grace of God, Queen of Jamaica and of Her other Realms and Territories, Head of the Commonwealth is the queen's official title in Jamaica. It's mainly a ceremonial one, but she still maintains the reserve power as constitutional monarch to dismiss Jamaica's prime minister or parliament. Even if the Rastas' earnest petitions to return to Africa reached the queen's ears, I doubted that she recognized the movement's authority enough to engage in dialogue. This, too, I kept to myself.

Shadrach's eyes shone. "One love. We just come to preach love, true love," he said. "We on a mission a show the world who the real Christ is. Jah is love. His blessed name we praise against abomination."

I felt comforted by his deep voice, either because he was lulling me in sweet paraphrases of Bob Marley or because by this point I was seriously high by proxy on the Rastas' good herb. The red, green, and gold of their accessories—Culture's wristbands, Reuben's pendant, Shadrach's belt, and the tricolor flags fluttering all around the compound—looked practically edible, like some Pan-African brand of Neapolitan ice cream. The fireflies, which they called peenie-wallies, blinked all around us like a legion of Tinkerbells from Neverland, and it seemed they were relaying the same message as Shadrach in Morse code: *I'n'I. God is Love. One love. One Heart. Let's get together and feel all right.*

I could hear the tune in my head. But this was not the song playing on the radio at that moment. A different song had picked up, more guttural, bass-heavy. I recognized it vaguely from the airwaves back home but had never really paid attention to the words. I was barely aware of the lyrics now, except that they did something to Shadrach. His affect turned on a dime, from relaxed to vexed. The old man pitched forward in his seat like a gambler at a dog fight.

"Fuck batty or suck pussy is abomination to de Lord! Shoot the batty man," he spat in tandem with what turned out to be the controversial and rabidly homophobic song by dancehall DJ Buju Banton. "Batty man" is the patois slang equivalent of "faggot," and the song promotes homosexual slaughter.

"Rasta no preach violence but the song speak truth!" It was as if Shadrach had been stung into a tirade by a wasp. His eyes went zany and full of scorn. He smacked the table and the scrawny chicken beneath it squawked and ran away. I felt, in the fashion of someone who'd been exposed to a far higher grade of kush than she was accustomed, that I'd been left behind in the wrong time signature. I was almost too slow to follow Shadrach's stutter when it sped into a staccato kind of machine-gun fire. "*B-b-boom, bye-b-bye in a batty b-b-bwoy's head. Rudebwoy no promote de nasty man.*'" He tore off the shoelace holding back his hair and shook out his impressive white dreadlocks. They looked vibrantly alive, like Medusa's head of snakes. Shadrach screeched, "Batty man him must dead! It what the good book say."

Reuben and Culture agreed with this doctrine. One love. One heart. Excluding gays, who are an abomination to the Lord and should be killed.

The folding chair beneath me asserted its metal. I realized that my throat and eyes were burning from the smoke. Every part of me was uncomfortable. Even in that Caribbean heat, I felt cold enough to wish for the loan of Shadrach's sweater.

"No disrespect," I interrupted, "but isn't that hypocritical?"

"Remember Sodom and Gomorrah, sistren," Reuben intoned. "In those days with the gays and lesbian, they was beheaded. It's against the Lord's work. We have a go off the Bible. Jamaica as a whole don't like gay and here it against the law for man to lay with man. They catch them doing that, they will shoot them and throw acid in their face and clap them in jail. We Rasta don't promote them gay but neither do we fight them. Homosexuality, that is not a part of God at all."

No Zion for gays and lesbians here then. I was profoundly disappointed, like a child who'd been deceived by her teacher. I felt a toddler's sense of outrage. I wanted to topple the card table, smash the radio, and throw a tantrum. Instead, I pinched my thigh to spur myself to leave. The eyes of Selassie, Garvey, and Marley followed me out the gate.

7

Roots Reggae

O N THE CONCRETE outer wall of the Bob Marley Museum at 56 Hope Road, just a stone's throw from the Twelve Tribes headquarters, someone had spray-painted the words LES-BIANISM & HOMOSEXUALITY = CANCER. DON'T BOW! DON'T SUCK HORMONE!

I wondered exactly what the slang meant. I'd begun noticing that the antigay slogans plastering the walls of Kingston were nearly as ubiquitous as the iconic images of Bob Marley and Haile Selassie. BATTYBOY MUST BURN. SUCK A PUSSY, GET A GUNSHOT. BUN DUNG QUEER! (Burn down queers!) Not that these sentiments don't exist in the States, but I was unused to seeing them so baldly and globally expressed. I was starting to think that the Rastas weren't the most "homeless" group in Jamaica. They were once an outcast community, "black heart" bogeymen, a despised underclass, but that condition was changed for good by Bob Marley, who put Rastafari on the world map. As fringe as the faith once was and as misunderstood as it remains, its trappings have become mainstream.

The Bob Marley Museum was a study in contradiction—simultaneously a Technicolor tourist attraction and a holy ground. There he stood, my saint, with his leonine dreads and electric guitar, at the center of the museum grounds. Just as with the Gandhi statue in New York's Union Square, there were leis of fresh flowers strung around Bob Marley's neck. An image of the I-Three, his backup singers, robed like the Fates, was painted on one side of the statue's base. On another side appeared Haile Selassie with his elaborate crown, and on another, a painting of apple-cheeked Marcus Garvey in his gold-brocaded uniform and white-feathered military hat.

In spite of his stature today, at the time of his death, Marcus Garvey was ridiculed as a failure. During his lifetime, this Harlemite from Jamaica built the largest Pan-African mass movement in history, referred to as "the Zionism of the Black Race." His brainchild, the Universal Negro Improvement Association (UNIA), aimed to unite black people with the vision of a common origin, a common destiny, and a common homeland—Africa. Speaking at a UNIA rally at Madison Square Garden in 1920, he said:

> We shall organize the four hundred million negroes of the word into a vast organization to plant the banner of freedom on the great continent of Africa . . . we say to the white man who now dominates Africa that it is in his interest to clear out of Africa now because we are coming . . . and we mean to retake every square mile of the twelve million square miles of African country that belongs to us by right divine.

They would get there the same way they left, by boat. But this time the journey would be a jubilant turnabout of the Middle Passage. UNIA's visionary Black Star shipping line was meant to capitalize upon a global African economy. In its aims to transport black goods and black people, the Black Star Line was branding Zion as both a geographical and a financial realm. The shipping line collapsed as a result of mismanagement and of sabotage by J. Edgar Hoover's Federal Bureau of Investigation. When that happened, both Garvey and the stock in his company were completely devalued. In the public eye, he morphed from champion to charlatan.

Before people stopped listening, Garvey preached that European colonizers had seized the African continent and scattered its population throughout the Western world under the yoke of slavery. He was considered a prophet by his followers, whose membership in UNIA was said to represent forty countries and number in the millions. He endowed them with noble titles, patriotic rituals, and a paramilitary legion, describing their spiritual freedom in the following words: "No one knows when the hour of Africa's redemption cometh. It is in the wind. It is coming. One day, like a storm, it will be here." A galvanizing orator, he told blacks to "look to Africa for the crowning of a king to know that your redemption is near." Africa would be the Promised Land for its scattered children. When Haile Selassie ascended to the throne a few years later, it seemed a direct fulfillment of this prophecy and the Rastafarian movement was born. Garvey was reclaimed after his death as a national hero in Jamaica. Bob Marley may be the world's most famous Rasta, but Marcus Garvey and Haile Selassie are the pillars on which Rastafari stands.

While our little tour group congregated in front of the shrine, a few Rastas sat getting high in the shade of the mango tree under which Marley is reported to have meditated. They studiously ignored us as we took out our cameras. We were in two separate but overlapping worlds—the sacred and the secular. In addition to myself, the tour group consisted of two giggling Dutch women in their early fifties accompanied by a pair of bleary-eyed "Rent-a-Dreads" (also known as gigolos, Rastitutes, and the Foreign Service) in tight pants.

Here I was, as close to Bob Marley as I'd ever come, but all I could think about was the problematic relationship between the Dutch women and their escorts. That and the inflammatory graffiti outside.

"What does 'don't bow' mean?" I asked Natalie, our guide. Natalie gave me a withering look. She was dressed like a park ranger. She smoothed the skirt of her brown polyester uniform and said, "It mean don't perform oral sex. Any other question before we go ina the house?"

"Yes," said the Dutch woman in the sun visor. She looked as though she'd been dunked in a vat of freckles. "I have a question. Where is the weed?"

"Ha!" laughed the other woman, with the fanny pack. These two girls were having a fine time.

Natalie had just shown us the healing garden next to the house where Marley lived from 1975 until 1981, the year he died. The garden was hemmed in by a dwarf picket fence painted the Pan-African shades of black, red, gold, and green, as was almost everything else on the property. It contained herbs I recognized with names I didn't: fever grass, sinkle bible, jack-in-the-bush, scorn-the-earth, bloodroot, comfrey, and cerasee, but no cannabis.

"Well, we did have a plant a life at one time," sighed Natalie, "but thieves them a-come and thieve it. Follow me this way if you please, up the marble stair."

Bob Marley's house, once home to the Tuff Gong record label he founded, was crammed with memorabilia and kitsch. His stage outfits and soccer shorts hung on a wall near his medals for the Order of Merit and the Merit of Distinction, Jamaica's third- and fourth-highest national honors, respectively. There was a photo of him holding hands with his teenage wife, Rita, on their wedding day, and a picture of his white father, "Captain" Norval Sinclair Marley, looking stern on horseback. The Awards Room displayed Bob Marley and the Wailers' silver, gold, and platinum records, including *Catch a Fire, Burnin', Natty Dread, Rastaman Vibration, Exodus, Babylon by Bus, Kaya, Survival,* and *Uprising. Exodus,* Natalie was proud to tell us, was not only named by *Time* magazine as Album of the Century, but featured a certain hit song voted by the BBC as Anthem of the Millennium.

She quaveringly sang the first line of "One Love, One Heart," then stopped and cupped her ear with her palm. "What the next line, people?"

The Dutch women sang with enviable gusto about getting together but I didn't feel exactly all right.

"Those ladies are shitfaced," I whispered to Natalie. It was ten o'clock in the morning.

"At least they're having fun," she admonished. "Are you?"

I shrugged. Still disappointed by the intolerance of the Twelve Tribes, I couldn't stop sulking.

"Do you know what is crazy?" laughed the Dutch woman with the fanny pack. "I even have this song in my mobile. Listen!" She withdrew her cell phone and turned on her ringtone. Sure enough, it played "One Love." "Isn't that so crazy?" she asked. "I am in love with Bob Marley. Don't be jealous," she teased her Rent-a-Dread.

"Cho, mon," he said. "You think you the only woman in love with Bredda Bob?"

Natalie led us through the Shot Room, where gunmen tried to assassinate the singer during the political turmoil of the 1970s. She made sure we observed the bullet holes in the walls to better comprehend the miracle of his survival. We were also shown a four-foot-by-four-foot stained glass window reproduction of the cover from the posthumous album *Confrontation*, depicting Bob as Saint George on a white steed stabbing a purple dragon in the heart.

"Bob Marley had two nickname," Natalie told us. "They call him the Tuff Gong because of the way his message resound and they also call him Skip, because of the way he a-move when he a-play soccer. He also kept fit by sprinting up and down the set of pitch-pine stairs you see before you, three and four at a time."

"*You* try it!" the Dutch woman in the sun visor urged her escort.

"Nah," said the Rent-a-Dread, crossing his arms.

"Sprint!" she ordered, playfully smacking him on the ass as if he were her private toy.

The Rent-a-Dread obeyed and we all walked up after him.

In the bedroom hung yet another portrait of the soulful-eyed emperor.

"Who is this Haile guy?" asked the other Dutch woman on the back porch, where two tremendous burlap backdrops from Bob Marley's stage shows hung before a hammock and a set of conga drums. One painted backdrop depicted Haile Selassie, and the other, Marcus Garvey. "I can't understand the Rastafarian religion. What is it exactly?"

"For Bob it was a way a life," Natalie said.

"It's a society," elaborated the woman's escort. His shiny black T-shirt had a coat of arms with two rearing sequined lions on it. "The younger generation them just a-grow their hair and smoke ganja, but the true Rasta is a honest, hardworking, self-reliant man. A righteous man. And that is the black God," he said, pointing at Haile Selassie.

"Any other question before you go to the gift shop?" asked Natalie.

"Yes," I said. "What does 'don't suck hormone' mean?"

"Hormone mean homosexual," she rushed. "Any other question 'bout *Robert Nesta Marley*?"

"Do you think Jamaica should pronounce him a national hero?" I asked.

I asked because around the time of the sixtieth anniversary of his birth, which was celebrated with great fanfare in Ethiopia, Bob Marley's estate started lobbying for the reggae icon to be granted national hero status by the Jamaican government. I had already visited National Heroes Park, a former racecourse whose grass was scorched by the sun. The park was desolate except for me, some grazing goats, and a pair of rifle-wielding Jamaica Defence Force sentries dressed in red uniforms like the beefeaters outside the Tower of London.

Marley wasn't memorialized there but I photographed the tombs of some of the others. When Great Britain granted independence to Jamaica, the two nations hadn't been embattled in a liberation war like those fought by Cuba, Haiti, and numerous African countries. Therefore, Jamaica's heroes were people involved in struggles against enslavement and racial or class inequalities during the colonial era—people like Nanny, the eighteenth-century leader of the Windward Maroons; Paul Bogle, leader of the nineteenth-century Morant Bay Rebellion; and Marcus Garvey, the twentieth-century Father of Black Power. But even after emancipation and independence, Jamaica, with its mountain of debt, devalued currency, and dependence on foreign goods, remains in thrall to the First World.

Many people consider Bob Marley a revolutionary for pushing the struggle forward in song, for hymning equal rights and justice in a way that made the world listen.

So did our guide think he deserved hero status? Natalie said, "I really don't think they should think twice about giving Bob the highest honor. Him do so much. The man was a right excellent prophet. Many of the things he sung about has come to pass."

"Nah, mon. Him bigger than Jamaica. Him a world hero," said the Rent-a-Dread in the lion shirt. "It be a insult put him in the park. The park too small for the man."

In the gift shop, handkerchiefs printed with neon-green marijuana leaves were stacked next to copies of Nelson Mandela's *Long Walk to Freedom*. A dizzying array of playing cards, sweatbands, shot glasses, lighters, key chains, alarm clocks, mugs, and tote bags were for sale, all of them stamped, stenciled, or silk-screened with Bob Marley's face. "Africa Unite" spilled from a speaker mounted above a rack of glittery Haile Selassie T-shirts. How was it possible for this song to be both a hymn and easy listening music?

I didn't get it. I picked up a pack of Bob Marley Mellow Mood Incense in one hand and a jar of Let's Dred Locks Maintenance Oil in another. Bob Marley described himself as an outsider and an outcast, but he became the face and voice of Jamaica. He said he was raceless, that he was on nobody's side, but he was a hardcore Pan-Africanist. He symbolized black identity but he said he wasn't black or white, and I suspected that, on top of his lyrics, this is part of what made him so popular. In his complexity, he reminded me of Barack Obama.

"Ease up!" cried one of the Rent-a-Dreads before I could continue that train of thought.

The Dutch woman in the sun visor was spraying him with a bottle of cologne called White Witch. The name refers to the owner of a sugar plantation in Montego Bay, a tiny, ruthless eighteenth-century woman named Annie Palmer who is rumored to have bedded dozens of her male slaves, murdered them, and buried them in unmarked graves. I didn't think of the Dutch woman as a white witch just because she'd purchased some human affection. In a sense, it was refreshing to see that men didn't have a monopoly on sex tourism and that an aging woman could be vibrantly sexual. But I truly disliked her. When her Rent-a-Dread tried to wipe off the sickly sweet scent and she laughed at him, I bristled at their interaction. Was she suggesting that he stank by trying to mask his odor? If so, somebody needed to slap her. Somebody needed to slap me too, for my fun-crushing sanctimony, but I didn't know it at the time.

"Rass bumboclaat," the dread muttered, storming out of the air-conditioned gift shop into the sweltering heat. Sadly, he couldn't even afford to curse at her in language she understood.

By the following week I had a mean sunburn. I was ashamed of this. It marked me further as an outsider, making me feel vulnerable and ridiculous. I seldom wore sunscreen at home and I'd been too relaxed about it here, hoping my skin would tan to a graham cracker color as it had every summer of my childhood. But I'd underestimated the wattage of the Caribbean sun. Now my face and shoulders were painfully pink and I needed to soothe them before the skin began to peel.

"Pepper, plum, tamarind, lime!" called a higgler in Coronation Market where I hunted for aloe vera. I wanted a leaf as fat as a baby alligator's tail like the ones I sometimes bought at Korean groceries in New York. I would break it open and wipe its cool clear jelly on my skin.

The crowded market was a chaos of color, a labyrinthine mini-village of zinc stalls, alleyways, open gutters, and noise, overhung with blue tarps strung together by ropes. They billowed like waves in the sea wind. I walked with my hands upraised to keep the blue plastic from brushing against the top of my head while the market women called after me to look at their wares. *Miss, miss!*

They sold fruits I had never seen with names I had never heard of: guinep, jackfruit, naseberries, star apple, soursop, and ortanique. They sold gungu peas, dasheen, and breadfruit. They sold flaming orange Scotch bonnet peppers, guava, papaya, plantain, and yam.

"Do you have aloe vera?" I asked an old woman with white cornrows shooing flies from her face with a tattered paper fan.

"Well, Miss, we a-call that plant sinkle bible here. You have fi see the obeah ooman for that."

I found the roots woman in a cramped tin shack filled with bunches of dried brown leaves and recycled liter bottles full of brown tinctures. She examined my skin, opened one of the bottles on the shelf, poured a bit of its liquid into the plastic cap, swished it around, tasted it to be sure it contained the right ingredient, and sold me a portion of the medicine.

Outside her shack a shirtless man with a machete tucked in his belt approached me. "Where you from, Miss? Italy?"

"New York," I replied.

"Me want go there. Me want fi see your country just as you're here fi see mine, but me no can get visa."

"I'm sorry," I said.

"Me stuck in this here bloodclot land. What you think of that, Miss?"

His ribs were showing and he was barefoot. "I think it's unfair," I said. What I didn't say was that even if by some miracle this man could get to my country, my country would be interested only in his cheap labor. He looked hungry so I gave him a hundred-dollar bill, thinking at first that I was being generous. I was still slow to understand the currency. One hundred Jamaican dollars is less than a buck fifty American, not enough to catch a subway ride in New York.

"Gimme thousand," the dread demanded. "Fi feed me children." He stretched out his hand. His fingernails were caked with dirt. I felt cornered. I'm reluctant to admit he looked less like a man to me than a goat on hind legs.

"I'm sorry," I repeated.

"Check your pocket, Miss."

"That's a lot of money for me," I said. A thousand dollars sounded just then like an astronomical sum.

"It not the same situation," he argued, and of course he was right.

"I don't have any more," I lied.

"A lie!" he exclaimed.

"Here." I gave him the change from the obeah. I had no idea how much it was. "That's all."

"You see that," he said, jingling the coins with relief and contempt. "*Money.*"

"Yes, I see." Even the interaction between the Dutch women and their Rent-a-Dreads seemed more human than this.

"Thanks, Miss," the man said, touching his fist to his heart and bowing slightly. "Jah bless." He turned on his heel and disappeared into the frenzied spectacle of the market.

I had sensory overload, I was hot, and I felt sick. I poured some of the brown tonic into my hand and wiped it on my white and burning face.

"Jamaica's an abysmal, God-forsaken place," said Rodney Turner, former manager of reggae star Peter Tosh and current musicology professor in the Reggae Studies Unit within the Institute of Caribbean Studies at the University of the West Indies. I guessed he was my father's age, somewhere in his early sixties. He wore a white linen shirt that matched his white beard. His skin was the color of a brown egg. I sat with him at a bar in the Pulse Complex on Trafalgar Road, drinking Red Stripes. Both of us were drunk.

"Rodney," I asked, emboldened enough by the beer to redirect the conversation, "can you enlighten me?" I asked him how a single faith could espouse both the righteous humanism of Bob Marley's "War" and the intolerant vitriol of Buju Banton's "Boom Bye Bye."

"Well, Jamaica is supposedly homophobic," he began.

"*Time* magazine describes Jamaica as the most homophobic place on earth," I pointed out.

"Maybe," he said, "but I tell you this. On the radio today they were talking about gay rights. I never could imagine such a thing happening here. I have said it from the time the Russians put two heads on a dog. I want to live to be a hundred to see what's going to happen to this festering dung heap."

Rodney was not Rastafarian and I was surprised to hear him referring to his nation as a dung heap when he'd devoted himself to promoting its musical culture.

"Do you feel this is Babylon, like the Rastas say?"

"We're still living in a slavocracy," he answered. "We hardly have any full whites left but their descendants still see themselves as masters. Mulattoes like you live up in those hills"—he pointed farther uptown—"and blacks who look like the Africans who came off the slave ships live down there." He pointed downtown.

What Rodney said about Kingston's contrasting neighborhoods was true. You can see the money fading the farther downtown toward the harbor you drive and the pigment fading when you drive uphill in the reverse direction. SPEED KILLS! warn the road signs. DON'T BE IN A HURRY TO ENTER ETERNITY!, as if everyone's life hangs at a rough juncture between heaven and hell. Birds of paradise, hummingbirds, and BMWs above; beggars, open gutters, and grit below. Halfway Tree Road cuts between the social classes like a belt. Smack dab where the belt buckle would be stands an emancipation statue of a gargantuan slave man and woman rising naked from a fountain to gaze up at some unfixed point in the sky.

"We live in two Jamaicas," he continued. "All you have to do is look who's at the top and look who's at the bottom to see these inequalities are about race, not class."

Just about every Jamaican I spoke with was as explicit about the lingering effects of slavery as Rodney Turner. The memory of slavery wasn't alive only in conversation, but in the landscape and in the imagination as well. The entire second floor of the National Gallery exhibited work about slavery. There was a slave gibbet—a head-to-toe iron cage with shackles at the ankles, wrists, and neck. I must have stood mesmerized for ten minutes before that rusty, horrifying device. You could see how the heavy exoskeleton would fit about your waist and ribs and how its nails would prick at the flesh of your throat.

Slavery was, of course, a topic back home, but for the most part only in conversation with other black people, in black museums, in black churches, in black neighborhoods, or in black books, none of which seemed very compelling to most white people, who didn't like to feel blamed. Here, where blacks were the majority, slavery was a majority topic. I found this liberating and distressing at the same time. I was like a wounded animal who'd finally been removed from a trap. I kept licking at the wounded area to help it heal but the action of my tongue was preventing the sore from scabbing over.

"Our music reflects the memory of the plantation," Rodney said, tonguing the same kind of wound. "And you cannot get to know Jamaica without knowing its music. '*Do you remember the days of slavery?*'" he sang. "'*And how they beat us / And how they worked us so hard / And they used us / 'Til they refuse us.*'"

"You have a nice voice," I slurred, finishing another Red Stripe. But really, I was growing tired of the conversation.

"That was Burning Spear. You know this tune? He sang a couple lines from "Concrete Jungle" about feeling bound in captivity, even without being held in chains.

"Bob Marley and the Wailers!" I cheered, as if it was a happy song. "Everyone loves that one."

"True," he said. "But that's some old-school roots reggae. Today the youth loves dancehall."

Dancehall was reggae's rude stepchild. I'd been to a dancehall show on a dark street in Jones Town a few days earlier. I'd arrived at four in the morning and the "sound clash" was still going strong. I placed myself between two towering speaker systems controlled by warring DJs mixing three and four songs together at once. "Respon' to dat!" one of them commanded, sampling Bounty Killer. Teenage boys roved in packs with matching jackets or sunglasses and syncopated dance moves. They raised their arms and pointed their forefingers in the air in a symbol of One Love, and alternately raised their arms with two fingers and a thumb in the air like the barrel and trigger of a gun. The young women wore skimpy stretch-fabric dresses in satiny copper, hot pink, and electric blue. They wore strappy heels and hair extensions and danced by humping the ground, or the speakers, or the boys, for a cameraman who dragged a long extension cord behind him like the tail of a rat. The sound was loud enough to liquefy my organs. I moved to the sidelines, unable to decode the lyrics, feeling distinctly middle-aged. I watched the libidinous spectacle until the sun rose and the market women returned with their wares.

"Pepper, plum, tamarind, lime!"

Although dancehall has had many socially conscious lyricists, like Luciano, Tony Rebel, Garnett Silk, and Anthony B, it was initially seen as a rejection of everything Bob Marley stood for—sexually depraved, morally slack, violent, gun worshipping, and lacking in uplift. And although it has had monumental crossover successes with the likes of Sean Paul, Shabba Ranks, Shaggy, and Beenie Man, dancehall hasn't met the level of international popularity achieved by roots reggae, in part because of homophobic lyrics. With pressure from the gay rights campaign Stop Murder Music and the Human Rights Watch, dancehall DJs Sizzla, Beenie Man, Capleton, and Buju Banton have all signed the Reggae Compassionate Act, a commitment to stop producing music and making public statements that incite hatred toward gay people. The Reggae Compassionate Act opens with a "dedication to the guiding principles of Reggae's enduring foundation ONE LOVE." It goes on to say, "Reggae has been recognized as a healing remedy and an agent of positive social change" and promises that the artists of the Reggae community will "continue this proud and righteous tradition."

I asked Rodney what he thought about the Reggae Compassionate Act.

"Our homophobia is based on the memory of being raped by other men in slavery," Rodney said. "On the voyage over the Middle Passage, slave traders released tension and desire with any man or woman down in the hold by bringing them up to the cabin and having their way. I have no doubt this also existed on the plantations."

I wanted to shake the man. "Do you *really* believe that's how homosexuality came to Jamaica, Rodney?" I asked.

"If it nuh go so, it nearly go so," Rodney reflected, slipping into a vest of patois and out again. "Homosexuality is almost unspeakable here. It's a third Jamaica—an invisible one we really don't talk about." He cleared his throat. "Once as a boy, after a cricket match, I and my rudeboy friends found a lesbian couple performing oral on the beach. We chased and heckled them for three miles. If they'd been two men performing anal we'd have stoned them to death." He looked at his hands resting near my tape recorder on the wet bar and confessed, "I'm not proud of this."

8

"An Island of Zion Is No Zion at All"

Is it true that homosexuality is illegal in Jamaica?" I asked activist author Thomas Glave. He had recently finished opening the Calabash International Literary Festival in Treasure Beach with a reading from *Our Caribbean*, the anthology of gay and lesbian writing that he edited. The Arts section of the last *Sunday Gleaner*, a paper his father once reported for, featured an article about Thomas. "GLAVE" MATTERS, the headline proclaimed.

"No," he clarified. "Homosexuality is not illegal here. That's a popular misconception."

Thomas had bright eyes, long thick dreadlocks, and an impeccable posture that reflected his years performing on and off for Dance Theatre of Harlem. (His teacher was Balanchine's fifth wife.) Born in the Bronx to Jamaican parents, he grew up in both New York and Kingston. Years ago, in a summer course for aspiring black writers at the University of Virginia, he'd been my teacher. He'd used big words, like "hermeneutics," and when I implored him to speak plain English, he said there were many kinds of English. If I wanted to be a writer, he advised, my task was to be fluent in as many Englishes as possible, for the sake of precision. I remember him gazing up from campus toward Jefferson's Monticello nestled in the soft blue-green folds of the Blue Ridge Mountains and telling us the landscape reminded him of Jamaica. I could see now what he meant.

"Being a homosexual isn't against any of the existing laws," he expanded, "but certain behaviors are. 'Acts of gross indecency' and buggery are against the law, and buggery is mainly interpreted as anal sex between two men."

What is the punishment for the "unnatural crime" of buggery? Article 76 of the Offences Against the Person Act states that "whosoever shall be convicted of the abominable crime of buggery committed either with mankind or with any animal shall be liable to be imprisoned and kept to hard labour for a term not exceeding ten years." Thomas explained that this and other articles legally justify the criminalization and persecution of male homosexuals in Jamaica.

In 1998 Thomas cofounded the Jamaica Forum for Lesbians, All-Sexuals and Gays, or J-FLAG. Due to the risk of being bombed or attacked, the address of J-FLAG's Kingston headquarters isn't listed. It is a secret place. I cannot describe where the office is, what its floors look like, what its windows look out upon, if upon anything at all. But I will say that Thomas sounded more like the Bob Marley of my imagination, "the stone that the builders refused," than did the Rastas. In 2002, J-FLAG made a historic presentation to the Jamaican Parliament's Joint Committee on the Charter of Rights. Their case for protecting Jamaicans from discrimination on the grounds of sexual orientation, an initial step toward changing the law, was denied.

"Our activity enraged the population," Thomas told me. "Anti-gay rhetoric has increased since then."

I told him why I'd come here; that I'd wanted a better understanding of the Rastas' sense of dislocation and homelessness in Jamaica; that I was originally drawn by Bob Marley's music to their dream of returning to Africa; that I related to his lyrics because I yearned for a feeling like home; that this was because I was a mulatto from a segregated country; that I was surprised to find I was a white woman in Jamaica; that perhaps my quest was a spiritual one; that I'd received a divine hug from a Jewish girl with Down's syndrome at the Kingston synagogue; and that the more time I spent here, the more I was beginning to think gay people were the most homeless of all.

"Not that it's a contest," I finished.

Thomas laughed.

"It seems like an expression of exile that a gay person from Jamaica must choose either to remain closeted or to emigrate," I said.

"That's right," Thomas agreed. "So many gays and lesbians leave with their talents. I call this phenomenon 'Jamaica's Hidden Brain Drain.' Of course, there is a vibrant gay subculture that exists here, tempered by the need to remain sequestered. I've been to those parties. They're held in upper-middle-class neighborhoods, where there's safety. I don't have it as bad as some because my family's middle-class. There's more room to maneuver. Life can be wonderful in the secret moment but you can't talk about that moment with straight friends. The worst censorship is self-censorship."

"How homeless do *you* feel as a gay Jamaican?"

"Jamaica is for me an ancestral and psychic home," Thomas explained. "Some of my most profound and enduring memories are in Jamaica as a child. But I feel incomplete and not at home here because not all of my person is welcome. I'm vulnerable to murder as a person whom others feel they have a right to kill."

I knew that Thomas had once been threatened by knife-wielding Jamaicans on Emancipation Day. They had held the blade to his neck but stopped short of slashing his throat after reasoning that a man could not be both Rasta and gay. He wanted to write about the attack but hadn't yet found the right words to unpack it.

"Truthfully, the ferocious level of violence and crime in Jamaica frightens me even more than homophobia," he said.

"What do you mean?"

"Homophobia is acted out with so much rage because of our violent social frame. It's symptomatic of larger rage that has to do with poverty and inequality of wealth. We're not the poorest country in the Caribbean. We're not as poor as, say, Haiti, but we have so much visible wealth in Jamaica that it drives poor people mad. Yes, gay men are butchered, burned down in their homes, but these exorcisms and eviscerations happen because of the level of rage. People will just as soon jump out and shoot you for bumping their car as they will chop you with a machete because you're gay. Gays are just scapegoated because of religious fundamentalism, literal readings of the Bible by Pentecostals and Revivalists, and other Far Right religions like the Jehovah's Witnesses."

"And the Rastas?"

"To an extent."

"Do you feel in exile?"

"No, I wouldn't use that word about myself because people use it too easily. Some are really in exile. I can go and come back any time I like because I have a U.S. passport as well. The larger question is really the general level of violence."

I asked Thomas what Zion looked like in his imagination.

"Zion is a myth, Emily," he said.

"I know, I know," I said, feeling childish, "but the search for it interests you, doesn't it?"

"Of course, yes. Zion looks like . . . I would take a total view. Freedom and total respect for everybody across class levels. Not this un-democracy where people can't read and make choices about government. I'm not just speaking of gay people's issues. Democracy would include freedom of access for everyone to fair trials and justice for the poor. Then this island really would be paradise. That's what I envision."

"Sounds lovely," I said.

"Listen, Emily. The search for blessedness has to start within."

"That's what a Rasta told me right before he said to kill the gays."

"So you take the part of what he said that accords with your sense of what is right. You make your own gospel. That's all any of us can do. We have to ask ourselves, 'What am I doing to make Zion possible?' Zion in Jamaica would be one thing but with the rest of the world tearing out each other's throat, an island of Zion is no Zion at all."

"If you look back in history, in every other part of the world, if you look which people are punished more, it's African people," said Ucal Ebanks, a barefoot Rasta in pinstripe pants who served me a breakfast of ackee and saltfish at an outdoor vegetarian Ital restaurant in the southern coastal town of Treasure Beach during my last week in Jamaica.

"I won't disagree with you," I said, "but have you ever considered that the gays might be the niggers of the world?"

"Nah, mon. Listen, here. You want fi take me hope, me glory. You kill a few of us with misery, oppression. You make war with me when there's no need for war. We come through slavery on slaveships fi do your dirty work, fi plant cane and such. Why you can't pay I'n'I for the work it take fi build you empire?"

I was sure Ucal saw me as a white woman and I wasn't going to disagree with him about that either. I would tip him a thousand dollars for his frankness and leave it at that. "I'm guessing you don't think of Jamaica as home?" I asked.

"Nah, mon." He brushed some sand from his rolled-up pant cuffs. "This not my home."

"Why not?" I asked.

"I'n'I a Rastaman. Rasta look forward from western hemisphere to our fatherland," he reasoned. "Jah love Africa more than anywhere else. He dwell there. We want meet him there. Rasta look to the king of Ethiopia. During the slave trade our ancestor and foreparent did come to Jamaica. We lost generation upon generation before Jamaica have independence. Something still missing from us, mon."

"What's missing?"

"Who I'n'I was in our soul before they did capture us. We of Rasta believe Africa is our fatherland and we long for home."

"Will you go back?"

"Yeah, mon. But before we a-repatriate home we must have reparation. Every man, woman, and child here before '62 is supposed to be rich with reaping royalties from what we sow. We appeal to the Queen of England for that reparation, but the whore a Babylon she deny us fi get our belly full when we hungry."

Ucal then disappeared into the kitchen to fetch the rest of my breakfast with the promise, "Soon come," which yawned into such a long interlude that I was able to read that day's *Gleaner* in its entirety. Much of the newspaper's content was about Barack Obama's acceptance of the Democratic Party nomination, and reading it I veered between breathless giddiness and cautious optimism. One article in particular caught my attention with the following paragraph:

> While there are some red-neck Americans and WASPs who bemoan "what America has come to" and see Obama's nomination as "America's shame," their blinding bigotry and crippling prejudice disables them from seeing that Obama's phenomenal rise to prominence in the American political system is a vindication of the long-espoused libertarian and democratic values of America; it is a fulfillment of John Winthrop's City on a Hill metaphor.

I hadn't thought much about that utopian metaphor since tenth-grade American history, when Tamar and I penned answers on the soles of our Converse high-tops to be able to cheat on exams. It was a reminder that just as Exodus was appropriated by slaves, it was also appropriated by white American preachers, politicians, and orators. They found in its story a wealth of metaphors to explain the nation's unfolding history. While black slaves cast themselves as the Old Israel, suffering bondage under a new Pharaoh, white Christians had represented their journey across the Atlantic to America as the exodus of a New Israel. John Winthrop, the leader of the great Puritan expedition to Massachusetts Bay Colony, set the precedent for this line of thought by linking America's destiny with God's will. The concept that the possession of land was contingent upon a moral covenant with God was drawn directly from Exodus.

These are the two stories about the birth of our nation and they're in fierce opposition, though they're both based on the book of Exodus. One says America is Egypt. The other says it's Israel. Amazingly, vexingly, both are right.

"What do you make of Barack Obama?" I asked Ucal when he finally returned with a plate of steaming johnnycakes. I presumed he thought of the candidate as a brown man rather than a black one, like the broom-selling Bobo Dred who explained when I first arrived in Jamaica that we came from different tribes. That Dred was speaking out of the nineteenth-century Christian tradition of dispensationalism. The tradition is still alive today and, to my mind, its obsessive eschatology is off its rockers. But back then, a strategy of black theologians was to critique America's pretensions of being the Promised Land. They saw Western civilization worshipping Anglo-Saxonism instead of Christ. This civilization corrupted Christianity by preaching racism and would destroy itself in the end-times. Dispensationalism appealed to them as a plan of divine human redemption. According to this notion, as certain blacks saw it, the role of Shem, the Semites, was to preserve the word of God. The role of Japeth, the Europeans, was to preach the word of God. Ham, the Africans, were the final dispensation. Their task was to put into practice the word of God.

"We don't know if them in power gonna make Obama rule," Ucal said, "but him a sign a hope fi bring white and black together as one."

My time in Jamaica was nearly through. I had to get back to my job, my life in the United States, and a man I liked who had asked me on a date. I was sad about leaving, as I always am when I travel. As I calculated how much money I would need to fund my next journey, I looked around, drinking a final long sip of detail—the cool lean of the palm trees, the taste of Blue Mountain coffee, the impossible turquoise of the sea. Why couldn't I be this awake to detail at home? These things were as exotic and delicious to me as they were mundane and humdrum to Ucal Ebanks. Maybe because I was his only customer, he sat down with me at the splintering table and picked up the thread of his reasoning to turn Babylon's logic on its bald head.

"Jamaica still run under queen. We no independent. Babylon build this state. Them say, 'I own this state. I own this land.' They master over us with a whip in our mind. They make our people become more ignorant. When Jah sent Moses to Egypt fi tell Pharaoh

'Set my people free,' Pharaoh became soft hearing the people sing. Music was given to every man, especially we the children of Zion. After Pharaoh set them free he got a grudge. 'If I let them go, how can my land flourish?' Rasta have to change the situation. We have to keep a fire burning. Jamaica is *not* our home."

My mind wandered. I watched a couple walking hand in hand down the beach: a young dreadlocked black man in cutoff jeans and an older white woman in a floppy sun hat. They bothered me, in part because they were a couple and I was not. I wanted someone to hold hands with. But I let it go because the sun felt good on the crown of my head and the food was decent.

Ucal sucked his teeth. "Him no true Rasta. Render your heart, not your garments. You don't have fi dread to be a Rasta. You have man with dread like this one not living up. The boy grow him hair for tourists. Good Rastaman hardworking like me, not hanging out on beach. Physically, you no can tell the difference, but when you talk to them you will know. You call them a wolf in sheep clothing. They don't have organized thought. Gigolo, them, mon. Them brain numb up."

He collected my empty plate. Before he bussed it to the kitchen, he said, "I'n'I hear lots of people say Jamaica is a paradise. They come a spend two weeks so they can party in Negril or Montego Bay. Those people them don't stop a consider maybe Jamaica is a hell for me. To me, I think of Jamaica as a sentence. I'n'I just upon a sentence waiting for the day to be free. If I have to die here I wouldn't ever be free. I have to reach back from this land."

As Ucal pointed out, there are two stories about Jamaica. The first says it's a paradise. The second says it's Babylon. Vexingly, amazingly, both these stories were also true. I began to wonder: What would Africa look like compared to Ucal's dream of Africa? Something like the paradise Jamaica seemed to tourists with its lush plant life, soulful music, and carefree people? Something more than that? Something less?

Would it be the Zion he dreamed of from an ocean away?

PART III: ETHIOPIA

AS LONG AS THERE IS BABYLON,
THERE MUST BE ZION

9

Jamaica Town

I BARELY RECOGNIZED THOMAS Glave when he knocked on the door of my room at the Churchill Hotel in Addis Ababa. We were in Ethiopia to attend a conference on black movements. He'd shaved his goatee and cut off his dreadlocks. Instinctively, like hands that want to touch a pregnant belly, I reached for his shorn head. I stopped myself before actually touching him. I didn't mean to be rude.

"Why'd you do it?" I asked.

"It was too heavy," Thomas said.

"And do you feel lighter now?"

"Yes." He smiled. His eyes were the same, big and bright as a child's.

"Your hair looks great, Thomas," I said, "but your feet look absolutely biblical." His feet were sandaled, dusty, cracked, and rough.

It was freeing, Thomas told me, to walk down Churchill Avenue and be mistaken for Ethiopian. He'd left his camera and notebook in his hotel room so that he could enjoy that feeling. It was freeing to be so far away from America and Jamaica, his two homes, in spite of how closely the haphazard little neighborhood in a half-mile ring around our hotel in Addis Ababa resembled Trench Town with its tin-roof shacks. The rusting, buckling rooftops were held in place with heavy stones, connected to each other in a web of laundry lines. Stacks of old tires collected rainwater. Women did the wash in buckets, squatted on stools to comb out their hair, called after their children.

The Churchill Hotel was just three months old. From my window Thomas and I could see all the way to the green Entoto Mountains beneath a drapery of rain clouds. In contrast with the slums below us, plenty of new construction was under way nearby. We counted six buildings of fifteen stories or higher being erected by scaffolding and cranes. Our hotel was even taller than those. The odd tagline on its business card read WHERE LUXURY GLAMOUR, and when the woman behind the front desk handed it to me along with my key, she was proud to report that if I visited again two years from now, the slums would be completely gone, to make way for a railroad that would run along Churchill Avenue, along with parking lots, businesses, and more buildings. This street was a major artery with great potential, she said. Churchill Avenue already had a hospital and a big post office. Its continued development would be good for the city. She sounded like a Harlem realtor arguing for the revitalization of 125th Street.

"But where will the people who live in those houses go?" I asked her.

"They'll be transplanted to more modern homes outside of the city. Don't worry, it will be better for them," she smiled. "Their children will have a better future."

These were the children who trailed Thomas and me in the following days as we walked the streets of the capital. Unlike Thomas, I could not easily be mistaken for Ethiopian. "Madam!" they called as they tried to sell us packs of stale Big Red gum, shine our shoes, beg a few birr. "Sir! Lady! Where are you from?" Unable to pin our origins, they tried catchphrases in several languages. When they thought we were American, they used President Obama's name as a begging trick. They were starting a football team called Obama, for example. Didn't we want to buy Obama a ball? Wouldn't Obama want us to buy them pencils for school? At times, when we found ourselves mobbed after giving a little something, Thomas switched into Jamaican patois or we spoke in broken Spanish. Still, they followed us past the coffin shops displaying velvet-covered caskets, past the gates of the obscenely ornate Sheraton Hotel with Beethoven piping from speakers in its rose garden, past the dated headquarters of the African Union soon to be replaced by a building of Chinese design, beneath the city's ubiquitous blue gum trees, and up the steps of the Derg monument, where we were stopped by a guard tasked with shooing away the children and charging us money to come closer.

"What is this?" I asked, pointing at the red star atop the phallic monument. I wondered what he would say about the Derg, the Marxist military junta that deposed Haile Selassie.

"Socialism," the guard shrugged, and left it at that.

When the conference wrapped up, Thomas and I flew north, along with a few other participants, to Lalibela, where we felt our way through dark tunnels connecting the underground churches, and then to Axum, where we woke before dawn to worship with the locals by circling the town, past the ancient stellae field, with long orange tapers in our hands. It was cold in the highlands. We wrapped ourselves in handwoven white *netala* and marveled at the weaving of the sacred into everyday life, Orthodox and strange to our eyes and ears, even as we could sense the quality of grace. It seemed always to be dusk or dawn, each day a holy day and every hour punctuated by a call to prayer in Ge'ez, a language that would take several lifetimes to comprehend. I didn't want to return home, even though that date I'd been on, after returning from Jamaica, had resolved in a serious relationship with a man I was falling for: Victor. I'd not felt so close to anyone since Tamar. He was a writer who loved horror movies and heavy metal, a formerly overweight man who still saw himself as big long after he'd lost the weight, working hard to be a catch without understanding he already was one. Victor was mixed too, though being five years older, somewhat less mixed up than I. I missed him but I wanted to see more of Ethiopia and Thomas was great company.

"Come with me to Shashemene," I begged Thomas when we'd finished touring the north. I'd extended my trip so I could spend a long weekend there, the third Wednesday through Sunday in July. I wondered how the Rastas had made this country theirs.

But Thomas hadn't come all the way to Africa to see Jamaicans. He could go back to Jamaica for that. "Maybe it's not like Jamaica," I pushed. "Maybe it's something else."

"Still looking for the Promised Land?" he asked.

"Still," I admitted.

I stepped off the bus from the capital at noon, or six o'clock in Ethiopia where the hours are counted from dawn, and hailed a *bajaj* in the driving rain. I was in Shashemene, Promised Land of the Rastafari, 150 miles south of Addis Ababa's ring of hills, scrim of car exhaust, thickets of eucalyptus trees, mass of Orthodox churches, and luxury hotels towering over tin-shack slums. Though Addis Ababa was hardly romantic, Shashemene was far less so.

"It's a truck stop," assessed Fekadu, the man who sat next to me on the long bus ride along the Cairo–Cape Town Highway. He meant it was a grubby place, a nothing place, a place between other places. Shashemene was known, he explained, for its leprosarium, its poverty, and its draught. Fekadu was perplexed that I should want to travel there rather than the hot springs of Wondo Genet or Lake Ziway, famed for its birdlife. "Where is your husband?" he asked, genuinely concerned. "Why does he let you travel alone?"

"I'm not married," I answered, a little too forcefully. Who was this guy to tell me I couldn't ride the dirt-cheap public bus to Zion? I told him I didn't need my boyfriend's permission to travel.

"Then surely he must not know how many thieves from Jamaica are in Shashemene," Fekadu chided. "What are you going there to study? Marijuana? Ha!"

I didn't laugh. I was growing more cheerless the closer we drew to my destination. July in Ethiopia was surprisingly cold and damp and I hadn't packed for such weather. Now my sinuses were swelling, my throat felt sore, and I had a slight cough. Either out of pity, or to make up for being a little judgmental, Fekadu shared his breakfast of *injera* and *wat*. We lurched along the rain-slicked highway past fields of teff, barley, wheat, and corn, and Dutch-owned plantations growing long-stemmed roses for the flower auctions of Europe. Along the way I learned he was a cameraman for Addis TV, on his way to record footage for a story about the adverse effects of the Dutch fertilizers upon the land and the lungs of the Ethiopian workers employed in the greenhouses. The land was sick, Fekadu said, and so were the people.

"Have you ever been assigned to film a story about the Rastas?" I asked him.

"They have a stupid religion," he scoffed. "When your deity is not happy with deification, you've got problems." He said he was unaware of anything positive the Rasta community had done for Shashemene, just as the *bajaj* driver whom I flagged to deliver me into its heart had never heard of my hotel, the Zion Train Lodge.

When I got off the bus I had to disagree with Fekadu. Shashemene was more than a truck stop. It was a bustling market town of one hundred thousand people, a good number of whom were hustling along the crowded main street where donkeys mixed with traffic, impervious to the rain shower. The driver zipped me around in his blue covered motorcycle dodging raindrops, trucks, and market women burdened with loads of firewood. There were restaurants, a post office, and an Internet café. These businesses looked sad through the mask of the rain, but so did everything.

Shashemene was just a trading post at the time of its foundation and it remains a hardscrabble, slapdash place. The town sits at a crossroads in the Rift Valley along an old trade route where spices, coffee, ivory, gold, and slaves were once carried. A railway ran along this route during the Menelik II era, between Addis Ababa and Djibouti on the Red Sea coast. Later, during the Italian occupation from 1935 to 1941, Shashemene was used as a garrison.

"Zion, Zion?" my driver asked the locals with increasing frustration. As we crossed a bridge spanning a dirty river, I began to wonder if there was such a place, if I'd imagined making a reservation, or if the hotel had simply shut down. The good people of Shashemene were shooing us out of town toward another place called Jamaica. That much, I understood. We followed their directions north along the main road for fifteen minutes and finally found the sign for the hotel propped on a pole the height of a gallows. The driver dumped me alongside it with my luggage and a look of condolence. The rain gave no sign of quitting any time soon and, like a putz, I'd left my umbrella next to Fekadu on the bus.

I looked up. Midday, and it felt like twilight. Bats would have fit the scene. The Zion Train Lodge's sign was in three languages—English, Amharic, and Orominya, for we were in Oromia Province. I looked down. The hotel was not beneath it. Nor was this sign in Shashemene proper but on its outskirts next to a gas station in the neighborhood of Melka Udo, which was, inarguably, a truck stop. The hotel was nowhere in sight. It was down a narrow road lined by huts made of wattle and daub the color of dung. In front of the huts half-starved dogs with skin diseases and distended nipples mixed with angel-faced children who were dressed in rags and had snot coming out of their noses. They seemed unbothered by the rain. Not one of them had on shoes.

"*Farengi, farengi!* Money!" they shouted with glee. They wore Coptic crosses on black strings around their necks to protect them from bad spirits and the evil eye, which, it is believed, has the power to transform people into hyenas in the night. Some of them pantomimed at their stomachs to indicate hunger. Some of them, practically babies themselves, balanced babies on their hips. Some of them stopped playing soccer with a battered moldy calabash to approach me.

I knew the rule not to give directly to begging children but to the organizations put in place to serve them. I knew that one such local organization, the Jamaican Rastafarian Development Community (JRDC), sought philanthropic donations for its kindergarten and elementary school, but I didn't know yet whether that school served any of these children, who were *habesha*, native Ethiopians. I swiftly calculated how much money I had on me and how I might divide it among so many.

There was no way. There were fifteen of them, then twenty, then forty. They came pouring out of the huts to gaze at me, the *farengi*, the foreigner, looking forlorn with my wet hair plastered down my back. A group of girls giggled at me and I knew I would have giggled at the sight of me too; that it was not malicious but rather inquisitive laughter. Their laughter was infectious, and laughing with them, I curtsied to make them laugh louder. If I'd known how to juggle, I would have. Whether or not I looked like a white woman didn't matter to me. I forgot, momentarily, that I felt sick. I was playing a goofy game with a bunch of kids, and laughing with them in the rain made me feel good.

Aside from the Antarctic peninsula, this was the most foreign land I'd ever traveled. I wasn't from here and I couldn't pretend to be one of its people any more than I could pretend to be an Adélie penguin. This obvious discovery didn't make me sad like I'd felt, to varying degrees, in Jerusalem and Kingston. How could I feel sad about my feelings of homelessness in the joyful *asmari bets* of Addis Ababa, the ancient stellae fields of Axum, the cryptic churches of Lalibela, or in the presence of these children? They crept closer, daring each other to see who might come nearest, and I loved them for their daring. Finally, the boldest boy grabbed my suitcase and I followed him, thankful that he hadn't run off with my belongings and trusting that he knew the way.

My escort led me down the muddy road for at least a quarter mile, my suitcase bumping against his skinny legs with every step. He had a shaved head and looked to be eleven or twelve, though he might have been fourteen and malnourished. "Are you here for His Majesty's birthday?" the boy asked in halting English. He must have been used to Rasta tourists and settlers who revered Haile Selassie as the living god. "Yes," I said, though more than that I was there to witness how the Rastas reconciled their reverence for the emperor with the dark matter of his dictatorship.

That Friday, the twenty-third of July, Haile Selassie would have turned 118 years old if he had gone on living. The Rastas do not believe he died. Because he is their Messiah, the day of his birth is a high holiday, like Christmas. And they believe that, like Christ, he will come again. They maintain that Haile Selassie disappeared one day in 1975 when the Derg announced his death.

Many Rastas, including Bob Marley's widow, Rita Marley, were present a quarter century later at the ceremony in Addis Ababa where Haile Selassie's bones were reburied in a state funeral. Citing the fact that the coffin was too large for the King of Kings, who barely cleared five feet, the Rastas refused to accept the corpse as his. Officials claimed the remains were contained in a smaller box within the oversized coffin, but the Rastas insist the bones were too long to belong to the emperor, Elect of God, Lord of Lords, Defender of the Faith—man of many titles.

"Bones lie," they said.

I followed the boy past the carcass of a donkey, its stomach being devoured by birds of prey. The donkey's innards were marbled with fat; its intestines were stretched in the beaks of the birds. We turned left at a desolate cornfield and then right onto a narrower, muddier pathway. Somewhere along that track, the mud sucked off one of my shoes. It was then I feared I'd made a mistake in coming to Shashemene.

This was the Promised Land the Rastas dreamed of? The relentless rain combined with the obvious poverty made this Zion appear despairing. Of all the remote places I'd ever been, it reminded me most of Cooter, Missouri. I stopped in Cooter once in my college days on a road trip to New Orleans, drawn off the interstate on a whim by the name on the side of the town's rusty water tower. A black boy, not much older than this one, spotted my Jersey license plates and begged me to bring him along so that he could have a crack at something other than a backbreaking sharecropper's life. Not even Cooter was as dispiriting as this.

Finally we came to a dead end and stopped before a tall wooden gate. Its doors were painted with twin guardian angels wielding swords. Soaking wet and shivering in the cold with mud up to my ankles, I looked at the boy for a clue. "Zion," he announced, smiling brightly, dropping my suitcase in a puddle, scratching a scab on his scalp, and holding out his hand for a tip. I gladly paid him this, along with the granola bar in my sweatshirt pocket and a hug that surely benefited me more than it did him. Then I rang the bell and the gates opened into what I can only describe as Swiss Family Robinson meets the circus.

The Zion Train Lodge was an explosion of color. Everything that could be painted had been painted red, green, and gold—the colors of the Ethiopian flag. Three round Sidamo-style guesthouses with bamboo walls and pointy grass roofs sprouted like mushrooms amid jacarandas, tiki torches, hot-pink hibiscus blossoms, and banana trees strung with hammocks made of hemp. Fat orange marigolds surrounded a vegetable garden bursting with radishes, tomatoes, and squash. To the right a small stable sheltered two donkeys, two goats, a brown horse, and a large round mound of hay. To the left, a guard snored in a watchtower that looked more like a tree house. In the center of the property, a caramel-colored boy with blondish dreadlocks practiced driving a carriage, drawn by a white horse, in circles, jingling the bells of the harness and shouting commands in French like a little lord. The canopy of the carriage was brightly painted with the likeness of Haile Selassie and Empress Menen in their ornate gold crowns and embroidered robes. There they were again decked out in their imperial regalia on the concrete water tank at the back of the property next to a chicken coop. The tank fueled an outdoor shower near a pair of red, green, and gold doghouses painted with the words ROOTS and CULTURE. I assumed these were the names of the two yellow dogs chasing after the boy in the carriage. Compared to the feral canines on the other side of the gate, these two were fat and happy. It occurred to me that, like Noah's ark, there were two of every animal on the property of the Zion Train Lodge. So where was the captain of this ship? I picked my way through the flora to the main house and found the proprietors inside.

Ras Alex, from the island of Guadeloupe, was a rail-thin black man with dreadlocks so long they brushed the floor. Sister Sandrine, his French wife, was a composed woman with porcelain skin, close-set blue eyes, and no eyebrows. In her white head-wrap she reminded me of Vermeer's subject in *Girl with a Pearl Earring*, aged twenty years. Their English was far better than my French. I came to understand from Sister Sandrine that several other guests would be arriving from France that evening for the holiday weekend, and from Ras Alex that the four-year-old hotel was the fulfillment of his dream to reach the Promised Land.

"Get on board the Zion train," he said as he welcomed me, pulling the chord of an imaginary steam whistle and tooting twice.

I told Ras Alex I thought it was a good catchphrase for his business and he nodded in appreciation. There were three other families in Shashemene from the francophone Caribbean, he counted, only fifteen people in total. They were a small minority in the Rasta community, which was itself a small minority, totaling only about two hundred permanent settlers (double that if you count the impermanent ones and triple that if you count the visitors who swooped in for high holidays such as this). He hoped more settlers would repatriate from Guadeloupe, Martinique, and St. Barths in time so that he could be more easily understood. Today he was joyful that his older sister's family would be among the other guests arriving. They lived in Paris but were building a house on the property next to the Zion Train Lodge. So whatever the state of the Rastafarian settlement at large, Ras Alex's homestead was steadily growing.

Shashemene was not only a home for blacks, he assured me, gesturing to his white wife. According to the couple's reasoning, Ethiopia was the cradle of humankind and therefore the shared ancestral home of every race. All of us descended from this Eden. Ras Alex wondered if I had visited the basement of Addis Ababa's National Museum to pay my regards to the hominid Lucy, whose bones were three million years old. I had. And was I a Rasta? I admitted I was not. Then what, he asked me, was I doing in Shashemene?

"I want to know if this is the home you dreamed it would be," I explained. How were the Rastas who settled here accepted by

Ethiopians and to what extent had they integrated into larger society? What impact did an actual, physical repatriation have on Rasta notions of Zion? Was Zion a state of mind? A physical reality? A combination of the two? Could the return to Zion, as one dream fulfilled, become an end in and of itself?

"*Êtes-vous journaliste?*" Ras Alex asked drily.

"No," I hedged. I wasn't a journalist. I didn't know exactly how to describe my role.

Skeptical of my aims, Ras Alex showed me a newspaper clipping from the French *Courrier International* and a short Italian newsreel, both of which ridiculed the Rastas' exodus, portraying them at best as outdated tribalists and at worst as clowns. Who in their right mind, these dispatches questioned, would emigrate to Ethiopia? Ras Alex said I was welcome here, but it would lie on my conscience how I chose to depict them. I understood what he was trying to tell me. He thought of me as a reporter and, as such, an agent of Babylon.

"*Je suis un chercheur qui écrit,*" I attempted. That seemed about right.

I am a seeker who writes.

Later that Wednesday evening, at a crowded dinner table in the main house of the Zion Train Lodge, I sat next to an old gentleman with a pocket square and a face as calm as sculpture. Sister Sandrine served omelets, a salad of garden-fresh lettuce tossed with yellow nasturtium blossoms, and, to soothe my cough, which was growing more phlegmatic by the hour, a slab of honeycomb floating in a hot cup of mint tea. The old man prayed over his plate before lifting his fork. Then he told me that his name was Ras Benedict and he came from the archipelago of Seychelles, near Zanzibar.

"It's a big place but a small country," he sighed. "I left there for France as a young man to find a better job, but I always knew Ethiopia was my true home and the place I should come to retire.

It's a blessing to be here. *Une bénissant*," Ras Benedict said, clasping his gnarled hands and tearing up. His eyes, clouded by cataracts, sought my own. "But what brought *you* here, mademoiselle?"

"I'm searching for Zion," I said, aware that I sounded like Ponce de León on the trail of the fountain of youth or one of those seventeenth-century mapmakers who believed Abyssnia was the land of the rich mythical Christian ruler, Prester John. But the Rasta from Seychelles didn't look at me askance. He simply nodded, as if the reasons for my quest were self-evident, honorable, and true.

A spliff passed around the table while our hosts went over the emperor's birthday itinerary. Friday would begin with a mass at the Nyabinghi Temple, followed by a parade in Shashemene, culminating in a big bash at the Twelve Tribes headquarters. Soon enough, I was high, much more so than I had been at the Twelve Tribes headquarters in Kingston; higher than I'd ever been in my life. After a bout of uncontrolled coughing, my mind began to dilate, then contract. I had the strange sensation of being inside a mismatched set of Russian nesting dolls. Here I was inside France inside Jamaica inside Melka Udo, which was not quite inside Shashemene, inside Oromia Province inside Ethiopia inside the Rift Valley inside the Horn of Africa inside a dream of the fatherland. After a while, the power went out, the candles were lit, and I gave up trying to speak French with the adults and crawled beneath the elegant dining table where Sister Sandrine and Ras Alex's son with the lion-colored dreads, and the children of the other guests, lay on their stomachs scribbling with crayons.

"*Où est votre enfant?*" Where is your child? they asked, unsure how to reconcile my solitude with my age.

"He isn't born yet," I told them. It seemed like the easiest answer so we could move on.

I showed them how to play "exquisite corpse" by folding the drawing paper in thirds and taking separate turns to draw the body's head, trunk, and legs, then unfolding the paper to see how these parts came together to make a whole. "*C'est grotesque!*" the children squealed in delight.

★ ★ ★

That night I listened to the patter of rainfall on banana leaves. My chest cold made it hard to fall asleep beneath the charcoal drawing of Haile Selassie mounted above my bed. *Ras Tafari*. This was his aristocratic name before he was crowned King of Kings, Power of Trinity, Lion of Judah, in 1930. He could not have known at the time that Ras Tafari would become the name of a new religion. There in the dark, the emperor's eyes were unsettling, watchful, liquid, and cold.

The other decorations in my room were a map of Africa and a poster from the Ethiopian Tourism Board that read THIRTEEN MONTHS OF SUNSHINE, which seemed sarcastic given the nonstop rain. The thirteenth month was a nod to the idiosyncratic time system based on the ancient Coptic calendar according to which I was seven years younger and the millennium had only just passed. Strange as that seemed, it was not as strange as the gaze of Haile Selassie, who ruled the country for nearly half a century. One of his physicians, a Frenchman named Sassard, wrote of his eyes: "They bespeak boredom as well as polite indifference, cold irony, or even anger ... The courtiers know these different expressions well and retire suddenly when the monarch's glance becomes indifferent, then hard. On the other hand, especially when he is dealing with Europeans, his eyes know how to be soft, caressing, affable—even sincere."

Credited with shepherding Ethiopia from a feudal to a modern federalist nation-state, Haile Selassie was the nation's first ruler to travel abroad. A talented and charismatic diplomat, he became fashionable in Europe as a forward-thinking African leader. He fought to be admitted to the League of Nations, abolished slavery, and built a centralized administration, a capitalist economy, a postal service, and an airline, as well as hospitals, roads, and schools, turning one of the royal palaces into the nation's first university.

Ironically, Haile Selassie's legacy was rejected by a socialist revolution fomented by student radicals whose education was his gift. In the 1960s they began criticizing his autocratic style of governing, his private hording of wealth, and the pace of his reforms. A popular Amharic proverb at the time ran, "The buildings are growing up and the people are growing down." Later, his international reputation was undone by a BBC film that exposed a famine the emperor shamefully denied. The damning footage spliced scenes of starving highlanders alongside scenes of Haile Selassie hand-feeding meat to his pride of pet Abyssinian lions.

You can visit one of the black-maned lions today in the halls of Addis Ababa University. The taxidermist did a fine-enough stuffing job, but the animal hasn't been well maintained. The lion's coat is mangy, its nose is peeling, and its glass eyes are frozen in alarm at his pitiful end.

When I'd visited the president of the university on the floor beneath the lion, he told me, "The hero worship of Haile Selassie by black Americans was a twisted irony."

Like Haile Selassie's, Professor Ashete's eyes took up half his face, but they were soulful and introspective rather than frightening and inscrutable. He was a dapper but slight, almost frail man, of my father's generation, wearing a black T-shirt beneath a navy-blue pinstripe suit jacket. As a young man, Andreas Ashete was one of the student radicals who supported the revolution. He'd gone to the United States in the 1960s to study philosophy at Williams and Yale. Under the influence of writers like James Baldwin, activists like Angela Davis, and fellow students in the Student Nonviolent Coordinating Committee, he became involved with both the Civil Rights and Black Panther Movements, taking part in protest marches and voter registration programs. The professor cited these American movements as inspiration for the Ethiopian students who brought about the emperor's downfall.

"We were very much influenced by the moral and physical courage of African Americans. We learned a lot from them," he reminisced, elaborating on an interview he'd given in the journal *Callaloo*. He talked with his hands. "Although they had no economic or political power, still they mounted this enormous movement, which shook the country. And it worked. It's not the same country anymore."

"No," I agreed. "But it's still not the country it should be."

"No country is the country it should be," the philosopher said.

I let that thought ping around in my head for a minute.

Professor Ashete's office sat next to the emperor's former throne room and below the royal chamber. I remarked that it was a paradox he should be here, ruling the roost he overturned, especially when the same American movements that inspired him to take down Haile Selassie came out of the very black tradition that put the emperor up on a pedestal in the first place.

The professor reflected on that paradox, working his fingers through his salt-and-pepper hair to massage his scalp as though his head hurt. Countless African Americans looked up to Ethiopia because of its prestige from the war, he said, and from the back-to-Africa movements. Haile Selassie seemed to reflect Pan-Africanism's imperative to resist white supremacy. They saw the emperor's international ambition and concluded that Ethiopia's fate was bound up with the freedom of all African nations. That was their logic, Professor Ashete allowed, but they had little sense of the Ethiopian masses' lives of utter misery or the hand the emperor played in that misery. "So the fact that we were opposed to the emperor and the imperial order to them was jarring—they considered him a hero-king. He regalized them even as he tyrannized us."

In 1974, Haile Selassie was arrested and driven along with his poodle, Lulu, from the Jubilee Palace in a Volkswagen beetle. It's difficult to imagine an exit more befitting his reduced stature. Once he was dethroned, his image was erased from the municipal offices and halls of government he'd built, replaced by that of Mengistu Haile Mariam, the army colonel who headed the junta that overthrew him. The Derg regime destroyed his statues and renamed the streets that bore his name. It was almost as if, like the Rastas uphold, the emperor "disappeared." To this day, it's difficult to find pictures of Haile Selassie in Ethiopia outside of museums. Unless, of course, you are, as I found myself now, in the settlement referred to by native Ethiopians as Jamaica Sefer, Jamaica Town.

10

Sons and Daughters of Ethiopia

SHASHEMENE, LIKE HAILE Selassie, goes by more than one name—the Ethiopians also call it Jamaica Town. Jamaica Town represents the largest organized community of Caribbean-born blacks residing in Africa. Most of the early settlers migrated here from Jamaica, though the land grant that brought them here was originally gifted by Haile Selassie not just to Rastafarians but to all "Black peoples of the West." The gift was a token of the emperor's gratitude for the overwhelming support of blacks throughout the Caribbean and North America who rallied and raised funds to help Ethiopia regain independence after its invasion and subsequent occupation by Italy from 1935 to 1941.

Ethiopia had long been the shining star of the black continent in the eyes of blacks in the diaspora. Their pining for Ethiopia was the main topic of the conference that brought me there. Abyssinia, as it was also known, was for these slave descendants a sacred symbol of antiquity, royalty, freedom, independence, and pride. Its legacy extended past imperial Abyssinia to the Axumite Empire born in the fourth century before Christ, one of the world's four major ancient empires along with Persia, China, and Rome. Ethiopia was lauded as the only African country with its own alphabet, one of the world's first Christian states, and the possible steward of the Ark of the Covenant. But for blacks in the West, it was beloved as an African realm that appeared again and again in the King James Bible, most notably in Psalms 68:31, which appeared to them as a royal forecast: "Princes shall come out of Egypt, Ethiopia shall soon stretch forth her hands unto God."

The enslaved ancestors of African Americans came from West—not East—Africa, but by the eighteenth century those slaves' descendants had adopted "Ethiopia" as a stand-in for the African continent at large, its apogee and crown jewel. Embracing Ethiopia as a nostalgic and spiritual point of origin soothed their feeling of exile and contradicted the notion that they belonged to a savage, inferior, uncivilized race. In the eighteenth century, poet Phyllis Wheatley, one of the first published African American writers, claimed her African heritage by referring to herself as an "Ethiop." In the nineteenth century, Ethiopia was plucked from the jigsaw puzzle of Africa and recast as a mythic realm of black solidarity and power. It grew sharper as an American metaphor, hardening into an arrowhead against the target of slavery. Frederick Douglass invoked Ethiopia in 1852 when he delivered the fiery abolitionist speech, "What to the Slave is the Fourth of July?" He declared: "Africa must rise and put on her yet unwoven garment. Ethiopia shall stretch out her hand unto God," paraphrasing Psalms 68:31, which had by now become, according to my father's estimation, the most popular verse in the history of African American religion.

By the turn of the nineteenth century, Ethiopia was a common icon of romantic race pride for black Americans. Poet Paul Laurence Dunbar earned national attention for his poem "Ode to Ethiopia," which opens, "O Mother Race! To thee I bring / This pledge of faith unwavering," and later asserts, "Thou hast the right to noble pride, / Whose spotless robes were purified / By blood's severe baptism." The poem was published in 1896, the same year the first Italo-Ethiopian War was brought to a bloody close in the landmark Battle of Adwa. Ethiopia's victory was adopted as a cause célèbre by blacks in the new world. Already dear to them as a dreamscape, Ethiopia lodged itself as a concrete example of strong black nationhood after this battle, wherein Haile Selassie's predecessor, Emperor Menelik II, and his wife, Empress Taytu Betul, had led an army of one hundred thousand soldiers to defeat the Italian troops encroaching on Ethiopian territory.

The Italians were latecomers to feast at the African table. They'd successfully colonized neighboring Eritrea and Somalia, but their failed scramble to possess Ethiopia was a humiliating loss, one they would try to recover from in 1935 with a second invasion. But as the first African victory over a European colonial power, the Battle of Adwa was seen by blacks in the diaspora as a proof of dignity and a model of anti-imperial defiance.

In the early twentieth century, back-to-Africa dreams reached their apotheosis in Harlem, itself a black Zion, in the charismatic figure of Jamaican immigrant and businessman Marcus Mosiah Garvey, whose grave I'd visited in Kingston. Ethiopian sovereignty was key to the Universal Negro Improvement Association, the grassroots organization he founded in 1917, which drew hundreds of thousands of members and raised millions of dollars. Using Ethiopia's success as an example of freedom for blacks in the Americas, Garvey conceived his Black Star Line, the shipping business that would, among other transports, repatriate black volunteers to the motherland. Although by this point black nationalism's biggest theater was Harlem and its destination Liberia, the image projected on its dream screen was Ethiopia. Culturally, spiritually, and politically, Ethiopia was looked at as an ancestral homeland much in the same way that Jews in the diaspora looked to Palestine.

Harlemites were captivated by Emperor Haile Selassie's coronation in 1930, which was broadcast on the radio and covered by the black newspaper, the *Amsterdam News*. *Time* magazine featured the emperor on its cover, reporting with surprise that though "the complexion and features of Haile Selassie, or Power of Trinity, resemble those of a Spanish Jew . . . the Negro newsorgans" were hailing the king "as their own."

Paradoxically, Ethiopia was both an imperial and anti-imperial empire. On the one hand, it was the biblical land of the Queen of Sheba whose last monarch, Haile Selassie I, claimed to descend from the Solomonic and Davidic throne. And on the other, until

Mussolini's Fascist occupation, it was the only African nation to remain free from white European domination and colonial rule.

Whether or not the emperor was a "negro," or ultimately a deserving spokesman for black liberation, Italy's second bid for Ethiopia in 1935 was an attack on the dream of the motherland for Africans in the Americas. The Italian invasion and Haile Selassie's subsequent exile in Bath, England, ignited a mass movement, fanning the flames of Pan-African sentiment and stoking international demonstration and support for the emperor and Ethiopia in its war of resistance. Thousands of Harlemites protested the invasion. They boycotted Italian businesses. They danced in the streets when Joe Louis, the Brown Bomber, beat to a pulp the behemoth Italian American boxer Primo Carnera at Yankee Stadium.

ETHIOPIA STRETCHED FORTH A HAND AND ITALY HIT THE CANVAS, reported the *Chicago Defender*, a popular black periodical. Joe Louis's win was seen as a victory for the entire race, just like the Battle of Adwa back in 1896. The Brown Bomber wasn't merely a black prizefighter; he was a personification of the Ethiopian cause. And the Ethiopian cause was more than an Ethiopian concern—it was a Pan-African one.

Marcus Garvey, who embodied the Pan-African sentiment, had planted the seeds for the Rastafari faith by interpreting the emperor's coronation as a fulfillment of Psalms 68:31 (recasting it as a biblical prophecy and prayer that "kings will come out of Africa"). In 1936 Garvey published a poem called "The Smell of Mussolini," which opens:

Let all Italians live and die in shame,
For what their Mad Dog did to our dear home:
Their Mussolini's bloody, savage name
Smells stink from Addis back to sinful Rome.

Haile Selassie wisely chose to harness the love of those blacks in the New World who mythologized Ethiopia as their "dear home." He understood the symbolic value and marketing potential of his empire, though he stopped short of claiming to be a god: "I am emperor not only of Ethiopia but all Africans, even those born under foreign domination," he said. The emperor sent his physician as an emissary to the United States to organize their widespread efforts under the official banner of the Ethiopian World Federation, Inc. (EWF), which still operates in altered form today.

The EWF's original headquarters were established on Seventh Avenue in Harlem in 1937, not far from the campus of City College, where I taught. Its media organ, the *Voice of Ethiopia*, urged the "millions of the sons and daughters of Ethiopia, scattered throughout the world, to join hands with Ethiopians to save Ethiopia from the wolves of Europe." Scores of African Americans tried to enlist to defend Ethiopia. Without the backing of the U.S. government, which was not officially in support of Ethiopia, they lacked the resources to get there.

Two pilots, however, did make the journey. They were John Robinson, the Brown Condor, of Chicago, a graduate of Alabama's Tuskegee Institute, and Hubert Fauntleroy Julian, the Black Eagle, of Harlem, originally from Trinidad, famed for his aerial circus trick of parachuting out of a plane while playing the saxophone in a red devil suit. The Brown Condor and the Black Eagle joined the Ethiopian Air Corps, made up at the time of a paltry three noncombat planes with which to outmaneuver an Italian air force made up of 140 aircraft.

Rabbi Arnold Josiah Ford, an early Garveyite from Barbados, made it to Ethiopia via Harlem as well. A musician who'd trained in the Royal British Navy, Rabbi Ford directed UNIA's choir and became famous for composing its national anthem. The song was sung at the start of every meeting and its lyrics hymned Ethiopia as a realm of black pride. In fact, "Ethiopian" was such an evocative, powerful, and historically rich term for Rabbi Ford that he argued it should replace "negro" as a referent to people of African descent.

I learned about Arnold Ford's journey to Ethiopia from his son, Abiyi Ford, who was born there in 1935, the same year his father died. The younger Ford looked a lot like a photograph I'd seen of the elder along with his congregation on 135th Street in Harlem, minus the white turban. He had the same kind, droopy, bloodhound eyes behind wire-frame glasses perched above a wide nose and sensuous mouth set in a large, heavy face. Abiyi Ford also resembled my step-grandfather, Royal Woods, a former priest who raised my father. My father, too, was born in the year his father died. Royal Woods was the man who'd baptized him, before he quit the cloth. I practically had to bite my tongue to keep from calling Mr. Ford "Papa Woods." They had the same walnut-shaped head, the same air of dignity.

"My father was not a Rasta but a man of the Jewish faith," Mr. Ford told me between music sets in the bar of Addis Ababa's Jupiter Hotel. The hotel was new and its bar was very cosmopolitan. We could have been at an upscale joint in Harlem, or black Atlanta. Abiyi Ford was a filmmaker, rather than a professional musician like his father, but the night we spoke he was playing percussion—conga drums, maracas, and a cowbell—with a jazz band, to unwind. "My father read a lot. He studied Hebrew and the Talmud, Arabic and the Quran. He tried to convince Garvey that the organization needed a spiritual direction and thought Judaism was the most appropriate avocation. It was easy to see the Zionist affinity—as Israel has suffered, so have we. He challenged the Western narrative of history and came to feel Christianity was a sham since segregation undermined its basic tenets."

Again, I thought of Royal Woods, who was also troubled by the un-Christian-like behavior of people who claimed to be Christians. His encounters with racism in the Catholic Church brought him to quit the priesthood, though he never left the faith entirely. Papa Woods was a strong presence in my childhood, a quiet, contemplative old man whose use of a walker and, later, a wheelchair dictated that the priest at our church had to bring the communion host to the pew where Royal sat. My Papa wasn't so disabled that he couldn't make the short march to the altar. As a child I thought him lazy and proud. But now I wonder if he took some satisfaction in making the priest wait on him. If so, it was a small act compared to the bold strides made by Rabbi Arnold Ford.

As a key progenitor of black Judaism, Arnold Ford lectured regularly in Harlem. In 1924 he founded the Beth B'nai Abraham Synagogue for Aethiopian (Orthodox) Jews in America, where he served as rabbi for six years. His was an ideology that became known as Ethiopianism, an array of thought that flowered into a bouquet of Jewish sects founded primarily by West Indian immigrants in the early decades of the twentieth century. They called themselves Abyssinians, Falashas, Rechabites, Essenes, Judaites, Canaanites, Hebrews, and Israelites. Most of these black Jews followed Marcus Garvey's back-to-Africa platform. In fact, UNIA's African Legion handbook of rules and regulations, which Rabbi Ford coauthored, was modeled after the Zionist Jewish Legion. Ford thought of the white Zionist back-to-Palestine movement and his own back-to-Ethiopia movement as parallel endeavors. He knew about the community of forty thousand black Jews already in Ethiopia who called themselves Beta Israel and were commonly known as Falashas, the people I'd learned about in Israel. Haile Selassie's coronation as black king of the last independent African country confirmed Rabbi Ford's sense that providence had a hand in the timing of his colony.

"But my father hit a brick wall," Abiyi Ford said.

"How so?" I asked, dreading his answer.

"The Christian component won out. UNIA had a strong arm that favored the Liberian model anchored in Christianity: going forth as missionaries to save the African 'heathen.' My father wound up leaving the movement because of that schism. He never wanted to go to Liberia. He practiced and preached a Pan-African model of Zionism. Beta Israel was his proof that Judaism wasn't compartmentalized to whites. His desire was to know Beta Israel in Ethiopia."

"But he made it here," I said. "He broke through the brick wall."

"To a degree," said Mr. Ford. He took a slow sip of whiskey and grew quiet.

Not long after Rabbi Ford showed up to find his Promised Land, Haile Selassie went into exile. I factored this into the equation of his journey. "The 1930s must have been a shaky time to arrive in Ethiopia," I guessed.

"Worse than shaky! It was anarchy. My father's aim was to move his entire congregation from Harlem to Addis Ababa and to build a school there with my mother, but the impending Italian invasion threw that out of whack. The law of order broke. My mother asked my father what to do. He said they'd come not to come to Ethiopia but to *become Ethiopian*. They decided to accept their lot and perish or survive with Ethiopia. My father died under duress but my mother was tough, liberated mentally beyond forces to destroy her. She wound up directing a school after all, just as she determined."

"And you?" I asked. "Did you 'become Ethiopian'?"

Mr. Ford laughed. "I like to say I'm African by heritage, Barbadian by parentage, Ethiopian by birth, British by registration, American by naturalization, and Ethiopian by repatriation. I disbelieve in geographic location. Here is my proof: you cannot tell me where Africa ends."

I smiled. He'd inherited the question of belonging from his father, as I had, but his hybrid identity was all his own. Mr. Ford paused to look at me in earnest. Then he asked me what *I* was.

"I've never liked that question." I squirmed.

He corrected me. "You mean you've never understood how to answer it satisfactorily."

"Okay, you got me."

"You've figured out by now that it's a trick question, haven't you?"

"I'm beginning to see that."

"Oh, I doubt very much you're beginning."

"Excuse me?"

"You made it this far, so you're somewhere in the *middle*." Abiyi Ford stabbed the bar with his index finger, causing my glass of honey wine to tremble. "My prognosis is that you're still looking for home."

"Good grief, is it that obvious?" I asked.

"It is to someone who understands the quest. Personally, I gave up on that long ago. I'm an old man, older than my father ever was. By my age, you'd better understand who you are in the world. Zion is a frame of mind only achieved, in my opinion, when you transcend false compartmentalization of humanity into black/white, Muslim/Jew. How do these terms prevail? They're nonsense. I believe God thinks we're crazy. I'll leave you with a metaphor," he said, before rejoining the band.

"Please," I said. I steadied myself for a bit of a dressing-down, something like what Papa Woods might have offered if he were still alive. "Pride goeth before a fall," I remember him telling me one cold day when I refused to wear my winter cap because of the frizziness it caused my hair. "Don't act the fool, fuzzhead," he'd cautioned me then. "Just count your sweet blessings you own a goddanged hat."

Mr. Ford surprised me by taking my hand before telling me what he thought I needed to hear now. "Two men with swords were trying to kill each other over a piece of land. Observing them, an old man begged them to pause while he checked with the ground. He bent over, put his ear to the dirt, and revealed what the earth had instructed: 'Tell them to sheathe their swords. They need not worry. They both belong to me.'"

"Thank you." I blinked, returning Mr. Ford's tenderness with a kiss on the cheek. I understood the old man's warning. It pointed to the unseemliness of my yearnings. The larger picture was not about this or that territory any more than it was about how my hair looked. I needed to check with the ground and listen.

While the band concluded its set, I wondered what Rabbi Arnold Ford would make of the son he'd never known, just as I wondered what my grandfather by blood, the man Papa Woods replaced, would make of my father and me. Albert Raboteau was killed by a white man in 1943, shortly before my father was born. He'd never left the feudal caste system of the American South, yet here I was, free as a sparrow, on the other side of the planet, thinking, as I so often did, of him.

Rabbi Ford's dream was to reinvent himself, first as Jewish, then as Ethiopian, light-years from the racial constraints of his time and place, but Abiyi Ford, beating the congas there in the lounge of the Jupiter Hotel, was something beyond Ethiopian, beyond the scope of his father's dream. Arnold Ford died before he could even discover for himself what being Ethiopian meant, but he must have considered himself one of the lucky ones for making the crossing. I, too, was one of the lucky ones.

Back in the 1930s, other blacks who wanted to support Ethiopia but lacked the means to get there were content to become members of the Ethiopian World Federation. Members were required to pay a joining fee of one U.S. dollar and dues of ten cents per week to help the Ethiopian cause. All members received a copy of the EWF's constitution and bylaws. Its preamble reads: "We, the Black Peoples of the World, in order to effect Unity, Solidarity, Liberty, Freedom and Self-determination, to secure Justice and maintain the Integrity of Ethiopia, which is our divine heritage, do hereby establish and ordain this Constitution." For African Americans at that time, the EWF's constitution was an inspiring alternative to the U.S. Constitution, with its rights that didn't extend to them. To be a member of the Ethiopian World Federation was to be a citizen of a nobler country, inheritor of a black kingdom. The first article of the EWF's constitution had as its objective "to promote love and good-will among Ethiopians at home and abroad and thereby to maintain the integrity and sovereignty of Ethiopia . . . that we may not only save ourselves from annihilation, but carve for ourselves a place in the Sun."

But what was it really to be Ethiopian? What was that "place in the Sun" supposed to look like? For that matter, what did "Ethiopia shall soon stretch forth her hands unto God" even mean? Unlike the book of Exodus, which made Israel a direct analogue for freedom,

Psalms 68:31 was harder for black Americans to interpret. Many of them assumed that Ethiopia stretched forth her hands unto God in order to be redeemed, as in evangelized. As Abiyi Ford explained, some aimed to emigrate to Africa as missionaries. Others, such as the writers of the EWF's constitution, posed Ethiopia as a physical place worth protecting, but also a spiritually ordained destination, a place that conferred "culture" and "manhood," a land to ideologically strive for.

Rabbi Arnold Ford's "Universal Ethiopian National Anthem" was declared the "anthem of the Negro Race" in UNIA's Declaration of Rights. It opens with an exultant commitment to defend that place:

Ethiopia, thou land of our fathers
Thou land where the gods loved to be
As storm cloud at night suddenly gathers
Our armies come rushing to thee!

The impassioned chorus continues, "Advance, advance to victory / Let Africa be free." The song suggests that to be Ethiopian, and African by extension, could or should ensure the ideal condition of freedom. But was it an empty metaphor?

Rabbi Ford, who at first supported himself in Addis Ababa by performing at local hotels, as his son was now doing for kicks, eventually managed to procure eight hundred acres of land on which to found his Ethiopian Zion. About one hundred individuals made it from Harlem to join him in developing it, alarming the U.S. State Department, which closely monitored their efforts. But by 1935, the black Jewish colony was at the brink of collapse. The drudge and gruel of farmwork sent most of them packing, and the imminent war with Italy scattered the rest.

It is said that when his utopia failed, Rabbi Ford died of exhaustion and heartbreak. He never fully arrived in the nation his anthem glorified. A few months after his death, an article by Robert Gale Woolbert ran in *Foreign Affairs*, offering a distinctly different perspective on Ethiopia as it prepared to engage in war. "Feudal Ethiopia and Her Army" opens with a series of contemptuous questions: "By what right does Ethiopia call herself an empire? How can a country where illiteracy is almost universal, where there are virtually no roads, and whose annual foreign trade is worth less than $25,000,000—how can such a land presume to arrogate to itself the most exalted of all titles?"

Still, when Ethiopia put out her palm, blacks in the Americas gave what they could. They continued to believe what Rabbi Ford had preached—that Ethiopia was their legacy. Their endowments, added to British aid, helped pave the path for liberation and the emperor's return in 1941. Seven years later, he bestowed five hundred hectares of fertile farmland in Shashemene should they wish to repatriate to their figurative homeland. Whether or not the land was the emperor's to bestow is another question altogether.

More than anything else, Haile Selassie's approach to land management led to his downfall. Combined with the holdings of the Ethiopian Orthodox Church, the amount of land controlled by the royal family totaled more than 90 percent of Ethiopia. As committed as he was to modernizing Ethiopia, the emperor was slow to end feudalism. Churchill Avenue, the main street of the capital, where Thomas Glave and I had stayed in the Churchill Hotel, may have boasted a national theater, a post office, and a hospital, but in the countryside the peasants continued to toil as they had in medieval times, often unable to coax enough from the land to survive. And this is still true today, as Thomas and I witnessed in the north, where farmers yoked oxen to plow the soil while their children milked Obama's name to beg.

"Land to the tiller!" chanted the 1960s student activists, Andreas Ashete among them, in their growing protest of the emperor's regime. Their revolts about the land fostered the communist revolution that ejected and finally erased the emperor. Under the red terror of the Derg, it was considered counterrevolutionary even to mention Haile Selassie's name.

These days, under the government of Meles Zenawi, who led the rebel army that ousted the Derg in 1991, the emperor's legacy has returned to public discussion. President Zenawi doesn't paint a rosy picture of his majesty's reign. When the emperor's bones were discovered beneath a latrine on the grounds of Menelik Palace, where the Derg imprisoned him, Zenawi's government distanced itself from the funeral proceedings by issuing a harsh statement: not only was Haile Selassie a tyrant whose brutal rule bred hardship and misery in its oppression of Ethiopian peasants, but the private fortune he'd disgracefully plundered from the people had been hoarded in foreign banks and the government was still working to retrieve it.

Even Marcus Garvey, who'd started out praising the emperor as a paragon of righteous black power, came in the end to criticize the emperor. Personally snubbed by Haile Selassie in England and distressed by the endless pageant of Selassie's diplomatic travels, which seemed intended more to ingratiate himself with white nations than to invigorate his own people, Garvey decided the man was not so holy after all. But it was far too late to retract his praise. Deep in the dirt of his native Jamaica, the seeds of the faith Garvey planted had taken root.

When I woke up on Thursday morning beneath the emperor's portrait, my cough had worsened and so had the weather. It was the day before the emperor's birthday and I had time to kill. Sister Sandrine lent me a red, green, and gold umbrella. I made my way to the Jamaica Rastafarian Development Community School, where I discovered Marcus Garvey's famous slogan painted above a fading mural of the African continent on the side of the light-pink lower school building: AFRICA FOR THE AFRICANS; FOR THOSE AT HOME AND THOSE ABROAD.

The Jamaica Rastafarian Development Community School was shut down for the summer, its playground swings whining in the wind over mud puddles from the rain that refused to yield. The JRDC has nongovernment organization status, like Habitat for Humanity or the Peace Corps, which enables it to do developmental work in the community. But unlike other NGO workers who temporarily come to Ethiopia from abroad, the members of JRDC mean to stay here for good. Subsidized by Rasta donors around the world, the school is the largest project of the JRDC. It serves some 450 students, the children of Shashemene's foreign-born Rastas and local Ethiopian *habeshas* alike. The curriculum includes a unit on the U.S. Civil War, Abraham Lincoln, and the Buffalo Soldiers. In the wider community, the school has a mixed reputation. On the one hand, it offers smaller class sizes and prized English-language instruction by native English speakers. On the other, its staff and faculty are criticized for their constant squabbles and internal strife. The campus was empty on the morning of my visit except for its bowlegged groundskeeper, Brother Leroy Anthony Bryan, whom I found guarding the gate in the rain.

Brother Bryan was in his mid-fifties and had the relaxed, loose-limbed, glassy-eyed manner of a man who'd been smoking weed all morning long. He wore scuffed black work boots, baggy jeans with ripped knees, an oversized houndstooth blazer with the sleeves coming unstitched at the shoulders, and his dreadlocks stuffed into a red, green, and gold knit cap. Knotted at his collarbone was a purple satin kerchief, a chic flourish to top off the vagabond look. He seemed not to notice, or to care, that he was wet.

Brother Bryan moved from Jamaica to Ethiopia at the age of twenty-two, "aspiring to pioneer." He arrived in 1976, just two years after the Derg that overthrew Haile Selassie came to power. He was eager to talk with me about the struggles of those early days, freely sharing the reasons for his coming and the ways he and the other Rastas had been less than welcomed into the Ethiopian fold.

"In my early days as a youth and a British subject I was a Boy Scout," he began. Now the purple kerchief around his neck made more sense. He straightened his posture, held up three fingers, and swore the old oath. "'For God, for country, for your personal self.' There's nothing wrong with being a Scout but I had to ask, a which country I swear allegiance? My eldest brother was already a Rasta of the Twelve Tribes. He taught that Ethiopia was our country. Here in Ethiopia, I a kind of a Man Scout," he said, proudly tightening the knot of the kerchief beneath his encrusted beard.

As we spoke, Brother Bryan guided me about the school grounds and what remained of Haile Selassie's original land grant. Today, the Rasta settlement spreads out on two sides of a major road the Rastas call King's Highway. At an intersection we passed by a bronze statue of Shashe, the market woman for whom the town of Shashemene is said to be named. A nod to local Oromo culture, she was recently commissioned by local authorities after they rejected the Rastas' petition to erect a statue of His Imperial Majesty in the exact same spot. Oromia State has control over the land under the present government, and the Rastas cannot build permanent structures without the permission of the local administration.

"They hijacked our plan," Brother Bryan complained. "We a-come here to build." He purveyed the dismal landscape, gesturing at enterprises that didn't exist, framing ghost buildings with his hands. "We had a plan to put a shopping plaza, offices, banks here, supermarket and thing there, but they reject it."

"Why do you think they did that?" I asked.

"They don't realize we Rastas are Africans," he said angrily. After a considered moment he added, "Ethiopians are a suspicious people because them have a lot of war and such." I thought the same could be said of Jamaicans. In three hundred years of British rule, Jamaica staged more rebellions, revolts, and insurrections than any other island colony.

We passed by the dead and rotting donkey on our walk. The corpse may or may not have been crawling with maggots. I don't know because I averted my eyes, glad that my congestion muffled the stench. We strolled past a string of businesses. They were small rather than the large-scale operations in the blueprint Brother Bryan described. Many of them were closed: the defunct Black Lion Museum, Dinky's Delicious Ice Cream, One Love Grocery,

Cryer's Tam Shop, the Lion of Judah Nix Nax Boutique. Only the Banana Leaf Gallery seemed to be open. I told myself I would visit it later.

While the land grant starts at the Melka Udo River and stops before the road leading south to the Bale Mountains, it was difficult to understand the contours of the Rasta settlement. This was in part because the Derg reclaimed the gifted territory as part of its broad and sweeping land reforms right before Brother Bryan arrived. It must have been a bewildering homecoming. His godhead had just been toppled, his Zion nationalized. *Land to the tiller!* Along with all rural lands that had previously been controlled by the royal family and the Ethiopian Orthodox Church, the Derg pronounced this land the collective property of Ethiopians. In spite of his fervent desire, Brother Bryan was not received then as an Ethiopian, and thirty years later he is still not. He has migrant status here, rather than citizenship.

"We just want our rights as Ethiopians who have come back after hundreds of years of captivity in Babylon," he argued. "His Imperial Majesty invite us back home. Selassie-I never forsake us." Under the Derg it could not have been savvy to say so unguardedly what Brother Bryan said next: "Jah Rastafari! He is the living God, the light and the flesh."

Somehow we had whiled away most of Thursday morning. By now it was nearly noon, the day before the emperor's birthday. I asked about another Rasta holiday, one I knew they celebrated with great fanfare in Jamaica. When Haile Selassie visited Jamaica on April 21, 1966, Leroy Anthony Bryan was just twelve years old. That day, which Rastas later came to celebrate as Grounation Day, was overcast and rainy, but the skies cleared when the emperor's plane touched ground. This was interpreted as a miracle by the joyful thousands gathered at the airport to receive him. Rita Marley, newly married to Bob and part of that enormous crowd, claims to have witnessed stigmata on the palm of the emperor's waving hand and was instantly converted to the Rasta faith. Similarly inspired by the emperor's sensational visit, Leroy followed his older brother in joining the Rasta mansion of the Twelve Tribes. There he was instructed to read the requisite "chapter a day."

"What we do, we read Bible like a part of us every day to expound ourselves. Start from Genesis to Revelation," Brother Bryan told me. "Jerusalem came down from heaven. If we forget Jerusalem let our tongue cleave to the roof of our mouth and make us dumb. It keep us reverent to think back and give us guidance for future action."

Selassie's visit to Jamaica made Ethiopia seem suddenly tangible, less abstract and more viable as a Zion that might be reached. But why were Grounation Day and the emperor's birthday bigger causes for celebration than Independence Day? I asked Brother Bryan why Rastas like himself hadn't come to consider Jamaica a potential Zion when the British relinquished possession of the colony, granting its political independence in 1962. Didn't that day bring on a newfound sense of freedom? Why hadn't he chosen to plant his own vine and fig tree on Jamaican ground?

"Jamaica is a island but it not I land," he said. "We were just shipwrecked on that forsaken shore."

"What was going on there when you left?" I asked. In 1976, then Jamaican prime minister Michael Manley had an idealistic vision of social democracy. Brother Bryan described how that vision was undermined.

"Well, Uncle Sam did have a plot to hobble us so we couldn't be as another Cuba. Jamaica don't manufacture guns but there was a gunman on every corner. Political gangsters with weapons from CIA. So much violence raining down you can't leave your house without catch a bullet. It was a kind of hellfire. The West removed the shackles and the chains but they still keep us bound up by economic slavery. But Rasta don't study politricks. I'n'I swear allegiance a Ethiopia. We just want come home."

Home. Again, the word made me feel blue, but this time with a kind of nostalgia for my mother. It was because of my cold and slight fever. I missed her care, how she nursed me on the days I stayed home sick from school, how she brushed and braided my hair so it wouldn't snarl up from a fevered head-sweat, how she laid wet washrags on the back of my neck to bring down my temperature. I didn't tell Brother Bryan that I felt sick. He struck me as the sort of man who talked more than he listened.

"Our leader, Prophet Gad, he said that we must go back home," Brother Bryan went on. "He aim to move the people to the land, even if not in a mass, we will still do like the Israelites of the Bible. We consider ourselves Israelites. We will go back to the original place. It's a opening for us, not only to repatriate but fi recognize it's the cradle of mankind, some part of the Garden of Eden. During those times, you get a number. When you reach that number, you were called to go. If you said no, they call the next number. The first Rasta of the Twelve Tribes called to go was Brother Cryer. My number was sixty-eight. So then my dream came to pass."

"Okay, but you didn't click the heels of your ruby slippers to get here," I said. "How did you finance the journey?"

"I'm not saying I was living up in Washington Gardens," Brother Bryan admitted, referring to an upscale Kingston neighborhood. "I was living down in Trench Town, what you call the slum. We depend on dues accumulated by Twelve Tribes. Bob Marley also lend us support."

Marley was reportedly underwhelmed when he visited Shashemene in 1978 at the height of the Derg regime. At that time a handful of his repatriated countrymen were struggling for permits to set up businesses and often quarreling over sectarian differences between the four houses of Rastafari. Of the four, only the Ethiopian World Federation, an iteration of the original EWF, had NGO status. Its ambiguous agenda as a nongovernment organization was to build Shashemene as a model city based on the cosmology and principles of Rastafari. But unlike King Lalibela, who modeled the city of underground churches I'd visited in the north on Jerusalem, the EWF didn't have the money, the power, or the slaves to pull it off. The community at large had heart but lacked cohesion, collaboration, and a sense of purpose. Observing this,

Bob Marley championed a psychological exodus—*free yourselves from mental slavery*—rather than physically repatriating himself. I couldn't see at first glance that much had changed since the time of the reggae legend's visit. Shashemene's Jamaica Town was a far cry from Jerusalem.

At some point during Brother Bryan's story, my mind began to drift on a raft of mounting frustration. Being under the weather made me crankier than usual, but it wasn't only that. Finding home seemed less and less likely the more I talked to people who, frankly, didn't have their act together. How many times had people tried to find Zion in Africa and failed? I was almost afraid to look back in black history and count.

Shashemene is not the first settlement of repatriated Africans by a long shot. Two of its historical predecessors are in West Africa and were created by white philanthropists to resettle freed black slaves and their descendants for vexing reasons. The Province of Freedom was the name British antislavery campaigner Granville Sharp gave to a settlement at the mouth of the Sierra Leone River. Sharp was a leader of the Committee for the Relief of the Black Poor, which sponsored the 1787 mission. A convoy of three English ships carried several hundred indigent blacks, only some of whom had volunteered to make the journey. The others were forced. Many of them died along the way. Part Promised Land, part penal colony, the settlement the survivors established in Sierra Leone was first called Granville Town, later renamed Freetown.

The land Granville Town sat upon was negotiated with a local Temne chief whose successor ransacked the settlement and enslaved some of the Black Poor. In an ironic twist, some of the Black Poor became slave traders themselves. In under three years, the Province of Freedom had miserably failed, annihilated by disease and abandonment. Granville Sharp remained undaunted. Back in

England he found new investors to back a second wave of settlers. But the next movement wasn't dispatched from London. Instead, the directors of the Sierra Leone Company recruited about three thousand distressed African Americans from Nova Scotia—the so-called Black Loyalists.

These freedmen had been slaves who earned their liberty by escaping to British lines and fighting on their side during the American Revolution. They served as musicians, laborers, cooks, and soldiers in the unsuccessful British war effort and were re-settled—evacuated really—to Canada, along with White Loyalists, when defeat became inevitable. In Nova Scotia they discovered wretched conditions—a rocky, untamed wilderness, brutal winters, poor harvests, and famine. They were free, but the farmland, legal rights, and opportunities the British promised in exchange for their military service were painfully out of reach. Most of them toiled on the rocky soil as sharecroppers, often without pay. Some of them were sold back into permanent slavery in the West Indies. Some of them starved to death. By the 1790s, the Black Loyalists had given up hope of a good life in Nova Scotia, so when the op-portunity to sail to a new homeland in Africa presented itself, they chose, overwhelmingly, to go. Those who survived the overcrowded crossing to the new Promised Land in Sierra Leone found more hardship when they arrived. The settlement wasn't surveyed, their leaders died, their resentments grew. But they endured. In 1792 the Nova Scotian settlers founded Sierra Leone's capital, Freetown.

The most prominent black supporter of the Freetown colony was political activist, abolitionist, whaling ship captain, philan-thropist, and Quaker evangelist Paul Cuffee, born free on Cutty-hunk Island, Massachusetts, in 1759 to a former slave father and a Wampanoag Indian mother. During the American Revolution, he petitioned the government of Massachusetts to end taxation with-out representation for African Americans and Native Americans. The petition failed but later influenced state legislation grant-ing all male citizens the right to vote. Cuffee, a ship owner who amassed a fleet of vessels that sailed the ports of Massachusetts, remained disillusioned about the rights of African Americans in spite of the fact that by 1811, he was both the richest black man in the United States and the country's largest employer of free blacks. Finding white hostility and hatred intolerable, Cuffee turned his gaze to Africa, believing an independent black nation led by returnees would prove a more promising home. Why not give purchase to that promise? He had the boats, the bankroll, and the brawn. He began recruiting free blacks to make the voyage back to the land of their forefathers.

Cuffee first set sail for Freetown in 1811 with an all-black crew, inspired by the fledgling colony in Sierra Leone. Once there, Cuffee helped establish a commercial trading enterprise he hoped would finance a mass emigration of free blacks who would help build the nation. In 1815, he brought thirty-eight black American pioneers along with axes, hoes, a wagon, and parts to make a saw mill. Before he could bring more people and provisions, however, his efforts were eclipsed by an organization with better funding powering its sails: the American Society for Colonizing the Free People of Color of the United States. Black emigration was its cause as well, but for very different reasons.

The pet project of the society, which was founded in 1816 by Washington's white elite and eventually renamed the American Colonization Society (ACS), was the colony of Liberia, "land of the free," south of Freetown. Some members were abolitionists who believed slavery was immoral and should end, some were slave owners who believed slavery should stay but that free blacks posed a threat and should leave, some were clergy who believed in the evangelizing potential of emancipated slaves to spread Christianity on the "Dark Continent." Whatever their motivations for sending blacks back to Africa, all ACS members shared the belief that free blacks could never succeed at assimilating into white America. As Southern congressman Henry Clay put it, because of "unconquerable prejudice resulting from their color, they never could amalgamate with the free whites of this country." He and the other founders, including Andrew Jackson, James Monroe, and Francis

Scott Key (newly renowned for composing "The Star-Spangled Banner"), drew up a constitution and fundraised, as the Ethiopian World Federation would do over a century later, by selling membership for the price of one U.S. dollar. They also lobbied Congress for support, and received it.

Over the course of its lifetime, ACS transported roughly twelve thousand blacks to Liberia. Of that number, two-thirds were slaves manumitted and conveyed to Africa by their masters for the "meritorious service" of ratting out the insurrectionary plots of other slaves. The first colonists sent by ACS in 1820 settled on Sherbro Island and swiftly grew sick with yellow fever. Within three months, a quarter of the settlers were dead. More settlers were dispatched from Virginia, but the community divided along lines of religious denomination and skin tone, setting the tone for Liberia's future. The settlers' motto? "The love of liberty brought us here." It wasn't meant to be ironic.

Though many nineteenth-century returnees fared poorly there, some of them did very well. Edward Wilmot Blyden, a so-called Pan-African founding father, was one of the success stories. Born in 1832 in the Virgin Islands, he was inspired by the local Jewish community and emigrated to Liberia in 1851, just a few years after the experiment had become an independent nation. There, he finished his education. He became a newspaper editor, a minister, a high school principal, a professor of classics at the new University of Liberia, and eventually Liberia's secretary of state. In the 1860s he toured the United States and Britain in a campaign to convince blacks to help regenerate Africa by emigrating.

Martin Delany was another black emigrationist, Pan-Africanist, scholar, and politician, but unlike Blyden, he ultimately dismissed Liberia as "a poor miserable mockery," a puppet of the whites who founded it. He argued instead for black Americans to emigrate to Central America. Dismissed from Harvard Medical School when his race was discovered, Delany was convinced the white ruling class would never permit blacks to get ahead. He argued there was no future for blacks in America in his book *The Condition, Elevation,*

Emigration, and Destiny of the Colored People of the United States, Politi-
cally Considered, published in 1852. By 1858, a good sixty years before
Marcus Garvey's Black Star Line materialized, Delany had schemes
for a black shipping industry. It would counteract the sickening pill
of the Middle Passage by carrying blacks to Africa, and the goods
they produced in Africa would be carried back to America in return. But when the Civil War broke out, Delany reconsidered the
place of blacks in America, a nation whose economy and society
they'd helped build. With renewed hope for his country, he joined
the Union Army and rose to rank as the U.S. armed services' first
black major. After the war he played an important role in South
Carolina politics. But ultimately, Delany's hopes were dashed by
the seemingly incurable white racism of the Reconstruction era,
by all those black men swinging from the trees. In his final days,
he looked again to Africa.

   I might have visited Sierra Leone or Liberia to see for myself what
kind of Promised Lands they had become. I might have spoken with
the descendants of the pioneering generations, the Creoles and the
Americo-Liberians. I might even have visited the stately old crumbling houses in Monrovia built to resemble the plantation homes of
the American South. But I knew a little too much about the civil
wars that had devastated both countries to take either of them seriously as successful utopias. And besides, I wished to speak directly
with the pioneers themselves, the ones who'd actually made the
exodus, the ones for whom the old place was still a living memory
and Africa, an aspiration. People like the Rastas of Shashemene.

11

I Land

"WHEN YOUR NUMBER was called, were you scared to come here?" I asked Brother Bryan over callaloo, rice, and peas at Joan and Family One Love Restaurant, where we sat down for lunch later that Thursday. A poster with the famous image of Malcolm X in suit, tie, and rifle was tacked to a community bulletin board on the wall behind him. LIBERATE OUR MINDS BY ANY MEANS NECESSARY, it read. It made me feel we were in a time capsule.

"Our history they taught in Jamaica was Africa is a land of cannibals," Brother Bryan remembered. "It was a head-decay-shun, not a education. I myself was not scared. If cannibals will eat us, why not go and see them? The Bible was our guidance. Remember that Moses sent spies to Zion—Joshua went fi scout if there was giants. I didn't find no giants. No animal eating us here."

"Still, it must have been hard to leave," I pressed, imagining the people he'd left behind and the people I'd be leaving behind if I were to move away from home. Not just my parents, my brothers and their wives and kids, my students and my friends, but Victor. It was growing harder to imagine leaving. I asked Brother Bryan if he'd been back to Jamaica at all.

"I not been back, sistren. You have to blank out everything, as I did. You have to have a lion heart. Some of us would have fi make that sacrifice. We came not blindly. Blanking out on family and friends you know is rough. I left six brothers, three sisters in Jamaica. And my grandmother that raise us, who was mother and

150

father both. Her name was Princess Stone. Most of what I miss is family and friend. Not saying I miss the bloodclaat place."

"And what did you find when you arrived?" I asked, knowing a little bit about the speed, control, and ruthlessness with which the Derg executed its land reforms, butchering suspected counter-revolutionaries in its wake.

"It was like Gaza. The Derg had vibes like Hitler's. Socialism is a mean force, man! Ten eating in one plate and if you talk bad about the food they a-come fi crush you with iron hands or a-shoot you in the head. During those days, the socialist government did nationalize the land. Most of our land they took back at harvesting time. Peasant Association confiscate our only tractor, reaped all the crops and plowed the land right up to our doorsteps to shove us out. Some of us were accused of drug trafficking and clapped into prison."

Persecution by the Derg police forced some settlers to flee— primarily to Ghana, an alternate Zion, where cultural assimilation was simpler for various reasons. English was spoken in Ghana, and securing business permits was easier. Non-Rasta settlers who'd been the first on the land were the first to go. Many Rastas followed suit, realizing this environment was inhospitable to their beliefs. Here was another paradox. The settlers who journeyed here in the spirit of anticolonialism were treated like colonizers upon their arrival. Still, several stalwart Rasta families remained, choosing to petition the Derg government on EWF stationary as a reminder of the land grant's historical integrity.

"They gave back land to eighteen of us. Five hundred hectares squeezed down to eleven. We still were not able to build. But tell them I say H.I.M. gave us this land for our organization fi we black people of the world could live here after our foreparents spilled their blood for the honor and glory of Ethiopia!"

I couldn't quite understand how the Rastas managed to justify the value of the emperor's land grant to the Derg, let alone the godliness of the emperor. Thinking about the local Oromia farmers who'd staged a new measure of independence by staking claim to the land during that socialist era, I asked Brother Bryan if he ever felt he was on the wrong side of history. But as a self-described "sufferer," this was not a leap he could take.

"Nah, mon. They persecute us. During those early days everything we built they stop us. Charge us money fi do this and do that. The thing Ethiopian pay twenty birr, foreign have fi pay one hundred. We pay foreign. They look upon us like tourists."

Clearly, it bothered Brother Bryan to be received as a temporary resident when he considered the land to be his. Migrant Rastas like Brother Bryan have to pay almost 400 birr to renew their residence, and getting business permits remains a challenge. Without business permits or citizenship, the Rastas' status here is precarious. I sympathized with Brother Bryan's plight, to a degree. It took grit to liberate his mind by journeying to Shashemene, but the means he deemed necessary to stay seemed to disregard the position of the people already here.

"They unseated your king and seized your land. Why didn't you go home if you weren't wanted?" I pushed.

"Rastaman don't give up. *This* was our home. We had intention to build," he reiterated.

I thought then of another well-known Malcolm X quotation: "Land is the basis of all independence." Both the Rastas and the Derg would have agreed with the statement, but not for the same reasons. Brother Bryan would never quit this territory. To do so would be giving up his freedom.

We left the restaurant and walked to Brother Bryan's home, still in the process of being built after all these years. He was proud to show me the house but explained that until he received more financing from Twelve Tribes members through Western Union, construction was stalled. A large satellite dish lay rusting in the front yard. Inside, the unpainted concrete walls had arched doorways and high ceilings. Compared to the wattle and daub dwellings of the *habesha* people around the Zion Train Lodge, Brother Bryan's house was a palace.

We encountered his Ethiopian wife in the unfinished sunken kitchen. The woman looked drained and depressed as she fed the youngest of their eight children from a breast that hung like a sock. Watching her nurse, I felt a twinge in my stomach, like a kitten kneading a blanket. It was not a sweet feeling, but an insistent tugging: Why are men allowed to dream while women's lives are a drudge-filled grind?

Back home, Victor was already hinting at marriage. The prospect seemed joyful and dreadful in equal measure. I was afraid that if I became a wife and then a mother, I'd have to quit traveling, in practice if not in theory. My father had been the traveler in my parents' marriage. He was gone a lot. He'd been to East Africa himself when I was little. He returned from that trip without the beard he'd always worn and I didn't recognize his face. The souvenir he brought my mother from Nairobi was a beautiful blue-and-white patterned dress cut to be one-size-fits-all. When he left her, years later, she bought back her maiden name for three hundred dollars.

My mother claimed to be satisfied by the adventure of raising my brothers and me. For the most part, I didn't doubt her claim. She'd performed a thankless job with contentment and grace. But every time she returned from the supermarket with a minivan full of groceries, she remained seated in the driveway for ten minutes of privacy. I remember her well in that posture, staring through the windshield into the middle distance beyond the bushes of forsythia. When I asked her, as an adult, what she'd been thinking in those moments, she confessed to a fantasy. It was to put the car in reverse and drive away from our house for good.

Lest I judge her, which I did not, my mother argued that this was nothing compared to her own mother's fantasy. Having popped out six kids in about as many years in true Irish-Catholic style, my grandmother's hidden wish was to go to prison, where she might have enjoyed reading a book from cover to cover, free from guilt. My grandmother had dreamt of becoming a writer. She craved solitude and had none of it. She'd spent a happy summer at the

Bread Loaf Writers' Conference before marrying my grandfather, a raging alcoholic. I have a photograph hanging above my desk of my grandmother there, in the company of Robert Frost. The year is 1941. She is twenty-three years old. In this picture, her smile is astonishing. Every time I look at it, I want to cry.

Brother Bryan brought my attention to a framed picture of his own. It was of his oldest daughter. He told me with great pride that she was studying law in the capital.

"What's her name?" I brightened, admiring the photograph.

"Ethiopia," Brother Bryan said.

I hoped Ethiopia would both work and dream. As for her mother's name, I never learned it. She didn't speak much English and barely nodded when I greeted her. Brother Bryan wasn't the only Rasta pioneer to take an Ethiopian wife when he settled in Shashemene; several of them had done so. I was curious about these women, whether the choice to marry outsiders had ostracized or isolated them from their communities, and what was behind that choice. I was curious too about their children who belonged to the so-called First Born-Free Generation. Were they accepted as more Ethiopian than their fathers?

"Do you speak Amharic?" I asked Brother Bryan, hoping he could translate for me.

"Amharic is good cultural thing. Language of Christ," he said, confusing it for Aramaic. "But a hard language to learn. Three hundred characters on the tongue. My mouth cannot shape it. And it take too long to speak such a simple thing! Instead of 'dawn' they say, 'when the earth and the sky separate.'"

"But that's a beautiful expression," I marveled, "and much more precise."

"No, mon. It take too long to say it."

In Amharic they have not one but *seven* kinds of silence, Brother Bryan complained, and the custom of greetings was endless. "First you have fi ask, 'Hello? How are you?' Then, 'Are you well?' And again, 'Are you fine?' when they just told you already they were fine. Then you have fi ask about their children, their parents, and their livestock. The things you say and do in the West in a half hour it will take you three days in Ethiopia, even a week."

"So how do you talk to your wife?" I asked.

"Sign language can work," he joked, leading me back outside. "I'm a walking sign man. Jack of all trades, master of most. When I came to Ethiopia I just started to try to pioneer myself. I started to do sofa, car seats, and like that. I did macramé, wood work, road authority, light company, garage work. I made afro combs from bicycle spokes and wood, coffee tables. It didn't bring much money but I survive. Some Rastamen come and cannot make it. If they cannot make it, they go to England, America, Ghana. But for me I still don't regret it. It's possible to make a better Ethiopia, better Africa. I'm glad I come fi be part of it."

"*Are* you a part of it?" I asked.

Even though the Derg's communist government didn't last, the federalist government that replaced it maintained communal ownership of the land, which means the bulk of Haile Selassie's land grant is still out of the Rastas' hands. The settlement was only ever a small fraction of Shashemene, even before the Derg took power. Its population peaked at two thousand. And now, as Ras Alex had informed me the day before, its population was merely one-tenth of that.

"The journey still not complete. A tree takes three and a half years to grow a fruit. Or, put another way, what you call a chicken in a shell suit?" he asked me.

"An egg?" I guessed.

"That's it!" he laughed. "Little by little, the chicken will grow a feather and it will fly."

Later I learned the Amharic expression he misquoted: "Little by little, the egg will grow feet and walk." At the time I just thought Brother Bryan didn't make much sense. After all, chickens can't fly much more than pigs. But maybe, indirectly, this was Brother Bryan's point.

He insisted on walking me back to the hotel for fear that the locals might steal my camera. His concern that I might be robbed by a *habesha* reminded me of Fekadu's concern that I might be robbed by a Jamaican. There was something adversarial in the way each side saw the other. They weren't natural blood brothers or kin.

Halfway back to the Zion Train Lodge, we ran into Takatl, the guard asleep in the watchtower when I first arrived at the hotel. He overtook us in the horse-drawn carriage carrying provisions from town. I introduced him to Brother Bryan who immediately asked, "You appreciate your job, young man?"

"Yes," Takatl answered. He wore the bored, sullen look of a teenager, an attempt at a mustache, and a T-shirt with a picture of Al Pacino as Tony Montana in *Scarface*. MONEY IS POWER, it said.

"You must appreciate the Rastamen here for hiring you. You must respect your *injera*," Brother Bryan advised. Then he gave me a photocopied invitation to the emperor's birthday celebration, which would take place the next night, and we parted ways.

"That man is always drunk," Takatl grumbled as I stepped into the carriage. He seemed miffed at Brother Bryan for pulling status. "You don't smell it?"

"I smelled something," I said. "I figured it was sweat."

"That man is not work hard enough to make sweat," Takatl corrected me. "The smell is *harake*. Do you know what is that? Hard alcohol. You take a little and it goes to the head." He glanced at the invitation in my hands, decorated with two doves holding olive branches in their beaks, and asked me to read it to him.

"The Twelve Tribes of Israel invites all to celebrate the one hundred and eighteenth anniversary of the birthday of H.I.M. Emperor Haile Selassie I. Devotion with theme songs. Stage show featuring Righteous Rebels, Heartical Spence, Sydney Salmon and Rodney Judah. Gates open Friday at 8:00 PM. Entrance: adults twenty birr," I read.

The invitation proclaimed to be inclusive, but the entrance fee was much more than the average local could afford, including Takatl, who in all his eighteen years had never once celebrated the emperor's birthday and did not revere him at all. Nevertheless, he asked me if I would please bring him to the party as my guest on Friday night. I said I would be happy to, while secretly wondering why he wanted to go. What did he really think about these Rastas who treated his land like it was their God-given right? I couldn't ask him this directly. They were his employers and he had to respect his *injera*. Instead, I asked Takatl what he thought made Leroy Bryan take to drink.

"He is missing Jamaica," Takatl assessed. We approached the dead donkey on the side of the road back to the Zion Train Lodge. This time I confronted it directly. The animal's entrails were now mostly eaten, its bloody rib cage swarming with black flies. I felt seriously unwell. I kept myself from vomiting and steadied myself by gripping the side of the carriage. The carriage wheels were slow to turn in the mud. The cloud cover was oppressive and promised more rain. We turned right at the desolate cornfield and arrived once again at Zion's gates. Takatl added, "*Harake* is like medicine for him because he don't find no Eden here."

After a nap I forced myself to go out again. I hadn't come all the way to Shashemene to succumb to a cold. I clomped through the mud to the Banana Leaf Art Gallery. The place was run by Ras Hailu Tefari, nicknamed the Banana Man for the artworks he fashioned from the multicolored bark of banana trees. He came from the island of St. Vincent, where he was called Bandy Payne. Eden was the name of the Banana Man's middle daughter. It was her sixth birthday, the day before the emperor's—an auspicious proximity, according to her father. Her party took place inside the compound of the Banana Leaf Gallery, which doubled as her father's house. The Banana Man invited me to join the celebration. Life in St. Vincent was "like playing football with no goal to kick to," he told me, whereas Ethiopia was "the capital of Africa, head of astronomy, philosophy, art, and religion" and could be considered "the gateway to Zion." He'd lived in Ethiopia for sixteen years. The man was irrepressibly enthusiastic.

MY GALLERY IS SMALL BUT MY HEART HAS ENOUGH ROOM FOR MY CUSTOMERS, read the welcome sign hanging on the door. The turquoise house possessed a garden that did look like a little slice of paradise with its canopy of tamarind, soursop, mango, and banana trees. The rain had softened to a drizzle. Little Eden flitted between tree trunks like a tropical bird in her red birthday dress, chasing two white corgis named Judgment and Jury, with several other children. She had dimpled cheeks and a round face.

So did Eden's mother, Abeba, who wore a lime-green dress. She was stout and looked happier than Brother Bryan's wife, happy, at least, to be celebrating her little girl's birthday among *habesha* neighbors and friends. Abeba asked me to join them on the veranda, strewn with grass and Abyssinian roses. A traditional coffee ceremony was under way, presided over by an old woman with blue-black crosses tattooed along her jawline and a fine white *netala* shawl across her shoulders. I wished my sinuses were clear enough that I could smell the brew—some of Ethiopia's finest coffee beans grow in Oromia Province. The old woman sat on a stool, roasting coffee beans over coals scented with frankincense. After grinding the beans with a mortar and pestle, she steeped the grounds in the boiling water of the slender black coffeepot. When the coffee was ready, Abeba served it in dainty porcelain cups along with plates of popcorn.

Ras Hailu stepped out of the house brandishing a bottle of roots tonic he wanted us to drink. Its label featured a muscular, barechested black man with his arms outstretched in the posture of Christ on the cross. "For the spirit and the strength," Ras Hailu crowed. "And also to give you children, even as an old man," he winked, as if the roots tonic was the key to his virility.

Ras Hailu looked less like an old man and more like the fit figure on the tonic label, although his waist-length dreadlocks were gray. They were drawn back from his unlined face by a black sweatband that matched his black tracksuit. Back in St. Vincent he'd been a cricket player. "Health is the best of all wealth," he said as he poured a small taste of the tonic for the man sitting next to me. He hovered there, expectant as a waiter allowing a diner to sample the house wine before committing to the bottle.

The Ethiopian sniffed the stuff and pulled back, as if bitten. *"Harake?"* he asked.

"No, no. No alcohol," Ras Hailu clarified, filling the man's glass and then doing the same for me. "It's organic." The stuff was awful. The Banana Man raised a glass of his own and said cheers in Amharic. It was one of the few words he knew in his wife's language, the lingua franca of Ethiopia.

"No Amhara. *Oromo*," the man next to me said pointedly, tapping his chest. That his ethnic identity be recognized as distinct was important to him, especially because some Oromo see the Amhara as invaders. Ethiopia isn't a homogenous country but a federation of different groups, and the Oromo people are the largest of seventy-two tribes that make up Shashemene alone. As I'd learned in Israel, Ethiopians don't think of themselves primarily as black, or even necessarily as African. They might, for example, be Amhara, Oromo, Gurage, Wolaite, Kombatta, or Tigray, just as Rastas might, for example, be Jamaican, Vincentian, Bajan, Trinidadian, St. Lucian, or Antiguan. I could see that it would be just as frustrating for this man to be thought of as Ethiopian as it would be for Ras Hailu, resident of so-called Jamaica Town, to be thought of as Jamaican when he came from an entirely different island nation. But while Ras Hailu would say they were all African because Afrocentrism was the taproot of his faith, the man on his veranda was no Afrocentrist. To his credit, Ras Hailu apologized and asked his guest to teach him the proper word for "cheers" in the language of Orominya. Yet in spite of his efforts to pronounce the new word, Ras Hailu couldn't get it right.

"I cannot make my tongue shape the sound." He gave up.

Eventually Ras Hailu and I retreated to the gallery where dozens of his collages decorated the walls. Many of them depicted scenes from Exodus—Moses on the mount, the Israelites crossing the Red Sea, the tabernacle in the desert. But most were portraits of the bearded emperor, either in royal vestments and crown or military uniform and oversized pith helmet. In each of these, the eyes dominated the face.

Ras Hailu said, "He not the God Michelangelo and Leonardo Da Vinci painted a picture of." I told him his portraits of the emperor reminded me of religious icons, meant to convey the divine light of Christ. I asked Ras Hailu to share his perspective about Haile Selassie's divinity. Did he really think of him as the Messiah?

"He come like a prayer in two different eras," the Banana Man began. "First time he come was two thousand years ago as Christ. Jesus Christ had a workshop of twelve, not a government. Second time he came not to change water into wine but to show us how governing must be done."

"What do you mean?"

"Sistren, let me school you on the works of the Lion of Judah. He was Organization of African Unity's first founding father and he had a great say in formulating the U. N. When he went to the League of Nations about his plight with Italy in 1935, he was the only black man to stand up. They booed him. He said, 'You have struck a match in Ethiopia but it will not burn Ethiopia alone. It will blaze across Europe. Today it's me, tomorrow you.' That was prophetical language. After that, World War Two broke out and Hitler was going through. So we say his word is of authority in this time."

I had expected Ras Hailu to exalt the emperor along more metaphorical lines and was somewhat surprised to hear him list concrete political accomplishments as examples of his spiritual righteousness. To Ras Hailu, these accomplishments were miracles but they were also historical facts. When the emperor went to Geneva to plead Ethiopia's just cause to the League of Nations, the great powers were indeed unwilling to help.

Like so many blacks in the West who were compelled to defend their spiritual home when the League of Nations would not, Ras Hailu was drawn to pick a spiritual leader with a face he could relate to. It mattered to him that God could have a black incarnation so he could see himself reflected in His image, just like the Rastitute back in Jamaica who told his Dutch escort that Haile Selassie was "the black God." It also mattered to Ras Hailu that he could pray to a contemporary face of God, a God who reigned in our age. As he said, "The King of Kings not dead. We reject that foolishness."

But most of all the Banana Man talked about Haile Selassie as a man to look up to. "If you could see someone of morality and good works that is pronounced, he should be an example. No world leader can stand in Haile Selassie's shoes. All his speeches is like modern Bible," Ras Hailu reasoned. "When Haile Selassie came he abolished slavery, he gave a chance for equal rights to be strong, he revised the constitution. He did so much, man. So we see him as the returned Messiah. You ask me for a proof but faith not about proofs. There is no thing as facts, only versions. The Buddhists have Buddha, the Muslims have Mohammed, the Christians have Jesus. Why should the Rastaman not have Ras Tafari? Nothing wrong with that."

"Maybe not," I said, though I wasn't convinced that admiration for a man with exemplary qualities at the expense of whitewashing his mistakes should lead to blind devotion. Still, as I listened, I couldn't help imagining the human mistakes history might have wiped clean from the lives of Mohammed, Buddha, and Christ. The closest person to the face of God in my realm was Martin Luther King. If there was one person in the United States we all revered as a practical saint, it was he. We understood that King was a man but his actions seemed governed by a higher power. It was considered almost traitorous in the black community to bring up his "sins," such as his infidelity. Likewise, Ras Hailu couldn't or wouldn't see the emperor's bad side. Yet his insistence that God could take on human form made me think he was aware of it.

"God is a man, He's not just a spirit. That was not a spirit that went on the cross. Blood came from Christ's ribs. God is not playing hide-and-seek. He showed His face to Adam, Eve, Moses, Jacob, and to us."

Looking at Ras Hailu's portraits of the emperor's face, I envied the firmness of his belief. I have always envied believers. Even when critical of their faiths, I have always admired their belief. Back in Harlem, I was the only one in my building who welcomed the Jehovah's Witnesses when they came to deliver "the good news." I made them tea, invited them to sit at my table, asked out of my periodic loneliness, "but how are you *sure?*," and later pored over the issues of *The Watchtower* they left in my hands, frustrated by the spelling mistakes, the corny graphics, and the clichéd prose that did not speak to my heart.

I realized there was no such place as Zion; that it was a metaphor at best. And I knew that I would never choose to live in Shashemene myself. But I also knew Ras Hailu and Brother Bryan weren't idiots. As concerned as Ras Alex was that I might paint them as buffoons, as concerned as I was becoming that their Zionist dreams had failed to incorporate the perspectives of the people already living in the Promised Land, including, perhaps, their own wives, I respected these men who had used the profound story of Exodus to alter their hard realities. It took balls to do that. It took temerity and commitment. It took a leap beyond reason.

"You said earlier that this could be the gateway to Zion," I reminded Ras Hailu. "But what is Zion really?"

"First Zion is the temple of the body. That is the essence that helps with spirituality," the Banana Man said. He touched his forehead. "It's up here, which commands senses, nose, eyes, and heart to overcome temptation and other thing. It's like a schoolroom. Earth was a beautiful place that got corrupted. Ego stepped in."

Eden crashed through the door right about then, fleeing Judgment, Jury, and her sisters. She clung to her father's long legs as if they were the home base giving her immunity from the chase. Ras Hailu swept her up in his arms and nuzzled her neck. I missed my father in that moment. He was seldom so physically free with me. Our moments of intimacy were usually about books or ideas. And that was the realm where I mainly lived—the mind. I recalled what Satan said about the mind in *Paradise Lost*:

The mind is its own place, and in itself
Can make a heav'n of hell, a hell of heav'n.

What did it mean in practice, I wondered, for Zion to be the temple of the body commanded by the mind?

"You!" Eden interrupted my thoughts. "Who are *you?*"

"My name is Emily," I answered, though I doubted my name was a satisfactory answer. I removed my necklace and stepped forward to put it over her little head. "I want to give you this," I told her. "Happy birthday." She squealed in delight, squirmed out of her father's arms, twirled on her toe, and skipped back out the door.

"She's beautiful," I told Ras Hailu.

"I do agree with you on that, sistren. But every John Crow think them pickney white. You no got no children?"

"Not yet." I stiffened.

He clucked his tongue and narrowed his eyes to signal I was out of focus. "A pity. Home is where your children are. The roots tonic could help you with that."

"No thanks." I blushed, scanning the gallery wall for a piece of artwork to take with me instead. I avoided the icons of the emperor and chose a small rendering of a faceless mother carrying a faceless child on her back.

"Good choice, sistren," Ras Hailu said, polishing its glass frame with his sleeve. He threw in two gifts free of charge—a pocket-sized copy of the Ethiopian World Federation constitution and, out of concern for my cough, a packet of dried rue, which he said was a good remedy for phlegmatic lungs, stomach trouble, cramps in the bowels, nervousness, hysteria, spasms, convulsions, the expulsion of worms, pain in the head, dizziness, insanity, colic in children, and sciatica pain in the joints. It would also relieve congestion of the uterus and suppressed menstruation. Later that Thursday night, the eve of the emperor's birthday, with the yipping of hyenas eerily near, I drank it as tea.

12

Birthday of the Patriarch

H AD I BEEN menstruating, I would not have been permitted into the Nyabinghi Tabernacle on Haile Selassie's birthday the following morning, Friday, the twenty-third of July, or the sixteenth of Hamle on the Ethiopian calendar. The Nyabinghi churchical order sees women as unclean most of the month— during the seven days before, seven days during, and seven days after their cycles. Wives may only sleep with their husbands on clean days.

The constant cloud cover of the rainy season had lifted for the emperor's birthday, but my cold had not. This mass at the temple would be the first of the day's celebrations. That afternoon there would follow a parade in Shashemene proper and, that night, the big party Takatl wanted to join me for. The morning service here at the tabernacle was scheduled to start at six AM with the sunrise but didn't get underway until nine. Forget the Ethiopian clock. We were on Caribbean time.

The priest began his sermon with an inverted math lesson. "Two and three is not five, it's one." The man was gangly yet broad-shouldered, like the letter *T*. He bounced to an internal rhythm as he spoke, whipping his head left and right to make divining rods of his dreadlocks. "We must work together. One heart, one love, one destiny. Burn down Babylon!" Striking a match, he lit the bonfire around which about twenty Rastas and I had gathered on the lawn outside the tabernacle. "Babylon, burn!" the priest called out.

Burn! the congregation called back. *Fire!*

Then came the Nyabinghi drums: the low bass pounding the first and third beats, the middle funde striking on one and two, and the high akette riffing an improvised rhythm. This was the locomotive sound of death and resurrection. It is said that the Nyabinghi inherited this ritual from the Maroons, warrior rebel slaves who beat drums up in the Jamaican hills.

"Give thanks for Jah-Rastafari on this His birthday. Let Selassie-I arise!" chanted the priest.

Rise up!

"Let all who hate Him flee before Him as the smoke is driven away. As the fire burn so let the wicked perish at the presence of Jah."

Rastafari!

King of Kings!

"Babylon is not a natural atmosphere and we cannot feel at home there."

Paralyze Babylon!

The fire grew hotter. I tried to suppress my cough.

"Bless the house. Bless creation. This is the Nyabinghi order chanting down Babylon kingdom full of war, corruption, and hate."

Too much violence!

"Bless Jah Ras Tafari, earth rightful ruler after fight a lot of battle against the greed and lust of manifest destiny, defend His people, defend Ethiopia."

Jah bless!

"Let His enemies scatter away. Let all who hate Him flee before Him. As the fire burn so let the wicked perish at the presence of Jah."

Fire hot, hot!

"As long as there is Babylon, there must be Zion," the priest intoned. It dawned on me then how oppositional the faith was, as dependent for oxygen on the idea of Babylon as heaven on hell. Or black on white. Having left Babylon behind, could Rastafari even survive in Zion? Apparently not without clinging to Babylon. It had only this sermon to preach.

By now the bonfire was taller than the priest.

"The way of the white man is evil. One who fights against justice fights against Nyabinghi!" bellowed the priest.

Nyabinghi meant "death to the whites," according to a propagandist with the Italian pseudonym Frederico Philos who meant to justify Italy's invasion of Ethiopia back in the 1930s. It was a secret society, he alleged, that had begun in the Belgian Congo with the aim of ousting the Europeans and had spread across the continent with a great fever and a fanatic zeal for Haile Selassie as its supreme leader. But Philos's propaganda had an unexpected result in Britain's colonial outpost: in notion and name it inspired a branch of Jamaican Rastafarians to become Nyabinghi. They had a visceral hatred of the white oppressor. The Nyabinghi sect was racially exclusive; their sessions might start with the rallying call, "Death to the white man."

This priest didn't say that. But at some point he did shout, "One who fights against the integrity of Black Supremacy then his portion is death!"

Burn down Babylon! the congregants called back.

For a moment I wondered if I should be on guard. I'd covered my hair and worn a long skirt, as Sister Sandrine advised, but aside from those gestures, I didn't really fit in. Even the red cloth wrapped around my head was the wrong color. Everyone else looked black and wore white. Yet they hadn't shunned me. They'd let me into the circle around the fire. Bundles of cannabis were wedged between the logs. As a by-product of that drug smoke, or the heartbeat of the drums, or the birthday spirit in the air, the feeling was joyful.

It was not just Haile Selassie's birthday, the priest proclaimed, but the birthday of every Rastaman born into the faith through realization of the true self. The flames, now fifteen feet high, were also meant to cleanse the impurities from our hearts. We circled the fire slowly as it crackled and smoked. Periodically, the priest read from the King James Bible, substituting "Rastafari" for the word *God* every time it came up. Finally, sweating from the fire's heat, we took our seats.

The tabernacle was a circular colonnaded structure with a conical roof built with support from Rastas in the United Kingdom and the United States whose purchase of a five-pound or ten-dollar building certificate ensured their names would be posted on its inner walls. Cannabis burned twenty-four hours nonstop in the Holy of Holies, the inner sanctuary. The priest paced the inner court in front of devotional paintings of the emperor in which his eyes were like cold embers. In one painting he sat bestride a steed in the posture of Saint George, stabbing a white dragon in the heart. I was instructed, as a non-Rasta, to remain in the outer court while the others gathered on benches in the middle court where the drumming and chanting continued.

Hear the words of the Rastaman say:
"Babylon, you throne gone down, gone down;
Babylon, you throne gone down."

This devotional song went on for about three hours, the message endlessly looping back on itself. In a trance, I grew hungrier and sleepier and might have passed out if I hadn't been startled awake by something like a spitball striking the back of my neck. It turned out to be a sunflower seed.

"Psst!" someone called. I spun around and looked down through an archway in the outer wall. There in the grass stood a young man with a neat haircut. He was wearing a crisp white button-down shirt and had a bag of sunflower seeds in his hand. He tossed one into his mouth, cracked it between his teeth, smiled, and beckoned for me to follow him past the dying bonfire and off the property. Having heard enough of the service, I did. The young man led me to a vending table on the other side of the gate with stacks of neatly folded, extra-large Haile Selassie T-shirts.

"Unless you buy one of these, my sister, they'll think of you as a government agent," he pitched.

I considered bringing one back for Victor but didn't want the gift from my travels to be some kitschy souvenir. Besides, he already had a kitschy Iron Maiden T-shirt that was more his style. "You're a good salesman," I told the man, "but I really don't want a shirt."

The guy looked crestfallen.

"Can I hire you to drive me into Shashemene instead?" I asked. I was starving for lunch, needed to buy cough syrup, and wanted to see the birthday parade scheduled to take place there in the afternoon.

"Yes," he quickly agreed. He opened the passenger-side door of his rusty Peugeot for me with a gentlemanly flourish. The car must have dated from the socialist era. There were holes in its floorboards almost big enough for us to poke our feet through to step on the road. "Where are you from?" he asked along the way, trying to read my face. "Morocco? Algeria?"

"New York," I answered. "What about you? Are you from here?" I couldn't place his accent. It was somewhere between Caribbean and *habesha*, and this made sense, because it turned out the young man was both. He told me his name was Mickey and that he was the son of an Ethiopian woman and Brother Cryer, who, having emigrated forty-five years ago, was among the "pioneer corps"— the first Rastas on the Shashemene settlement.

"So, you're one of the 'First Born-Free Generation'?" I asked Mickey.

"If you must call it that," he smirked. He confessed he didn't feel all that free. He just wanted to go west, like any other Ethiopian youth in search of opportunity, but he didn't have the money to get there. He had a bachelor's degree in accounting but couldn't afford to follow it up with a master's and, even if he could, there was no such thing as a PhD on offer. He couldn't get as far here as he wished. "That's Africa," he sighed. "The ceiling is as low as your knees." His dream was to go to business school and get rich in the United States.

"What does your father think about your dream?" I asked. "Hasn't he told you the West is Babylon?"

"Yes, but that's not how we see it." Mickey was articulate and sympathetic about his father's point of view. He understood why his father saw the West as he did. When he was Mickey's age he was a second-class citizen in another man's country. "But in this country we were never colonized," Mickey said. "I respect what my father passed through to come here but he cannot respect why I want to leave."

Businessmen were respected everywhere, he elaborated, men who dressed in formal attire like the shirt he was wearing, and not like the ones he was trying to sell, emblazoned with the emperor and Bob Marley and marijuana leaves. As a businessman, he knew his market, but he also knew that those who wore his products would be perceived outside Jamaica Town as heretical, lazy, land-poaching drug addicts. Most people in Shashemene were Orthodox Christians, he told me, and some were Muslims, but, in either case, they thought the Nyabinghi Tabernacle was a pagan temple. That is, if they knew about it at all.

In a way, Mickey was the fulfillment of his father's freedom dream: leave Babylon, inherit Zion. He was a child of Ethiopia. He had no concept of the white man as his master or of Babylon as the place where he was humiliated and scorned. But as a consequence of that relative freedom, he couldn't understand or uphold his father's faith. The dream started and stopped with Mickey.

"So I'm guessing you're not a practicing Rasta," I said. "You don't believe Haile Selassie is God?"

"Have you visited the museum at Addis Ababa University?" he asked in reply.

"Yes," I said, recollecting the sorry state of the stuffed lion in the hallway of the former palace.

"Then you tell me. Would God let you visit His art deco bathroom and look upon His toilet?"

"I doubt it. But who knows? Isn't that one of the parts of your father's faith that makes sense—that the Rastas wanted to praise a living God they could see and touch?" I asked, thinking about my talk with the Banana Man the day before.

"No," Mickey argued. "It's nonsense. First, Haile Selassie is not living, but dead. Second, he was not in touch with the people at all. Last, he was not God."

Haile Selassie and the long line of monarchs before him were crowned in Axum, at the church complex where I'd tried unsuccessfully to witness the Ark of the Covenant. When I pleaded with its guard to describe what it looked like, he swore if he did so I'd burst into flames. He steered me instead to a ramshackle collection of weighty gold and silver crowns studded with diamonds and emeralds. The crowns looked heavy, ostentatious, and incredibly impressive. Standing before them I'd thought two things: "This was why the revolution was necessary," and, "They should really protect these better." Behind the dusty glass cases where the jumbled crown jewels gleamed, a pair of Selassie's tiny gold-threaded blue velvet shoes lay crumbling with a slow and steady rot.

"So who *was* the emperor?" I asked Mickey.

"Just a very small man with a very big crown."

"Just that?"

"No more, no less."

As we rolled into town, the "Rastaman Chant" from the tabernacle was still thrumming in my ears:

Babylon, you throne gone down, gone down;
Babylon, you throne gone down.

But the fact remained that the throne gone down had been the emperor's.

"If they love the emperor so much, why they didn't save him from the Derg?" asked Genene Tasew, a schoolteacher who joined me for a tall glass of avocado and, strawberry juice at a sidewalk café on Shashemene's main street. He wore a bright yellow T-shirt, a black baseball cap, and, now that the sun was finally out, a pair of mirrored sunglasses. He was dubious about the Rastas' commitment to Ethiopia. "If they love Ethiopia so much, why they didn't aid in the famine? Why they don't help develop the country?" he asked. Despite being born and raised in Shashemene, Genene hadn't even come face-to-face with a Rastafarian—not at school or at church or in the market—until he was in his thirties, when he took on a translating gig for Dr. Erin McLeod, the Canadian scholar who'd put us in touch.

Dr. McLeod's fieldwork brought Genene into contact with local perspectives about the Rastas and with Jamaica Town itself. She'd shown me a translation of a pamphlet handed out a few years back at the Africa Unite concert in honor of what would have been Bob Marley's sixtieth birthday, had he gone on living. "As Ethiopians we speak to you Rastafarians; don't pretend you love us . . . Celebrate your events anywhere but not here. Don't come here claiming that our former emperor is God and don't call our nation Zion, for we are not," it read.

"Shashemene don't trust them," Genene said. He listed the adverse effects of the Rastas upon the land and its people, his voice thickening with derision. "They drink more. They smoke more. They grow drugs. They make bad influence on the boys to be lazy. They have relations with high school girls. Stay away from their party tonight. Please."

"I'll be fine," I coughed.

"No. They will look at you with no respect. The ladies join them to use drugs and dance, just for the matter of fun. Also, you are sick."

"But some *habeshas* have married Rastas," I pointed out, trying to redirect the conversation to the ways the Rastas had integrated.

"Ethiopian women, the majority are poor. Look." He gestured at the women transporting plastic canisters of brown water from the river, where other women stooped over to scrub their loads of laundry. "Do you see them? They are miserable. They see Jamaicans are foreign people. They think they have the opportunity to leave the country with them. Or if they stay, they make dance, drink, smoke drugs. Compared to hard labor it's a good life."

Genene could have sought the good life himself, or at least a more opportunistic one, in the neighboring resort town of Awasa with its acacia trees bordering a lake full of flamingos and hippopotami. He was an educated man. Yet he'd chosen to stay put in Shashemene. As its native son, he was committed to its development. To him, the Rastas were an invading poison like the Dutch fertilizers on the rose plantations along Trans-African Highway 4.

"What about the JRDC school?" I asked. "Isn't it a productive contribution to society?"

"One school in thirty years is not a lot," he shrugged. "They should invest more, but they never finish what they start. They can't organize. They say they would build a great hospital for the town. Where is it? They say they want a stadium in the name of Bob Marley but it never comes."

"I understand they can't get building permits," I said.

Genene nodded. "They don't show us they can build good businesses. A good business serves the people, but who do they serve? A false God. We will never give Shashemene for Jamaica. They want to help Ethiopia but they can't do it. They should go home. Doesn't Jamaica need help? Let them have their Africa over there in Jamaica. Here they are living illegally on land they don't own," Genene complained, as if this were the biggest grievance of all. "This is *Oromo* country." The Rastas would have debated him about that, but I had to agree it was disturbing to witness the wide gap between the lush grounds of the Zion Train Lodge and the dung-colored huts surrounding it. I told Genene about the poor children who'd greeted me when I arrived on Wednesday, how I'd wanted to help them but wasn't sure how to do it.

"Those children are not poor," Genene said.

"Tell me you're kidding," I said.

Sadly, he was not. "Tomorrow, if you are feeling up to it, I will show you the poorest children, and we can choose the one you can send to my school," he said.

On Saturday, Genene drove me on the back of his red motorcycle under the bridge that spanned the river; he parked the motorcycle in the mud. Then he extracted a boy from a pack of orphans. Abu was a wide-eyed, red-brown six-year-old with a mop of curls and a smiling mouthful of loose baby teeth. I couldn't help the selfish impulse—immediately, I wanted to bring him home. Not that he was up for adoption. Abu's mother was alive but sick, her body wracked by a hacking wet cough far worse than my own. She eked out a living selling roasted corn on the side of the road. The two of them lived in a crooked one-room shack that, like the other crooked shacks in the region below the bridge, had a sheet for a door and newspapers pasted to the walls for insulation. The shack seemed to be sinking at a cockeyed angle into the riverbed. But at least Abu and his mother had shelter. A lot of these children were homeless and parentless. They slept in a huddle among the bridge's stone pylons.

Sending Abu to school would not be enough. I told Genene that my boyfriend might like to sponsor a child. And my mother, my brothers. Aunts and uncles. Coworkers, friends. "Good. Take out your camera," he said, as if my idea had been his design from the start.

Then, like Oskar Schindler compiling his list, he marched through that slum, selecting this child and that, passing over the half-naked ones with crooked limbs or crawling head lice or goop coming out of their eyes—those he intuited could not be considered cute by Westerners—and tapping the heads of the ones who looked hungry but otherwise healthy. Those he commanded to smile.

"Shoot him," he directed me. "Shoot her."

Discomfited, I hid my face with my camera and shot.

All of that would happen on Saturday, the morning after the emperor's birthday. But on Friday afternoon, when I was still focused on the Rastas from the perch of the sidewalk café, I shot the parade. It consisted of a float—one single flatbed truck blaring Buju Banton's song, "'Til I'm Laid to Rest." His was the same guttural voice behind the homophobic battyboy song that turned me off in Jamaica, but here it was purely plaintive:

Africa for Africans, Marcus Mosiah speak;
Unification outnumbers defeat.

What a day when we walk down Redemption Street,
Banner on heads, Bible inna we hands.
One and all let's trod the promised land . . .

There were Sister Sandrine, Ras Alex, and their caramel-colored son waving the Ethiopian flag and dancing in the bed of the truck along with a crew of other ecstatic Rastafarians. I waved and snapped their picture but it came out a blur.

"You blink, you miss it, and the rest is Ethiopia," said Genene, polishing off his juice. The tiny motorcade flashed across the lenses of his mirrored sunglasses and then disappeared from their frames altogether.

As I watched the truck roll down the street and around the corner, the Ethiopians on the street either looked on in amusement or didn't look at all. The kids, as young as Abu, went on selling lotto tickets, gum, and packets of tissues, or shining shoes. The women went on arranging their avocados and oranges in pyramids on their mats on the sidewalk or, like Abu's mother, fanning ears of corn on charcoal grills. The men went on pissing in the gutter. The love song grew softer and thinner in the air—

Oh what a beauty my eyesight behold
Only Ethiopia protect me from the cold

—until it was gone.

I did not heed Genene's warning. Friday night I went to the emperor's birthday party, and I went alone. Takatl was not allowed to accompany me in the end. He was needed to guard the Zion Train Lodge from theft since it would be empty while its owners and guests attended the celebration. I didn't see Sister Sandrine and Ras Alex at the Twelve Tribes headquarters. I didn't see Ras Hailu, the Banana Man, or his wife, Abeba. There was a blackout. It was too dark to see. The air was skunky with smoke and testosterone.

In the crush of bodies trying to get in the gate, I felt a bony hand dig its way into my pocket. I removed the hand and returned it to its owner, a young *habesha* man with *harake* on his breath who demanded I pay his entrance. "I'm from here," he growled. "I'm allowed." There must have been forty or fifty men close behind us.

"Let her be!" Another hand clutched my sleeve and I was yanked inside the headquarters. "You all right, sugar? You irie?" It was Brother Bryan, working security detail and admission at the gate. He was also drunk or still drunk, and still wearing the magnificent purple kerchief around his throat.

"I'm fine," I said, brushing it off, though I wasn't. I had a fever and a bad craving for the company of women. I was out of luck. The headquarters was nearly at capacity, its acreage spilling with hundreds of guests, Rasta and *habesha*, African and a few Europeans, but they were mostly men. They milled about like shadows with a mounting edge for the power to come back on so the party could get started. Finally, it did. The stage lights popped on and there, again, was the emperor, painted on a canvas backdrop, coolly surveying the scene. Seated on the stage before the patriarch were twelve men in self-styled multicolored robes: silver, yellow, purple, brown, pink, gray, green, white, black, and so on, each man belted by a red, green, and gold lariat and sporting a knit snood on his head. These were the Rasta pioneers. In that moment they looked to me like an ancient order of Smurfs.

The one in red rose to address the crowd. "We would appeal to our people to behave ourselves and enjoy the one hundred and eighteenth birthday of the two hundred and twenty-fifth heir of Solomon and Sheba, Lion of Judah, Emperor Haile Selassie-I, the first. Give thanks!"

I heard a bottle smash and a scuffle erupt nearby. The men onstage seemed not to notice. They stood up, faced north, placed their hands on their hearts, and began to sing a version of Rabbi

Arnold Ford's Ethiopian national anthem. *Ethiopia, land of our fathers, the land where our God wants to be . . .* The crowd surged forward and I was pressed between bodies . . . *like bees to a hive swiftly gather, God's children are gathered to thee.* Something ground against my leg. A beer bottle, a hard-on, I didn't want to look. I couldn't breathe. I tried to push my way toward the edge of the property where there seemed to be more space, and found myself cornered against a wall by another young Ethiopian. *With our red, gold, and green floating for us, and our emperor to shield us from wrong . . .* The whites of his eyes were bloodshot. He was weaving on his feet. *"You,"* he hissed. "Buy me a beer."

"Buy your own damn beer," I said.

He laughed crazily, leaned forward, and slapped his palms against the wall on either side of me so that I was trapped between his arms. He brought his face inches from mine. I could see a green bit of his dinner caught between his teeth.

"You! What are you doing here?" he demanded. A fleck of his spit landed on my cheek. My pulse quickened. At the same time, I was spookily calm, the way I always become when I know something bad is about to happen.

"Let me go," I said.

"Farengi girl," he snarled. "Give me money."

Ethiopia the tyrants are falling, who once smote thee 'pon thy knee . . . Without thinking, I lifted my knee as hard as I could directly into his balls. Incredibly or not, it worked. He clutched his groin and dropped to the ground like a tree that was already halfway felled. Once he was down I kicked him. It wasn't necessary but I did it. His head was hard but yielded against my foot like a pumpkin. And then I ran. Propelled by adrenaline, I shoved and elbowed my way back to the gate. I heard shouting behind me and the lusty anthem crackling from the loudspeakers . . . *to advance with truth and right, truth and right; to advance with love and light, love and light . . .* By the time I made it out to King's Highway I was as sick of Rastas and Ethiopians as they were of each other. And I was sick of myself. Why the fuck did I come to Shashemene? I did not stop running.

At the sign for the Zion Train Lodge I turned onto the muddy road, breathing hard as I sped past the squalid houses toward the desolate cornfield. I neared the dead donkey. Its final bits of fur and flesh were being shredded by the eyeteeth of a pair of mangy speckled dogs. One of them raised its dark muzzle to watch me as I approached. It seemed to be smiling. The animal's proportions were worrisome. It was strangely muscular; its back sloped downward from front haunches as large as a linebacker's. Its ears were alert, too far back on its skull and round as a bear's. Worst of all, it had the leer of an evil clown. With a flick of its tongue, it licked its chops. That beast and its mate were not dogs at all.

Hyenas.

Were hyenas hunters or simply scavengers? I didn't know but I didn't doubt they were faster than I was and I didn't want to die in this place. I scanned the ground for a rock but in the end, a weapon wasn't necessary. The hyena broke its stare, lowered its head, and rejoined its partner in feasting on the donkey's remains. Slowly, softly, and without turning my back on the animals, I crept on to the hotel.

Takatl opened the gate with a pout. I presumed he was sorry to be missing all the fun.

"Don't look like that," I said. "You should be glad you didn't come to the party."

"The old man said that also," sighed Takatl.

"What old man?"

Takatl pointed toward the banana trees by the water tank where Ras Benedict, the gentleman from Seychelles, had stretched out in one of the hammocks to gaze up at the starless sky. I wove through the garden, sank into the empty hammock next to him, flung my leg over the side, and used it to rock myself to and fro. It was going to rain again. I could feel it in my knees.

"*Avez-vous eu une bonne nuit?*" he asked.

"No," I answered. I was shaking.

"You didn't find what you were looking for," he said. It wasn't a question but a statement, and he spoke it very sadly.

"What about you, monsieur?" I asked. "I didn't see you at the party. Did *you* have a good night?"

"No," he confessed. "Someone pick my pocket so I left. This Shashemene is not a good place."

His hands were folded on his chest directly over his heart. He looked smaller than I remembered from two nights before when he'd told me he dreamed of retiring here. He lay sunken in his hammock like a mummy in a sarcophagus.

"I'm sorry you were robbed," I said.

Ras Benedict reached over to pat my knee and I was grateful to be so gently touched. I put my hand on my navel and felt it rise and fall until my breathing was normal again. I tried to envision the stars behind the rainclouds above us, the constellations it was just as hard to see in New York City. Just because we couldn't see them didn't mean they weren't there, punching through the dark. I wished I could sweep aside the clouds to reveal their glory: Pegasus, the flying horse; Aquarius, the water bearer; Cepheus, a king of Ethiopia. After a while I asked, "Will you stay in Ethiopia, then?"

"I don't think so. *C'est trop difficile.* You can't get inside the culture. The people are too desperate and closed. But when I left Seychelles as a young man I told myself I would never return. It was a hell. I can't return to Seychelles."

"Does that mean you'll go back to France for your retirement?" I asked.

He cleared his throat. "I don't wish to die there. I am not French. I wish to die in Africa."

"So where will you go?" I asked.

"I know some people in Ghana," he said. "I believe it will be better there."

My mind bent toward Ghana.

Before venturing to Shashemene, I'd watched their final match in the first World Cup ever to be held in Africa. By then Ghana had already beaten the U.S. They were the last African team in the running. Cameroon, Côte d'Ivoire, and Senegal had fallen. I stood in a crowd of taxi drivers in Addis Ababa's Meskel Square where the game was broadcast on a wide screen, hoping desperately they would win. "The Black Stars are carrying the dreams of the continent," the announcer whooped. "This time for *Africa!*"

All eyes were fixed to the screen, all muscles tense. At halftime Ghana was in the lead. When the announcer enjoined us at the start of the commercial break not to budge because the Black Stars were in flight, we didn't. Some thrilling nationalist sentiment froze us there, breathless, together. It wasn't just the game. It was an idea of the black family.

In the end, Ghana lost after a grueling overtime and endless penalty kicks, but that sense of unity flushed back to me now like a shot of hard alcohol. It seemed too long since I'd felt it. Maybe I'd just made the mistake of trying to find it here, in Shashemene. And maybe I was, in the final analysis, a foolish optimist. What kind of person travels so far to trace something as ephemeral as a *feeling*?

"Have you been to Ghana, sister?" asked Ras Benedict.

I closed my eyes, dreaming already, again, of the star sparks veiled by clouds.

"Not yet," I said.

IV: GHANA

WHO WILL INHERIT YOU
WHEN YOU DIE?

13

Daughters of Obama

"EH! ARE YOU the daughters of Obama?" an old woodworker called from his stall in the art market on the road to Aburi. I was traveling in Ghana with my friend Kaya and I was somewhat taken aback by the question. Black friends back in the United States who'd traveled to Ghana before had all been called *obruni*, and been stung by it. They warned me to expect the same thing. In the language of Twi, among the most common of the seventy-five tongues spoken in Ghana, *obruni* means more or less the same thing as *falasha*: stranger, outsider, foreigner. It also means "white person"—a rude awakening for black folks who've come here in search of their roots, though Kaya, who lived here for a time while researching a book about indigo, explained that *obruni* is seldom meant maliciously, and can even be used as a term of endearment.

But so far on this visit, nobody had called us *obruni*. Instead, this wood-carver questioned if we were Obama's daughters. What did the old man mean by it? For a moment, I wondered if he was asking us if we were mixed race. Both Kaya and I, like Obama, have a black parent and a white parent. I decided it was more likely that the old man wanted to know if we were American. Clearly, we were not Ghanaian. But how did he know we were not Egyptian? Or Pakistani? Or Syrian? Or Tuaregs from the Sahara? Maybe our clothes or our cameras gave us away. Maybe it was our accents. Or maybe, ours were American faces. For the first time, somebody had guessed my identity correctly, and for the first time I wasn't reluctant to admit it.

"Yes!" I answered. I understood that in the asking, all the wood-worker really wanted to know was if we had money to spend on his wares. Nevertheless, I was proud to say it: "Obama is our father."

"Eh heh," beamed the old man. He wore a long, loose Cleveland Indians jersey that fell nearly to his knees. Beneath the frayed cuffs of his jeans, his feet were bare. The dirt they stood on was the same red as Mississippi soil. "What do you think of this man, your new president?"

"As a president, I like him," Kaya said. "As a black president, I love him."

"White people voted for him too!" the woodworker crowed, as if this fact were a miracle. "They want to try a black man for America. Some of us Africans know how blacks fought there. I studied history," he began. "I know about the Black Panthers and this man, Booker T. Washington. Also, W. E. B. Du Bois. In those days, if I am right, they weren't admitted to school. Isn't it?"

"Well, not exactly," I said. "They went to separate schools. Schools that weren't as good."

"And that situation hasn't really changed," Kaya pointed out.

"But you will surely agree it's a long journey for a black man to be in the White House," the woodworker said. "We are proud that Obama is there. People came from Kenya, Nigeria, all over Africa to see this man. But he chose to visit this our Ghana above those nations because in all of Africa our democracy is strongest. We have learned from American history. 'For the people, by the people.' Who brought democracy? Abraham Lincoln, isn't it?"

"No," I said. "You might be thinking of him as the one who brought the slaves to freedom?"

"Yes. Excuse me-o! Freedom is the thing."

"But it's more complicated than that . . ." I started, remembering Lincoln's pronouncement that there "there is a physical difference between the white and black races which . . . will forever forbid the two races living together on terms of social and political equality."

"Are you sure?" the wood-carver challenged me. "They shot the man dead in a theater for bringing that institution!"

"Freedom?" I asked.

"Freedom! All that time, the White House was meant for the KKK. I did history. I know—from 1600 on. We built America four hundred years ago."

I could not say I knew as much, right or wrong, about the history of Ghana before its first black prime minister and then president, Kwame Nkrumah, came to power in the 1950s. I was impressed by the woodworker's knowledge. I was also touched by his use of the pronoun "we," with its implication of kinship. Ghana already felt more familiar than Ethiopia had.

"We are black and we are proud, say it loud!" the woodworker shouted. I smelled his breath suddenly and recognized that he was drunk, overeager. This was, after all, a market, and he had souvenirs to sell. I steadied myself for the hustle.

"Have you heard of Martin Luther King? He said one day we will all be judged not by the color of our skin but by the content of our character. Now what he said has come to pass," he reasoned brightly, clapping his hands. I thought him a very good salesman in that moment. I expected him to begin showing us the masks and stools he'd carved. Then came the pitch.

"Do you want an African man?"

"No thanks," Kaya laughed.

"Our husbands wouldn't like it," I added, though I was not yet married to Victor and Kaya was going through a divorce.

"How many children have your husbands given you?" the woodworker demanded.

"My friend here has a boy and a girl. I have none," I confessed. He scrutinized me. "Not one?"

"Not yet."

"Nonsense! Then your husband has no portfolio. You must go and take my son here. Ekow!" he called back into his little stall. A young man in a brown silk shirt with white polka dots emerged from behind a towering stack of mancala boards. His lower lip was dyed luxuriously purple. It was a beautiful brushstroke, like a bright tuck of plumage on some exotic bird. I gazed in wonder at that purple while he stared flirtatiously back at me. Meanwhile the woodworker began unbuttoning Ekow's brown silk shirt to demonstrate his pectoral muscles.

"What is this—the African Chippendales?" I asked Kaya. The old man was so playful, I knew this striptease was partly in jest, but I also felt we had turned some dark corner. I was afraid to see what he might do next to prove his son's value and strength. Would he open his mouth to show me Ekow's teeth and gums? Wasn't that what the traders did at markets when exchanging a human life for brandy, gunpowder, baskets of cowrie shells, Venetian glass beads, or lengths of patterned cloth?

"He is a good worker," the old man pitched. "If you take him to America and get him a job, he'll bless you with many children."

"Your son is beautiful to look at but I'm not looking for a man," I rushed, trying to keep the situation light. "How about I take a mancala board off your hands instead?"

Kaya and I moved on, but later, with the mancala board tucked beneath my armpit, its pebbles chattering inside like a rattle, I couldn't stop thinking about the mysterious purple shine of Ekow's lower lip. That peek of color seemed to represent the wide cultural divide between us, which the woodworker had so winningly tried to bridge. There was a reason his son's mouth was purple, and even if I couldn't kiss it, I found it beautiful and wanted to understand it. Was it a mark of his tribe? Asante, Ewe, Krobo, Ga? I asked Kaya if she could explain the purple's significance. She burst out laughing and said, "Honey, that was gentian violet, for infection. The boy probably had a herpes sore."

Kaya left me to go off on her indigo trail, but not before introducing me to her friend Kati Torda, a bead designer who was kind enough to let me stay with her in Accra for a few days. A generous, pleasantly plump, no-nonsense woman whose eyes smiled even when her mouth didn't, Kati owned a bead shop in the neighborhood of Asylum Down. The shop was a rainbow of ropes and strands and bins of beads in powder glass and Baoule brass, plastic and bone, bronze and bauxite, lapis lazuli and cowrie shell, imported amber and freshwater pearl. In zigzags and swirls, big as babies' heels and small as termites, round as marbles and flat as buttons, long as pen caps and short as grains of rice, these beads shone brighter than candy. I didn't know how Kati resisted the temptation to fist them into her mouth and suck them for their color. Her dimpled hands were quick and sure as a surgeon's with the tools of her trade—the flat-nose pliers, the tweezers, the thread cutters, the wire nippers, and the beading awl—yet her method of design was meditative and slow. It involved spreading unlikely pairings of beads across a desk blotter and listening until they told her who belonged with whom.

I sat with her in the back room of the shop, where she allowed me to use her office phone to make a call. I'd come to Ghana with the phone number of a critical contact. As I waited for an answer, I looked at the small YES WE CAN! Obama campaign poster tacked to the wall behind Kati. She'd given the Obama daughters a beading lesson on their father's first visit as president to sub-Saharan Africa. Sasha and Malia had been very shy and sweet in their matching dresses, Kati told me, amidst strict security at the hotel where she helped them to craft ankle bracelets. The Obamas had left only two weeks before I arrived in Accra, and their trace was everywhere. You couldn't take a tro-tro ride without passing by a shiny yellow billboard plastered with Barack Obama's face. Usually he was pictured next to Ghanaian president John Atta Mills against a backdrop of the U.S. and Ghanaian flags, the red and white stripes of the one dissolving into the black star of the other, but you might also spot Obama smiling on Independence Avenue or Liberation Road with Michelle by his side, perched above CHRIST IS IN ME FASHIONS, BUT FIRST SEEK THE KINGDOM OF GOD CONSTRUCTION WORKS or NAKED I CAME CHOP BAR.

CHANGE HAS COME, the billboards announced.

And also, AKWAABA. Welcome Home.

"Hello?" A tired voice finally answered the phone.

"Dr. Robert E. Lee, I presume," I said.

Kati laughed at my Livingstone reference but Dr. Lee did not. Instead he asked who the hell was calling. Before I could answer, he explained that I'd woken him up from a nap and anyway, he was all talked out. "I'm an old man now. I'm in my nineties," he coughed. "I don't know what you all want from me. I swear I've done an interview every week since I came here."

I did the math in my head. Fifty-two interviews a year multiplied by fifty-two years would have equaled over twenty-five hundred interviews. Yes, his voice sounded like a ragged whisper in my ear, but surely the man was exaggerating.

"Please," I pressed. "I came all the way from—"

"No, young lady. You listen to me. I'm retired. You hear? From Martin Luther King to Malcolm X, every one of you negroes who comes through Ghana tries entering through the same two doors: the door of no return, or *me*. I'm talking to one of you about Africa tomorrow. I'm supposed to talk to one of you about Africa next week. I've talked so much I'm all talked out."

But I didn't actually want to talk to Ghana's unofficial ambassador for African Americans about Africa. I wanted to talk to him about America. Why did he leave it just as the Civil Rights Movement was taking shape? And how in God's name did a black man come to be named after the father of the Confederacy?

But Dr. Lee cut me off before I could ask about his past. "If you really want to learn about your roots, try talking to an African," he wheezed and hung up the phone.

Kati Torda looked up from her beadwork with her eyebrows raised. "Sorry-o! No need to tell me the dentist won't see you. Your face betrays your disappointment. I beg you please, make your long face short and sweet before Mrs. Mills arrives." Then she went back to work attaching three long strands of fat orange and red beads to a gold clasp for Ghana's First Lady, Mrs. Naadu Mills, who would be picking up the necklace later that afternoon.

I returned Kati's office phone to its cradle, smarting at Dr. Lee's accusation that my quest was a cliché. Yes, Ghana is a major site of roots tourism, attracting roughly ten thousand African Americans every year, far more than any other nation on the continent. Yes, many of us are drawn by the nightmare of history to the coastal castles, through which our ancestors may have passed on the slave route across the Atlantic. And yes, I wanted to see the slave castles too—how could I not? To satisfy such cravings Dr. Lee himself had established a foundation to restore the castle in Elmina. But more than all that, I wanted to talk to African diasporans drawn back to Ghana by the myth of return.

Under the Right of Abode, any person of African descent in the diaspora can live and work in Ghana indefinitely. Roughly one thousand African Americans live in the nation's capital today. Unlike in Israel, Jamaica, and Ethiopia, in Ghana there was no fixed community of "black Zionists" to visit, no confined movement, utopia, or plot of land, but rather a motley crew of "returnees," some old, some young, some here for good, some just for a week, some a part of a diplomatic corps, some here to do research or because they were travelers, like me, on one of many stops.

Having lived there the longest, Robert Lee was the undisputed elder statesman of this community. He and his late wife, Sarah, both dentists, repatriated in 1957, at the invitation of Kwame Nkrumah. Nkrumah called for skilled black professionals from all over the world to help strengthen the newly independent country. In fact, Lee and Nkrumah had been classmates at Pennsylvania's historically black Lincoln University in the late 1930s when Ghana wasn't yet Ghana but still the British colony known as the Gold Coast.

I liked the ring of the phrase: Right of Abode. It wasn't as poetic or official as the Right of Return. Yet the sanction was somehow parallel, a Promised Land of another kind. I'd been envious of my best friend Tamar's legal right to return to Israel even as I was critical of her choice to make aliyah and become an Israeli citizen. She had a country that wanted her, a people and a place where she ostensibly belonged.

Though I'd grown up without feeling the same was true for me, things had changed in the three years since I'd last visited Tamar in Israel. I had fallen in love with Victor, a born New Yorker with little interest in living anywhere else. He'd recently proposed on a trip we took together to Buenos Aires and I'd said yes. We were not only getting married but looking to buy an apartment, giving new and concrete purchase to the word *home*. I was now thirty-three years old. I still wasn't sure I wanted to live in the United States, but the restlessness and unease of my twenties were fast giving way to the drive to settle down. Politically, things had changed too, or on the face of things, they had. The shameful Bush years had come to an end. Obama was our new president and his face looked something like mine.

I wasn't sure what that meant for me and other black Americans with complicated feelings about our citizenship. For those like Robert Lee and his wife, pioneers who'd had the guts to tear up roots and plant them here in Ghana, what did home look like now?

"Dr. Lee said I should seek out an African." I sulked.

"Good advice. You are in proper Africa after all," Kati replied, holding the First Lady's necklace up to the light to check for flaws. As she worked, the long, loose sleeve of her purple kaftan fell to her elbow, revealing a heart-shaped sankofa tattoo on her forearm.

In Akan, one of seventy-five languages spoken in Ghana, sankofa literally means "go back and take." As a philosophical concept, sankofa is better defined by the proverb, *"Se wo were in a wosankofa a yenkyi,"* which translates, "It is not wrong to go back for that which you have forgotten." It's been poetically expressed by African Americans as, "We need to look to the past to understand the present." This is exactly what the longing backward gaze to Africa is all about.

When I was in high school in the early 1990s a sankofa, or what appeared to be a sankofa, was discovered during a building excavation in Lower Manhattan. The symbol embellished the wooden lid of a coffin belonging to one of 419 colonial-era Africans unearthed at the site, now known as the African Burial Ground. The coffin held the remains of an unknown black man between the ages of twenty-six and thirty-five, who died at some point after 1760.

For many African Americans, these unknowns represented questions of personal history—*Who was* my *great-great-grandfather? What was his name? Where did he come from? How did he live and how did he die?*—painful questions to ask because, so often, their answers couldn't be found. For some, that pain was softened by the sankofa driven with cast-iron tacks into the coffin labeled BURIAL 101. It was interpreted as a rare and triumphant symbol that African culture did survive the yoke of slavery. I remember reading about its discovery in a current events unit in social studies class. I traced its curving lines with my fingertip and wondered about my own grandfather, of whom I knew almost nothing. He was not a slave but he was killed in Mississippi for being black. I didn't have the vocabulary for it but I felt there was a link between my grandfather and Burial 101.

Archaeologists estimated that twenty thousand other slaves were buried in a six-acre tract under the streets of New York City in the area we now call Ground Zero. That is over seven times the number of victims of the September 11 terrorist attacks on the World Trade Center. The archaeologists unearthed some of the dead and dispersed them for study. During careful examination, the archaeologists identified other artifacts of African origin in the unmarked graves—shells, rings, and beads like the ones for sale in Kati Torda's shop. But the sankofa captured the black imagination more than these trinkets ever could. It was a bridge. It was an invitation.

The archaeologists spent years studying the contents of the burial ground. Once they were finished, the sankofa was invoked during an elaborate ceremony to return the remains to their resting place. So many black people wanted to make peace with their history that, before going back underground in New York, those bones went on a traveling circuit. The ceremony lasted six days, beginning at Howard University in Washington, D.C. "We give thanks for the opportunity to connect with our past and our future," intoned Bernard L. Richardson, the dean of Howard's chapel where thousands had gathered to pay respects to their African ancestors about whom they knew so little. "Oh God, you have made these bones live again."

Similar ceremonies took place in Baltimore, Wilmington, Philadelphia, and Newark, where the remains were placed on boats chartered for Lower Manhattan that docked at the spot where slave ships once sailed to port. There I stood, in the light autumn rain, with a crowd of onlookers at South and Wall Streets, once the site of the second-largest slave market in America, where we had gathered to pay our final respects. We marched the coffins and caissons up Broadway, back to their burial place north of City Hall. The funeral was a feat of improvisation—two parts mourning, one part circus. There were drummers in dashikis; red, black, and green flags snapping in the wind; the blessings of a Yoruba priest; and speeches by Mayor Michael Bloomberg and the poet Maya Angelou. Vendors hawked sankofa T-shirts, sankofa key chains, sankofa buttons.

Later, the sankofa was chiseled into a black granite stone memorializing the site, and when the African Burial Ground became a national landmark, the sankofa became its logo. Recently, however, historians are in a debate about whether the adornment on 101's coffin is in fact a sankofa or just merely, and heartbreakingly, a heart.

To witness the black sankofa inked on Kati's forearm was culturally confusing, though I suppose, given the Japanese character tattooed on my left shoulder blade, I shouldn't have been surprised. Technically, Kati wasn't any more African than I was Japanese. In fact, she was Hungarian. At this very moment, she was streaming music from a Hungarian radio station and humming along to the tune. Yes, Kati Torda, master African beader, was a white woman.

After her recent divorce from a Mr. Dagadu, a Ghanaian engineer she met in Hungary when she was just nineteen, she'd reclaimed her maiden name, but everybody still referred to Kati as "Madam Dagadu." Madam Dagadu or no Madam Dagadu, I didn't at first think of Kati Torda as an African. She may have married one and followed him to Ghana where she learned Ewe before English, raised two daughters, now grown, and lived here for over thirty years, but I didn't think of her as being really *of* this place, mainly because she didn't look it.

"Naadu Mills is African enough for you," said Kati, as if reading my mind.

I'm embarrassed to admit that later, when Ghana's First Lady arrived at Kati's shop in a Mercedes Benz with a driver and a bodyguard, the only thing I could think to ask was, "What did you think of Barack Obama?" Mrs. Mills touched the curls of her stiff copper-colored wig and gave such a politic answer I forgot it as soon as it came out of her mouth. Kati was freer to speak her mind. She said, "Whosoever sells hope is in business. Lotto, church, or president."

"I'm more interested in talking to African Americans. Or Rastafarians," I told Kati. "You know, the descendants of slaves who came back here in search of a homeland. Zion. I want to know if they found it."

"Oh-ho. If it's Zion you're hoping to discover, my friend, then good luck-o, as long as your spirit carries you on that journey. Rather you should pray for the small earth in front of you. But as for an African American, there is always Mary Ellen Ray. I will give you her number, but first dash me small *kele wele* from across the road."

"Excuse me?"

"*Kele wele.* Go and come. You must please just follow your nose." Kati pointed her eyes at the door with no further explanation.

Outside, the smell of open sewers fought the smell of open cookfires. A cloth seller at Jesus Is Alive Fabrics dozed in the tropical heat, framed in her stand by bolts of electrically bright patterned cloth—one of them commemorating Obama. A tailor sauntered by with a beautiful antique Chinese butterfly sewing machine on his head, a hot-pink measuring tape around his neck, and a large pair of scissors tied to his belt loop. He was ready to hem a pair of trousers on the spot. A young mother with a sleeping baby bound to her back carried a tin basin full of bladderlike plastic baggies of drinking water, the size and shape of breast implants. She gracefully straddled the gutter and squatted to pee without removing this burden from her head. In fact, everyone carried their loads on their heads, and half of them were selling those loads: boiled eggs, smoked herring, charcoal, bundles of dry broom grass.

"Egg, sister?"

"You are welcome, sister," the people called. "Come and have a look."

Why weren't they calling me *obruni*? Maybe it was by design. So many tourists flock to Ghana from the diaspora with a roots agenda that its Ministry of Tourism had recently renamed itself the Ministry of Tourism and Diasporan Relations. One of its efforts was to shift the image of African Americans in the minds of Ghanaians from rich travelers to long-lost brothers and sisters. There was big profit to be made from this our slave past. For a price, Africa's lost children could be reunited or reborn in an African naming ceremony, a captivity reenactment, or a "door of no return" ritual. Surely *obruni* like me would spend more money in this Promised Land when that word wasn't used?

I wouldn't have minded being called by that name. If I'd left Jamaica with any lingering sense of belonging to a black family unified by the memory of slavery, then East Africa had knocked it out of me for good. I was white in Jamaica, *farengi* in Ethiopia, and *obruni* here. How could I claim to be of a place I had never been? I couldn't even balance a book on my head.

"Sister," called the young mother who had finished peeing in the sewer, "I can see that you are thirsty! My water is safe for your mouth."

"No thank you, sister," I answered. "I already have enough to drink."

I took in my surroundings and thought of one of the first books I learned to read, about a peddler who carried a towering stack of caps on his head, crying, "Caps for sale! Fifty cents a cap!" I was as delighted by my dislocation here in Accra as I had been by that book. I was lost, but I trusted myself to find my way. What was it Kati asked me to find? Since I did not yet begin to know how to read this place, I did as she suggested. I followed my nose. The closest cookfire glowed across the red dirt road, fanned by an old woman in a loose batik wrapper. She sat close to the ground on a two-legged stool that resembled the symbol for pi.

"Hello, Auntie!" I greeted her as I'd learned to do as a mark of respect for older African women including Victor's mother, who came from Uganda. "Is that *chale wate*?" I pointed at the tempting plantains frying in red palm oil with what smelled like ginger paste and hot peppers.

"Eh!" The old woman slapped her thighs and laughed from her belly at my mistake. "You like my foot too much. Is that right?" She lifted her legs and wiggled her toes, pointing at the dusty plastic flip-flops on her crusty feet. "These *chale wates* are not for sale-o! Make you chop this *kele wele* instead," she said, ladling the plantains out of the boiling oil and into her bare hand. She served me a portion of that deliciousness in a cone of dot matrix printer paper—a kind I hadn't seen since the 1980s—and took two cedis in return. "Eh!" she called as I turned to go. "Are you the daughter of Obama?"

14

"Nigganese"

Y OU LOOK LIKE my mother!" shouted Mary Ellen Ray when I showed up at dusk outside her peach-colored one-story cement house in the middle-class neighborhood of Osu. The house had been difficult to find. The streets were nameless or changed names several times; the buildings went unnumbered.

Down the road an outdoor funeral party of 150 guests, dressed entirely in white, feasted on *joloff* rice with goat, drank Star beer, and danced to highlife music pumping from two enormous speakers. With shyness and longing, I had stopped to photograph some children at the party kicking up red dirt as they chased a terrified rooster in circles. The women in their white *kaba and slit* had the silhouettes of mermaids. I hoped to catch a glimpse of the deceased in one of the glorious painted coffins I'd seen a carpenter carving on the road to Teshie—a coffin shaped like a hammer, a sardine, an ear of corn, an airplane—but these were obscenely expensive, reserved only for the very rich.

Mary Ellen opened her metal gate. She was seventy-nine but looked considerably younger. A whorl of thin gray-brown dreadlocks rested on the crown of her head like a sparrow's nest. She wore sandals, khaki shorts, and an extra-large T-shirt that swallowed her small frame. TRO TRO DRIVER, it said.

"You look like my aunt Alise!" I shouted back over the music. Mary Ellen laughed. Maybe we were both pleased to discover a family resemblance in a place where we were such obvious outsiders.

A sandy, big-pawed puppy bounded toward me and chewed at my shoelaces.

"Shoo, Tut!" Mary Ellen said. "He's new. We've always had dogs instead of children. And they always disappear when the neighbors poison them. We'll see how long Tut lasts . . . Well, come on in, child, before one of these mosquitoes gives you the malaria. I just hope you haven't come here to interview me about Africa. Seems like every black Tom, Dick, and Harry who comes to Ghana knocks on our door."

I liked Mary Ellen immediately. It was more than the smell of gin on her breath, the dark humor, the fact that she was childless, and the large brown eyes that gave her face the appearance of a wood sprite that reminded me of my aunt Alise. It was her house. Whether she'd closed the shutters against the funeral noise or the mosquitoes, Mary Ellen's house was dark and stifling as a mauso-leum, smelling faintly of mildew and urine.

My aunt Alise's house in Compton was similar—one story, shaded by a palm tree, peach-colored, and depressing. The first and last time I saw that house was when my father and I flew to Los Angeles to pack it up after Alise's husband disappeared. Uncle Curtis, who suffered from dementia, turned up later, raving in a Safeway park-ing lot, wearing nothing but his underwear. While he was gone, Alise took a hard fall and broke her hip. Neither of them was old enough for this to be happening to them. Alone and too weak to reach the phone from where she'd fallen on the kitchen floor, Alise spent two days tap-tap-tapping on the aluminum trash can with her wedding ring until the repetitive, troubling sound caught the attention of a neighbor.

"I apologize for the dirt," Mary Ellen said, leading me into a bright yellow kitchen where she began cracking eggs for an omelet. "This is John's dinner. He's resting," she explained. "I'm a terrible cook. I was already menopausal when I got here—too old to learn to cook new things."

As a high school student in Chicago during the late 1940s, Mary Ellen wanted to be a foreign correspondent but didn't believe her dream was possible for a black woman. Later, she took a job fundraising for the DuSable Museum of African American History. That's where she met her husband, John Ray, a self-taught photographer and sculptor, who was then an artist in residence. By the time he met Mary Ellen in Chicago, he had already spent several years in Ghana as part of a sophisticated expat community that variously included Maya Angelou, Nina Simone, and Richard Wright.

Those years, the late 1950s through the 1960s, were a golden, voguish time for the African Americans in Ghana. In 1956, when Louis Armstrong blew his silver trumpet before a crowd of one hundred thousand at the racecourse in Accra, he heralded the handover of power from colonial to independent rule. In 1957, the Gold Coast followed Sudan as the second sub-Saharan African nation to elect a black leader.

Ghana was born.

The nation was a lodestar for hundreds of African Americans who visited and settled here. Malcolm X made the journey in the same week as Muhammad Ali. Martin Luther King Jr., who flew in to celebrate Ghana's independence, is reported to have wept when its flag was raised. The crowd beneath the flag's black star was five hundred thousand strong and the word it cried was "Freedom!" The same word was being cried across the water in the name of civil rights.

"How does it feel to be free?" Vice President Nixon asked a group of ecstatic blacks in a popular but probably apocryphal story about the independence ceremonies he attended as a U.S. delegate. "We wouldn't know," they answered him, drily. "We're from Alabama."

With its new leader and its new name, Ghana was more than a magnet for these visiting Americans in their own long tug-of-war for freedom. Here as there, the political struggle had a spiritual dimension. But whereas the United States was marching toward integration, equal rights, and justice in a system that would remain dominated by a white majority, Ghana had ousted its white colonial oppressors and won the right to rule itself. It appeared to be a black Utopia, a New Jerusalem.

Kwame Nkrumah had studied religion at Lincoln University back in the United States, where he delivered charismatic sermons about the ills of the British Empire rather than the miracles of Jesus Christ. He knew well the power of biblical language. Now that he embodied the promise of the fledgling republic and, like Haile Selassie before him, the continent at large, Nkrumah was hailed as *Osagyefo*—"redeemer" in the Twi language. He was promoted as the Messiah and his Convention People's Party was portrayed as the Party of God. Nkrumah hoped that Ghana would serve as a shining example for the rest of the continent. It would motivate change and inspire revolution. A union of independent black republics would break free from colonialism and rise. Ghana would be free, Nkrumah believed, when all of Africa was free.

John Ray was one of the hundreds of black émigrés, known to Ghanaians as "the Afros," who shared that belief. Born in Mississippi to sharecroppers, he had served in the U.S. Air Force during the Korean War and went on to teach African art in the newly minted African Studies Program at U.C. Berkeley in the 1970s. Mary Ellen was immediately attracted to John when she met him in Chicago. He struck her as a bohemian raconteur and she couldn't get enough of his stories about Africa. Eventually, he invited her back to her "ancestral home." The journey appealed to Mary Ellen's wanderlust and desire to break free from the limitations she felt in the United States. In 1976, they celebrated America's bicentennial by going into exile. They sold their belongings, bought a van, and planned an elaborate gypsy route of return from California through Central America along the Pan-American Highway where they would catch a ferry from Panama to Bogotá, Columbia, drive through South America, and, finally, look for passage to Ghana on the Black Star Line.

★   ★   ★

In their sunflower-yellow kitchen, Mary Ellen now handed me
a bottle of Fanta and apologized again, this time for not having
a drinking glass to offer me. "We've only got two and they're
both dirty. John wouldn't let me buy new ones when the others
broke. 'We can't have our possessions possessing us.' That's what
he says. I'm more or less of the same mind. The more we have,
the more we think we should have. That's what our American
culture of rugged individualism nurtures—the compulsion to
possess. Don't you think?"

"Yes," I agreed, though I was embarrassed to admit then just how
much shopping I'd been doing in Accra. Overtaken by a hunger
for color, I felt compelled to buy this fertility fetish, these gold
earrings, this pretty cloth with the bird print named "Money Flies."
I was losing track of how many cedis I'd spent in the markets, at
the trade fair, and at the antiquities dealer. Each night I draped
my cloth collection on the bed so the color would be near my
skin—the gold of the kente, the blue-black indigo, the purple
from Mali. Now that I knew my way around well enough to have
left Kati Torda's house, I'd had to buy another suitcase to haul my
mounting load to Chez Lien, the hotel in Osu where I had taken
a dark little room and gotten into a battle with the man at the
front desk over lightbulbs. Only one of the room's four lamps had
a bulb, strong enough to illuminate the clouds of mosquitoes but
not strong enough to read by. The man was exasperated when I
asked for more bulbs. "Light, light, how much light can this woman
need? If I wanted to hear such complaints I should have stayed at
home in the company of my miserable wives."

"Anyway," Mary Ellen said as she flipped the omelet, "we've got
to be able to travel light when we leave."

"You're planning to leave Ghana?" I asked, surprised.

Mary Ellen dropped her voice. "I want to."

"Can I ask why?"

She spoke under her breath as if concerned about John over-hearing: "Water shortages, public urination, potholes, con artists in the market giving us *obruni* prices, cutting two yards of cloth when you've paid for three. The power's more off than on and *oh*, the litter."

In spite of herself, her voice grew louder. "Accra is drowning in those plastic bags they call rubbers. It wears on you. Don't get me wrong, Emily. It's a lovely little country." There were plenty of rich natural resources, she went on, and land producing two to three crops a year. But with all its timber, bauxite, cocoa, and gold, there was still so much poverty to lament. "Half the kids aren't even in school ... I used to think, 'If only we could import several thousand industrious and creative, take-charge black Americans to build this nation.'"

By now she was almost shouting. "We've certainly had enough experience building America!"

Mary Ellen's idea that African Americans could save Ghana struck me as patronizing. But I also knew she was speaking out of a Pan-Africanist tradition. If she came here believing it was her destiny to help build the nation, it was in large part because when Nkrumah came to power he had invited skilled black Americans to do just that.

"What about the AAAG?" I asked about the African American Association of Ghana housed at the W. E. B. Du Bois Memorial Center for Pan-African Culture on Cantonments Road. Of all the African Americans to emigrate to Ghana, Du Bois was the most esteemed. The founder of the National Association for the Advancement of Colored People was ninety-three years old when he renounced his U.S. passport for Ghanaian citizenship. With one foot in the grave and the other planted at last on African soil, he devoted his final days to penning the *Encyclopedia Africana*, a sweeping compendium of the black world that furthered his long quest to attain a black Zion. Decades before, while in Paris to or-ganize the Pan-African Congress of 1919, he announced that "the African movement must mean to us what the Zionist movement must mean to the Jews, the centralization of race effort and the recognition of a racial front. To help bear the burden of Africa does not mean any lessening of effort in our problems at home." The encyclopedia was a tireless attempt to define black peoplehood, so it was no wonder that the Center in Accra, where Du Bois was buried, was a gathering place for returnees.

"Are you a member?" I asked Mary Ellen.

"I was at one point," Mary Ellen sighed. "But it's a potluck group, not an activist organization. Its practices are even more disappointing than its aims." She turned off the flame under the frying pan.

"Why should it be an activist organization?" I asked. There was a part of me that thought a potluck group sounded more fun. Especially for someone like Mary Ellen, who cooked eggs for dinner and had only two drinking glasses.

"The fact that so many of us came to Ghana to build a new home speaks of a sense of purpose that should form the basis for a strong and unified group. Yet we can't seem to bring our disparate talents together. Of course, everyday survival in Ghana takes an incredible amount of energy, but we have to find a way to work together with all our differences for the benefit of us all."

Mary Ellen reached to the shelf above the stove, pulled down a chipped plate, and inspected it for ants. She continued. "At best the AAAG should be operating like one of the Lebanese merchant associations, providing business liaisons and contacts for expats and also services for visiting brothers and sisters like you—meeting folks at the airport, organizing tours, setting up accommodations. Instead, it's splintered into factions. Some members accepted backing for the Du Bois Center from the U.S. government and others thought it was dirty money—the very thing they were distancing themselves from by coming to Ghana in the first place."

I was about to ask Mary Ellen if she could explain what she meant to distance herself from by coming here when a heavy thud sounded from the back room, like a duffel bag hitting the floor.

"What are you two niggers talking about?" slurred a loud voice.

"Watch your mouth, John Ray," Mary Ellen called. "We've got company. Use good English."

"I ain't talking English, woman!" he yelled. "This here is my house. I'm talking Nigganese."

Tut began to bark.

"This is *our* house!" Mary Ellen shouted back, like a woman who could dish it as well as she could take it. She slid the omelet onto the plate. "Now mind your manners and come and eat your dinner before I burn it to spite you." She bent over and swiped the yapping puppy on his wet nose. Whimpering, Tut retreated.

"Should I leave?" I asked, even though I didn't want to go. Things were getting interesting.

"No, dear. Please stay," Mary Ellen said. "You'll see—he'll be so glad to have a visitor from home."

John shuffled into the kitchen. He was tall and thin as a pencil and missing some upper teeth, but in his prominent cheekbones and rakish grin you could still see the devilishly handsome man he must have been. An ascot and smoking jacket would have seemed more fitting than his pilly brown bathrobe. Immediately, he spotted my digital camera.

"Leica?" he asked.

I nodded.

He gestured for me to hand it to him. I did.

"Look out," Mary Ellen warned. "You'll be leaving here without it."

John squinted at the viewing screen, scrolling back through the shots I'd snapped, as if to discover what I was looking for. He passed my pictures of the conical eight-foot termite hills, the malnourished child with her hair gone patchy and blond from kwashiorkor, the kora player with his head thrown back in song, and the Homowo festival where the red-robed chief and his entourage posed under umbrellas decorated with skulls. Finally, John paused at a picture of a seller at Makola Market carrying a tin basin full of groundnuts arranged in a flawless pyramid on her head.

"Not bad," he assessed.

"Thanks," I said, eager for his praise.

"This one's better." He scrutinized a picture of a very unofficial-looking hand-painted sign: BIRTH AND DEATH: KINDLY PASS TO THE NEXT GATE. Something to do with birth and death certificates, Kati had explained.

"I know where that is," Mary Ellen said, peeking over John's shoulder. "That's outside the American consulate. If you passed by there, Emily, then you've seen the lines. Throngs of Ghanaians are plotting for travel documents to enter the gates of the 'Land of Opportunity.' Not to mention the brain drain. Whether they're educated or not, your average Ghanaian's got serious get-outta-Ghana genes. They make no contribution to their nation's growth but can't stop talking about what's wrong with Ghana. They're definitely not foot soldiers. So, you see? We're not the only ones who want to leave. No one wants to stay here."

"I'm not going anywhere but the grave," John objected. "I'm an old man."

"Oh, hush. You're going to the living room to eat these eggs I made you, that's where you're going. Come, Emily. Let's sit."

We moved to the living room, where the walls were streaked with water stains from past rainy seasons. It smelled of mildew and bug spray. A small TV rested on a metal stand in the corner, its rabbit ears rigged with tin foil. Later on, Mary Ellen and I would watch one of her "stories," a South African soap opera called *Generations* whose twisted plot I could barely follow through the TV's screen of snow. But for now my attention was caught by a few of John's black-and-white prints hanging above a worn couch. He was reluctant to tell me about his work and confessed that most of his photographs were stored away in a trunk, probably growing mold. Whether or not he was still active as a photographer, he was inspired by my camera.

"I'll give you two hundred bucks for it," he offered.

"It's not for sale," I said. "I'm sorry."

"Two-twenty. Final offer."

The camera had cost me five hundred dollars, half my rent in Harlem. "No way."

John looked disgusted. I wished I could let go of my camera so easily; that I could see it for the possession it was and offer it freely, but it was too important to me. I wanted to give Mary Ellen and him something else. I realized too late that I'd been ungracious to show up empty-handed. "Here," I offered lamely, handing John a commemorative issue of *Time* magazine with Michael Jackson on the cover. The king of pop had died just before I left the States.

It was the worst gift I could have given.

"Just look what America did to this little brother's face," John spat, tossing the magazine aside like a dirty tissue. "And you wonder why we left that twisted piss hole of a country?"

"He did that to himself, John," said Mary Ellen.

"He did that to be *loved*," John corrected her.

"The women here bleach their faces too. They look like cadavers. It's no better here in Ghana. It's worse. I'm telling you, I want to leave."

"But where will you *go*?" I asked, somewhat exasperated. All this ceaseless wandering—my own, theirs—all this self-conscious navigation was exhausting.

"We're too old and broke to retire anywhere else," John huffed, sitting on the couch with his plate balanced on his bony knees. Tut sat begging at his feet, his tail swishing the floor.

"We talked about Belize and Tobago," Mary Ellen parried, recalling their gypsy days, "and I used to want to go to Cuba." She lowered herself next to John on the couch. I sat opposite them in a rattan chair next to a small bamboo shelf with a collection of small sculptures, a jade ashtray, and a pipe.

"But, to tell you the truth, now I just want to go home," Mary Ellen added. "Some people view returns as a sign of failure, but me, I want to go back."

"You mean to Chicago?" I asked.

"Well, for the last twenty years I've had strong urgings tugging at me, saying, 'Go home,' but where was home?"

"My wife waxes on and on like an amateur poet these days," John grumbled. He tucked a napkin under his chin and took a bite of his omelet. "She got bit by that Obama bug. Please don't get her started."

But she had started already. "I didn't think home was Chicago anymore," she continued. "I just had this longing—"

"You been to the Slave Coast yet?" John attempted to change the subject.

"No," I answered. "I plan to."

Mary Ellen kept talking as if John hadn't interrupted her monologue: "—this shapeless, persistent, intrusive longing . . . "

"The coast is usually the first place folks go," John said.

"At first we thought my parents would join us here, but my daddy balked. He said, 'That's why I left South Carolina when I did—no indoor plumbing, no electricity. If I thought sharecropping was backwards, then why should I go to *Africa*?'"

"Do you two visit the castles anymore?" I asked, trying to draw their two streams of conversation together.

"Please," scoffed John.

Mary Ellen said, "After Daddy and Mother died, I realized how homeless I was. Wherever I went, I thought I'd be misplaced." I sensed she was stuck in the same note of this song, like a record needle skipping in place on scratched vinyl. John had either stopped listening or pretended not to hear her.

He had his own song of disappointment. "The last time we went to Cape Coast, we were cornered by beggar children," he spat. "I could have slapped them upside their nappy heads. They sent us away in chains, we came back in planes, and they're still hustling. They should be filthy rich from selling us into slavery." The hurt in John's voice held more heat than the last bite of eggs on his plate. What did he want from those children? Kinship? Compassion? Contrition? Respect? And what did they see when they looked at him? An African? An American? A tourist? Or, as he put it, "an ATM"?

"You see what the West reaped from all those years of bloody trade in human misery? The birth of capitalism! But what did the

Africans earn for our souls? A bunch of beads and trinkets. And just look where that junk got them," John finished, defeated.

"But just look where we are now," Mary Ellen announced. Her face shone with pride. "In all my life, I never thought I'd see the day."

I knew she was referring to Obama. My neighbors of her generation all said the same thing on Election Day. I'd walked around Harlem photographing them with my Leica, impervious to the November cold. Nobody wanted to be inside. There was a charge in the air. We felt it. A black president! The church ladies in their ankle-length furs and whimsical hats outside Abyssinian Baptist Church, the trumpeter trilling "Battle Hymn of the Republic" triple-time on Speakers' Corner, the Vietnam vets sipping out of paper bags at the oblong base of the Adam Clayton Powell statue on 125th Street, the New Black Panthers in their dark sunglasses, outside the Studio Museum, and the old man hawking Obama buttons, essential oils, and shea butter across from the Apollo Theater—they all said the same thing: "I never thought I'd see the day."

They said it as if pinching themselves to be sure they weren't in a dream. But we were awake. This was happening in our country, in our lifetime. Swept up in the reverie, I bought an Obama button and pinned it to the shoulder strap of my bag, his face marking the spot where my right hand would go in the Pledge of Allegiance, in the appropriate region of my heart. Sure, he was unproven. He wasn't as radical as any of us wished. But he was a metaphor and, like the sankofa, the metaphor mattered.

I told the Rays about that night—how Victor and I watched the polls come in at the Shrine on Lenox Avenue; how packed it was; how at a certain point the proprietor stopped charging for drinks, turned off the volume on the TV, and put on Bob Marley; how we all knew the lyrics; how we danced to "Buffalo Soldier" and couldn't stop laughing; how we ran outdoors when it was clear he'd won and flocked down to 125th Street like it was the throbbing center of the universe, like we were the vestiges of a long-ago Garvey parade; how folks danced on cars and rooftops, setting off firecrackers and shouting his name, "Obama!," which was verb, adjective, and noun; how the crowd of thousands hushed its riotous noise; how our upturned faces watched his acceptance speech on a jumbo screen outside the Harlem State office building; how the ones who never thought they'd see the day openly cried tears of joy.

"Oh, child, you've made me homesick," Mary Ellen marveled. "John, I *told* you we should have been there that night."

John didn't answer. Somewhere in the middle of my story, he had either passed out or fallen asleep. Tut was now snuggled up next to him on the couch, happily licking the plate on his lap.

"We should have been in Chicago. We should have been right there with Obama and the people in Grant Park," Mary Ellen sighed.

I'd chosen not to mention the loud woman standing directly behind us in the crowd who said, "Let's not forget he's got a white mother, people. Now if we can get it together to elect a brother with two black parents, we can form a *truly* black nation," because at the time she'd struck me as a spoilsport and I didn't think the nation she imagined would embrace me as a citizen any more than Ghana had embraced Mary Ellen and John Ray.

"Well, it was a great day in Harlem but maybe I'm being overly sentimental," I admitted. I thought about the group of African Americans on my flight from JFK who'd knelt down to kiss the hot tarmac when we landed at Kotoka International Airport. I would have felt silly doing the same, but I understood the gesture. This trip wasn't a simple vacation for any of us, it was a vexed pilgrimage.

Mary Ellen said, "You can't help it, Emily. You're obviously a romantic; otherwise you wouldn't have come. Ghana attracts a lot of dreamers. Funny thing, since this country is so inhospitable to dreams."

She gathered Tut in her lap and stroked his yellow back. "When I came here, I suppose I was looking for family. I used to call myself African American. I don't call myself that anymore."

"What changed?"

"I realized I'm not African. Four hundred years away made me something else. I'm black. My neighbors here don't think of me as family at all. What hurt me the most was that the women didn't embrace me as a sister. They're materialistic," she said. "Most of them assume we have an inside connection to get them a U.S. passport. Or that because we're American, we're rich. They have the audacity to think we're fortunate. Half of them are jealous that their ancestors weren't sold into slavery too. Can you believe it? They think they'd have better opportunities that way."

"Are they wrong?"

Mary Ellen waved her hand. "Slavery was an opportunistic in-stitution for slave traders and slave owners but not for slaves. And worst of all, the Ghanaians still practice it here, more or less. I sometimes wonder who gave lessons to who when it came to brutality and inhumanity—whether the colonialists taught the Africans or the Africans taught the colonialists."

I'd never heard that said before, not by a black person. I asked Mary Ellen if I'd heard her correctly.

"Just go inside my neighbors' compounds. Domestic help is the custom here but that owner-slave mentality makes me uncom-fortable. The madam brings her housegirl to Makola, points at the items she needs. The girl carries that load on her head. What is the madam carrying? Money, car keys, and self-righteousness. She complains, 'These people are lazy and shiftless.' Ah, shades of America! The servants' quarters are stashed from view like the photos of plantations where the slaves' quarters are out of sight."

"You really think it compares with slavery?"

"If you don't believe me, just pay our neighbor Abena a visit. She runs a shop a few doors down. See for yourself what you think about her housegirls. They have a saying here: 'The ruin of a nation begins in the homes of its people.' I used to think, this can't be so, not in Nkrumah's country known across the globe for spearheading Pan-Africanism. I was naive. Naivety's a charming quality in a girl your age, but sugar, at my age it's just a pretty word for foolishness."

We laughed until our laughter ran out and then we sat in silence, listening to John's labored breathing and the sounds of the highlife at the funeral across the road, which seemed an ocean away. I looked at Mary Ellen and saw a version of myself, or how I might be in the future if I didn't stop dwelling on the provenance of my blackness. *Misplaced* was the word she'd used, a more delicate choice than *displaced*. It was not so much that she lacked a home but that she'd been put in the wrong place and then forgotten. "I don't think you're foolish," I told her.

"Maybe not, but my thinking is warped," Mary Ellen confessed. "My daddy was brown-skinned, like John here. My mother looked so much like you. She could have passed for white. When they drove in their Packard, he used to have to pretend to be her chauffeur so they wouldn't get stopped by the police. You grow up in a world like that, boy, does it mess with your head."

I thought I understood. My head was messed up too.

Mary Ellen lovingly wiped a line of drool from her husband's chin with the napkin folded in her hand. Something in her gesture made me worry he was dying. And indeed, by this time next year, he would be dead, cremated, and memorialized in the courtyard of the Du Bois Center. The tableau in which I now sat with the Rays would be restaged there to depict John's life—the rattan chair, the little rug before me, the thirsty-looking potted plant, and the bamboo shelf to my left with its jade ashtray and black pipe. His photographs would be unearthed and, just as he suspected, many of them would be freckled with mold.

"I'm sorry if I've taken the moon and stars out of Africa for you," Mary Ellen said softly, scratching Tut behind the ears. But how could she have done that? Robert E. Lee, who would pass away within the same week as John, was right. I hadn't yet spoken to an African. I was very tired suddenly. I missed Victor. I wanted a foot rub or a stiff drink and didn't know what else to say.

"Stay awhile," Mary Ellen begged, as if sensing I wanted to escape their claustrophobic house. Then she reached to turn the dial on the TV. "My stories are coming on."

15

Kindly Pass to the Next Gate

THE NEXT DAY I took up Mary Ellen's challenge and visited Auntie Abena's compound. It was open and bright where the Ray's house was private and dark, a pop-up picture of something Kati had expressed: "In Ghana the houses are strictly for sleeping. Life is to be lived outdoors!"

One half of the gate was flung open, and the other half was in use as a drying and display rack for long wet batik cloths. At least a dozen people worked in the courtyard at various tasks—pounding fufu, feeding children, dunking cloth in bathtubs of deep purple dye. More batiks, six yards long and wet as tongues, hung over the chocolate-brown walls or stretched out to dry on the ground both inside the courtyard and outside on the sidewalk. When I arrived, I had the delightful sensation of making a grand entrance on a red carpet—or, more accurately, a series of patterned carpets—ochre, azure, chartreuse, and orange. I couldn't really tell where the street ended and Auntie Abena's property began.

"Akwaaba!" Auntie Abena sang from the door of her shop, To-getherness Spot, which fronted the compound at one side of the gate. "You are welcome." One of her shopgirls produced a stool and a sweating bottle of Coke. Before I knew it, I was resting inside the shop at Auntie Abena's side with the cold soda in my hand. At first I wasn't sure what to say. I knew better than to ask if her servants were her slaves, and certainly not while she was busy running what looked like a miniature version of the bodega on

147th Street and Amsterdam where I sometimes bought orange juice and a bagel on my walk to work.

Togetherness Spot was no bigger than a walk-in closet, yet, like Mary Poppins's carpet bag, contained far more bounty beneath its tin roof than seemed logically possible. Heinz baked beans, cans of concentrated juice, rolls of Mentos, sanitary napkins, Voda phone cards, bottles of Malta and Fanta and shampoo, toothpicks, tins of margarine, Ajax powder, Ovaltine, sewing needles, insecticide spray, fat yellow bars of soap, plastic canisters of hard candy, packets of biscuits, and bunches of zippers neatly crammed every inch of every narrow shelf. The thick gold bracelet on Auntie Abena's wrist twinkled as she siphoned sugar from a large bag into several smaller plastic bags and twisted them closed. She had done the same thing with millet and cassava flour, and, in this way, turned a larger profit. I noticed that her steady, if slow, stream of customers bought items in tiny portions, one or two eggs instead of a dozen, four slices of white bread instead of a loaf, one stick of gum or a single cigarette instead of a pack.

"How many children do you have?" Auntie Abena wanted to know, just like the woodworker. I'd been so busy watching that I was surprised to be seen. But her question didn't much surprise me. Somewhere inside my years of travel it had replaced "What are you?" and "Where are you from?" as the surest means to fix me on some kind of map.

"No children yet," I told her.

Auntie Abena paused to study me over the frames of her rectangular glasses. She was a widow somewhere in her fifties. Originally from the hills of Akropong in the southeast, she had a quick, gap-toothed smile and high, wide cheekbones. Her thick black hair was permed straight, parted on one side, and curled up at the ends in a 1960s-style flip.

"No children?" Her eyes were smiling but concerned.

"Not *yet*," I stressed.

"Papa!" she exclaimed, crossing her arms over her ample chest. "Then who will inherit you when you die?"

This was a new question. Who will inherit me when I die? I wasn't planning on dying anytime soon. There was still plenty of time to have kids, I hoped, and doing so seemed ancillary to the task of figuring out where I should make my home. But it struck me as somehow connected to her question that death was near enough to hit with a stone. Christiansborg Castle, the Danish slave fort (now the office of President Mills), was on the beach just a short walk away; the Rays' house, which had felt like a tomb, was just down the road; and almost directly across the street, last night's funeral was still raging. Even louder and larger, it now included a buffet spread over a white lace tablecloth.

"In Ghana we adore the dead. *Abusua do funu*. It means 'the family loves the corpse,'" Auntie Abena told me. "Weekends are for funerals." There were professional mourners, she explained, grievers hired to wail with sufficient force to deliver the dead to the spirit world. If the dead weren't properly glorified, they would curse the living from beyond the grave. But I didn't notice anyone crying among the revelers across the road. These people were dancing.

Auntie Abena said that her neighbor had died forty days before, at eighty-four years of age. It was a good death because she'd lived a long life and borne many children, grandchildren, and great-grandchildren, all of whom were in attendance. This was why the mourners wore white and celebrated. If she'd died young, of unnatural causes, they would suspect witchcraft and tear out their hair. Auntie Abena unrolled a copy of the old woman's funeral poster and showed it to me. A cross between an obituary and a concert flyer, it listed the pertinent details of the woman's life next to a recent photograph of her face. Scrolled across the top in bold cursive lettering were the words: CALL TO GLORY.

"As for me, I have five children," Auntie Abena said proudly, rolling the poster back up and using it like a conductor's baton to point through the rear door of the shop. Peeking back into the busy courtyard, I couldn't tell who belonged to the family and who served the family. All of them worked and their work seemed woven into the fabric of the household. I envied that closeness even as I didn't think I could stand the lack of privacy.

"Which are your children?" I asked.

"That one is my oldest daughter, Naa." Auntie Abena pointed the baton at a woman in a matching batik skirt and blouse. Naa had thick eyelashes and her hair was in short twists like a crown of exclamation points. "A design school graduate. This batik is her business."

Naa's batik shop stood on the opposite side of the gate fronting the compound, twin to Togetherness Spot and equally tiny. Stocked with finished cloth, it was closed for the moment while the new pieces were being designed in the courtyard. Later on, I would buy a batik and bring it to a tailor to have it fashioned into a dress, but for the moment I watched as Naa painted wavy wax brushstrokes on blank white cloth.

Four young men assisted her at wide wooden tables. Two of them dipped brushes into a black pot of boiling wax and copied Naa's pattern. The third used a woodblock to stamp Adinkra symbols, including the sankofa, on cloth that had already been dyed, and the fourth folded and stacked the finished batiks into tidy piles after smoothing them with an iron heated by coals. These men were Naa's apprentices, Auntie Abena explained, not relations.

"Are they paid?" I asked.

"No. They are working for the benefit of learning a craft."

That didn't seem so bad. I'd been an unpaid intern myself. It wasn't the same thing as slavery, even if it was slavish.

Auntie Abena pointed next at a pretty toddler with the face of a middle-aged woman. "That is Naa's daughter, Baaba." Little Baaba, in waist beads, played *ampe*, a jumping and clapping game, with the shopgirl who'd given me the Coke. Finally, Auntie Abena pointed at the infant bound to the shopgirl's back: "And the baby is Nana, Naa's son."

"Your grandchildren are beautiful," I said, and it was true. Baaba and Nana had their mother's eyelashes, designed to shade their eyes from the equatorial sun.

Auntie Abena beamed.

"What about those two?" I asked of the two sweet-faced teenage girls in front of a clothesline hung with brassieres and synthetic hair extensions. Both girls wore their hair natural, cropped close to their scalps. One pounded fufu with a wooden pestle as long as an oar. She gripped it with both hands, lifted it above her head, and brought it down with a thud by lowering her arms and bending at the waist. The other had faint Hausa scarification markings on her cheeks, like cat scratches. Crouching astride the giant wooden mortar, she deftly added water and pieces of boiled cassava from a cookstove, then turned the stretchy fufu like pizza dough every time the pestle lifted, pulling her hand out of its way just in time for the pestle to fall. *Thud, thud, thud.*

"What are their names?" I asked.

"Gifty and Rebecca."

"Your housegirls?"

Auntie Abena nodded. "Eh heh."

"Are they paid?"

"Their parents couldn't feed them. We give them food."

"That's how you pay them?"

"Sometimes we help their families too."

"Do they go to school?"

"No."

"Do they live here with you?"

"No, apart from Adolay. We adopted her." Adolay was the girl playing *ampe* with Baaba, the one with the baby on her back.

"Oh?" I brightened.

"But we can't keep her much longer. She has just begun her menstruation and could become pregnant from one of these rough boys. Another mouth to feed-o!" Auntie Abena clucked her tongue. *Thud, thud, thud.*

Was Mary Ellen right? Was this a kind of slavery? It seemed wrong to import that concept when I knew so little about the backgrounds of these girls, the context of their labor, and its relative benefits to them. Besides, Auntie Abena and Naa, the businesswomen at the top of the household's pyramid, were working tirelessly hard themselves. But it also seemed wrong for children to be unschooled, working without compensation or foreseeable prospects. Where did Gifty and Rebecca live if not here? And would Adolay really have to leave as a consequence of puberty? Where would she go next? Would she sleep at Makola Market on sacks of rice like the vulnerable *kayayo* girls, porting fermented *kenkey* wrapped in banana leaves or charcoal briquettes on her head for pennies? Or would she be married off? What was I doing at fourteen? Complaining about having to practice my clarinet, comparing my development to the diagrams in *Our Bodies, Ourselves*, occasionally babysitting for five dollars an hour, and, on Thursday nights, watching *Twin Peaks* at Tamar's house with heaping bowls of ice cream on our laps.

It was nearly impossible for me to comprehend, with my limited understanding of slavery, that there was any other kind of bondage. I knew about field slaves and house slaves and thought of them mainly as tied to the plantation, deep in the past. To my mind they were chattel without rights, commodities who could be bought, sold, and inherited, property who were not considered human, people whose children inherited their status in perpetuity. Until I read the book *Lose Your Mother*, whose author, Saidiya Hartman, had visited the Rays before I did in her journey to retrace the transatlantic slave route, I didn't know the many words in Akan for "slave," the particular shades of meaning for Ghana's own peculiar institution. *Akoa*—a subject, assistant, or vassal; *awowa*—a bondservant pawned for a relative's debt; *akyere*—a peon enslaved as punishment for a crime; *domun*—a captive of war; *odonkor*—a person for sale in the market. This was the book my eyes strained to read in the weak light of my hotel room. I hadn't known that of these words, *odonkor*, closest to what we mean by "slave" in the West, was the only one colored by stigma and shame, a brand of dishonor that made the topic of slavery, as I understood it, utterly taboo to discuss with Ghanaians. And I wouldn't know until later about the scope of contemporary slave traffic in Ghana—grand enough to land it on the Tier 2 Watch List of the U.S. State Department's 2009 Trafficking in Persons Report, which opens:

> Ghana is a source, transit, and destination country for children and women trafficked for the purposes of forced labor and commercial sexual exploitation. Trafficking within the country is more prevalent than transnational trafficking and the majority of victims are children. Both boys and girls are trafficked within Ghana for forced labor in agriculture and the fishing industry, for street hawking, forced begging by religious instructors, as porters, and possibly for forced kente weaving. Over 30,000 children are believed to be working as porters, or *Kayaye*, in Accra alone. Annually, the IOM reports numerous deaths of boys trafficked for hazardous forced labor in the Lake Volta fishing industry. Girls are trafficked within the country for domestic servitude and sexual exploitation. To a lesser extent, boys are also trafficked internally for sexual exploitation, primarily for sex tourism . . . In 2008, the UN reported that a form of ritual servitude called *Trokosi*, in which young girls are subjected to forced labor and sexual servitude, continues in at least 23 fetish shrines.

These practices are so entrenched in Ghanaian society today that in 2007, when former president Rawlings announced the nation would commemorate the two hundredth anniversary of slavery's abolishment in the British Caribbean on Emancipation Day, Ghanaians responded, "Has slavery ended in Ghana?"

When I arrived in Ghana, my narrative of slavery was one of black victimhood and white violence. I was vaguely aware that some Africans had colluded in and profited from the international slave trade, but not that in a system similar to serfdom, Africans had enslaved Africans for centuries before the Europeans arrived. If they assumed the European system was the same, they were sorely mistaken. Unlike the slaves who would work the plantations in the West, domestic slaves in Ghana could own property, inherit their master's wealth, specialize in artisan crafts, marry, and bear children, and they were rarely sold. But had those Africans who sold Africans to Europeans (and who had no concept of racial ideology, or of themselves as African) foreseen the brutality of chattel slavery or the magnitude of the millions dispossessed and dead, would they have had moral qualms about the trade? Probably not, as long as they stood to profit from it. For a long, long time, it was perfectly legal, and besides, they weren't selling their own. The people they exchanged were spoils of war won in battles with different tribes who spoke different languages and prayed to different gods.

I didn't know that domestic trade in slaves continued through the tail end of the nineteenth century, decades past the point when the transatlantic trade had been officially abolished. In that century there were more slaves in Africa than in the Americas. In West Africa, these slaves and their descendants made up somewhere between half and three-quarters of the entire population. The largest slave market in Ghana wasn't run by Europeans on the coast, where I would make the compulsory errand to wrestle with the crime of slavery, but by Africans in Salaga, which sat poised below the Sahel and above the Volta River. Tens of thousands of captives were bought and sold each year of the nineteenth century in Salaga at the perfect crossroads to feed the ravenous appetite of the trans-Saharan, transatlantic, and African slave trades.

I didn't know much of anything about the history, complexity, or semantics of slavery on the African side of the Atlantic. So is it any wonder that when I watched Gifty, Rebecca, and Adolay at work with an eye to understanding their status, or tried to talk to Auntie Abena about what had brought me to Ghana, as Mary Ellen and Robert E. Lee had respectively tasked me, I hardly knew where to begin? I was shamefully unequipped.

Auntie Abena interrupted my thoughts. "You are too sober." She looked at me with bemusement and pity.

"You're right," I conceded. "I am too sober."

I hoped she'd caught me looking ponderous rather than critical. I knew that there was a grave conceptual error in peeping at Auntie Abena's household through the goggles of slavery, that she had never sold a slave into the dungeons at Cape Coast, that the racism of my homeland was not her responsibility, and that my confusing alienation should not be her burden. Besides, I was enjoying her company and watching the world pass in and out of her permeable gate—customers, relatives, mourners, a girl selling sugarloaf pineapples, a fisherman hawking fresh mackerel to be cooked into *red red* with black-eyed peas and palm oil in Auntie Abena's bottomless outdoor cook pot. This was the small earth in front of her. I admired how contentedly she sat on her well-polished stool in Togetherness Spot with its view of the family compound, full, fulfilled.

"Let me help you," I offered, attempting to twist the end of one of her little bags of sugar into a knot.

"Help? With those soft hands?" Auntie Abena laughed as I fumbled at the simple task. Then, with winning goodwill, she called me sister, pinched my stomach, and told me I needed to wear waist beads. "Tell your man to count the beads one by one at night with his tongue if it pleases you! It will give you a sex feeling. And then you may get a child."

I agreed to give it a try.

"You should try it so many times as it takes you until the child arrives!" she laughed. Then she squeezed my thigh and invited me to "come and discover some fun at this my neighbor's funeral."

The funeral. I got so swiftly drunk on fermented palm wine that all I can remember is a feeling of increasing bliss as we danced to highlife until it was dark. Whether it was a trick of the equator or a trick of the drink, the darkness was sudden and absolute. It was day and then it wasn't. This night was extravagant. Probably the dead woman's family had bankrupted themselves for her glorious send-off in order that she should be respected in the next life. But even I could see that four hundred bodies dressed in lambent white, dancing themselves into a dizzy galaxy, was a priceless celebration of this life and life in general, the outrageous gift of feet and knees and hips and wrists. If you allowed yourself to forget yourself, you could be at home anywhere. The air stank, sweetly, of sweat. My heart drummed in my chest. Our feet drummed on the ground. *Thud, thud, thud.* I danced, it grew dark, and I was glad my muscles hurt. When I stumbled home and blacked out beneath Naa's batik in my bed at Chez Lien, I was smiling and unconcerned about who might be whose slave and the pitiful lack of lightbulbs.

The sun glinting off the white walls of the slave castle seared my eyeballs. It was high noon and the heat was unforgiving. I had no shadow and neither did the castle. I glanced at it sideways, unable to look upon it directly. My stance reminded me of a dear friend who once drove me in his jeep along Route 64 where it chases the churning Rio Grande. Not once did he turn his head from the road to look directly at the water. When I asked him why, he told me he was cowed by the river's majesty. But it wasn't for its majesty that I couldn't look upon the castle.

Of the sixty trade castles and forts dotting Ghana's three-hundred-mile coastline, I'd chosen to visit the one in Elmina because it was the most notorious. Being the first permanent European settlement in Africa, it was also the oldest. The Portuguese began construction on Fort São Jorge da Mina in 1482 with stones imported from Portugal. It was designed to defend against attacks from the local people and from other Europeans, but in the seventeenth century it was captured by the Dutch. In the nineteenth century it was purchased by the British. Now it is a World Heritage monument.

In the castle's early days Europeans didn't think of themselves as European any more than Africans thought of themselves as African. The Dutch weren't betraying a European bond when they captured the Portuguese castle, just as the Mandinke weren't betraying an African bond when they captured Ayuba. Nor, in the castle's early days, was the structure a slave castle. Like most of the fortifications built after São Jorge by Holland, England, Denmark, Sweden, and the state of Brandenburg, the castle was built to promote and protect the trade of goods, not people. The Europeans bartered brandy, brassware, beads, and guns for African pepper, ivory, and gold. These were the treasures warehoused in the castles.

But by 1700, the face of African commerce had changed. Holland and Britain needed labor on the plantations they were laying in their Caribbean and American colonies. Year after year, more and more slaves exchanged hands until they'd tipped the scales of balance and replaced gold as the most lucrative commodity of all. At the peak of the slave trade in the eighteenth century, nearly a million slaves were shipped to the New World from Ghana alone. In 1730 a report from the Dutch West India Company tells us that "the part of Africa which as of old is known as the 'Gold Coast' . . . has now virtually changed into a pure Slave Coast." Someone had to pick all that cotton, till the soil, cut the cane.

Richard Wright wrote of the castle's battlements as "awe-inspiring," their form as having "a somber but resplendent majesty." How should I describe the sprawling São Jorge Castle? Its canons were erect. Its towers rose two hundred feet in the air. In places its walls were thirty feet thick, punctuated by embrasures like black keys on a grand piano. It exuded a crumbling grandeur. Its edges and corners were rounded by time. It was ringed by palm trees and, in a postcard, might have been mistaken for an elegant resort hotel.

But to me the castle just looked like a wedding cake made out of pigeon shit.

I'd arrived carsick and hungover from the funeral, having driven the hundred dusty miles from Accra with a young goateed driver named Elolo who couldn't comprehend why I wanted to go there. He was Kati's nephew, through her ex-husband, Mr. Dagadu. "At least let me take you to Akosombo Dam or somewhere beautiful instead! Elmina is no good. Only black Americans come across the water to cry about that place," Elolo offered, assuming I was something other than a black American. I decided to play race spy rather than try to convince him of my blackness.

"You must guide them often," I prompted.

"Of course. They have big money to spend on their tears. But with all that money, what are they crying for?"

"For their ancestors," I said. If Elolo made something near the national average of two dollars a day, why should he sympathize with people who could afford to pay more than he could make in two years just for the airfare to come and grieve for ancestors they couldn't even name? The baldness of his car's tires made me sad. The vehicle was held together with duct tape, rubber bands, and grit. Every time we hit a rut in the road or had to stop for a herd of cattle, its engine shuddered, choked, and stalled, on the verge of dying altogether. I had no doubt his foreign passengers complained. But given that he'd been raised in such a rich mourning tradition, I wondered why he wasn't more sensitive to the pain that brought the black diaspora to Ghana. "They're honoring the souls of their dead," I said, somewhat defensively. "They come here to pay their respects."

"But they don't respect *us*," Elolo objected. "These black people-o! They keep saying they are Africans like us. 'We are one people.' 'One Africa.' But all they do is criticize us. Why won't these blacks leave somebody alone? They say, 'You are using the wrong fuel in your car. The air is dirty. The gutter stinks. It is unclean to cook near a gutter, therefore your food is dirty. Also you are dirty. You must wash yourself more frequently.' They disapprove of how we live."

Queasy from last night's palm wine and the ruts in the road, I rolled down the passenger window to clear my head. The air rushed in, hot as a steam room, cloudy with red dust, and seething with diesel fumes. I quickly tried to roll the window back up but the crank broke loose in my hand. Flashes of life scrolled past: TRY JESUS DIGITAL PHOTO CENTER, PRINCE OF PEACE MOTORS, GOD BE THE GLORY BEAUTY SALON. Ghana was, in Kati's words, a "rabidly Christian" country, which by no means meant animism was dead, just that devotion and praise to God as key to success was often expressed in signs like these. We passed a CLAP FOR JESUS BLOCK FACTORY and an ironically empty fruit stand called LITTLE IS MUCH WHEN GOD IS IN IT. I saw thatch-roofed mud huts made of dung and straw with sheets strung in their doorways, a herd of goats in the shade of a calabash tree, a woman bent over a basin washing her hair, a gang of children tossing garbage onto a tire fire, a man holding two roasted grasscutter rodents by their naked tails. I would have liked to photograph these scenes but, just as Mary Ellen warned me not to, I'd left her house without my camera. For all I knew, it was still in the pocket of John Ray's brown bathrobe.

Elolo griped on about the gripes of black Americans. "And even if they are spending their nights in the biggest hotel in all of Ghana, they cry, 'It's too hot here. Where is the air-conditioning? Where is the toilet paper? This bed has fleas. The water doesn't run. The TV is broken. The power is out.' Eh, my sister, you should see them! They think they are too fine."

"That's entitlement for you," I said, shaking my aching head. "I bet they believe lightbulbs grow on trees."

"Yes! You have understood me. When a man's coat is threadbare, it is easy to pick a hole in it."

"But not all of them are like that, Elolo."

"Are you sure?"

I hesitated. "Yes."

"How would you know?" He sucked his teeth. "These blacks truly expect too much. When you go to a new country, you can't expect to belong to that place. Here, everybody knows where they are from, but these American blacks are lost here. They will hire me to be their guide in Africa, but truly they intend to guide *me* to become a better African. They should not come in here thinking that they are on a God-given mission to change Mother Africa. They want us to love them, not as our neighbors but as our superiors. So I ask you this: How can we weep with *them*?"

The castle hove into view. "We are seriously approaching," Elolo remarked. "Slavery is not the only story about black people. It's only a small story! Don't they know that if tomorrow a slave ship arrived at Elmina to carry us to America, so many Ghanaians would climb on board that this ship would sink to the bed of the ocean from our weight?" he laughed. I couldn't help laughing, myself. But who was the butt of the joke?

I'd been to the Annual Tribute to Our Ancestors of the Middle Passage celebrated every June in Coney Island, where people tossed roses and oranges into the surf while the Wonder Wheel spun behind them. Here I was on the flipside of the tragic Atlantic. From the drawbridge of the castle I could see that the beach was being used by the local men and boys as a public toilet. Once I crossed over the moat and into the mouth of the castle, I could no longer make out the sound of the waves. The auction hall was silent, vast, and bright as sin. Blinding white. Whiter than cowrie shell, white as bone. There was no shade. It was hard to see.

The first thing I saw was a marble plaque engraved with these words:

IN EVERLASTING MEMORY
OF THE ANGUISH OF OUR ANCESTORS
MAY THOSE WHO DIED REST IN PEACE
MAY THOSE THAT RETURN FIND THEIR ROOTS
MAY HUMANITY NEVER AGAIN PERPETRATE
SUCH INJUSTICE AGAINST HUMANITY
WE, THE LIVING, VOW TO UPHOLD THIS

The scale of those words was too large for my mind to contain. I could see pieces of the castle, such as the heart-shaped plastic funeral wreath of flowers someone had placed beneath the plaque, the iron balustrades decorated with the initials of the Dutch West India Company, and the skull and crossbones above the door to the male dungeon. But like one of the blind men in that Indian parable about the elephant, where one feels the tail and says it is a rope, one feels the belly and says it is a wall, one feels an ear and says it is a hand fan, one feels the trunk and says it is a tree branch, and one feels a tusk and says it is a solid pipe, I could only grasp at the castle's details, not understand its shape as a whole. If I had been hovering above it, viewing it from a helicopter at a cold distance, or reading about it in a dispassionate history book, I might have been able to discern its magnitude, but I was swallowed inside it, wandering its entrails on a guided tour of hell.

As Elolo had predicted, the others in my tour group were black Americans. An elderly couple from Brooklyn, a family of five from

Baltimore, and two middle-aged sisters from Pasadena who peeled off halfway through the tour for Cape Coast when they realized that was the castle the Obamas had visited, not this. "I heard he cried," the one using a kente-print umbrella as a sunshade said by way of explanation. "But they won't show *that* in the news," added her sister with the knockoff designer bag, and they were off to replicate the president's purported trail of tears, leaving the rest of us shading our eyes in the Dutch West India Company trading hall where, our guide explained, a male slave in 1750 worth six ounces of gold could be traded in equivalent goods such as: one thousand beads, four pieces of fine linen, two muskets, or one anker of brandy. If he was missing a tooth the slave was worth less, though smearing his skin with palm oil was a useful trick to make him seem strong and young enough to fetch the full price.

"God almighty," said the father from Baltimore, shaking with rage.

I wanted to feel angry too, but I felt nothing aside from dizziness, not even in the dank female dungeon, which was humid and swarming with flies. The Dutch word for this storeroom was *hoeregat*—whore hold. One hundred and fifty women at a time were imprisoned for as long as it took for the ships to arrive. One month, three months in the barracoon. It's hard to say how they crammed so many women in. As many as 15 percent of them died here before the ships arrived, mainly of dysentery, from lying in their own waste. The accretion of menstrual blood, excrement, urine, sweat, and tears combined over time into a carpet several inches thick upon the stone floor. I believed I could still smell it, the compacted issue of those women's bodies. I wanted to smell it. Something stank but it may just have been the green beard of algae on the dungeon walls.

A rope ladder led through a trapdoor from the female dungeon up to the governor's private quarters. He could descend and choose whichever woman in the whore hold he desired. The governor's quarters, which overlooked the sea, were breezy and palatial. Attached to his chambers was a worship space where the soldiers,

225

lieutenants, clergymen, bookkeeper, and governor had prayed. What did the company men pray for in that lofty room? Within a year of their arrival from Europe, most of the white men died of "climate fever." They died between the harmattan and the monsoon, between the Tropic of Cancer and the Tropic of Capricorn where there were no seasons, where the humidity turned their wigs to mold. They died of hepatitis, guinea worm, typhoid, boredom, malaria, and yellow fever. For the most part they were too weak to penetrate the interior. They simply sat in their fort and waited for the slaves to be brought to them. The castle must have been a hell, a higher circle of hell than the hell of the dungeons and the belly of the boats, but a circle of hell all the same. The officers could not have seen Africa as the utopia many Europeans envisioned it to be during the age of discovery, a tropical Eden before the Fall. This was the Fall. What did they think in the chapel above the dungeons when they read the psalm I discovered high up on the wall?

Zion is des heeren ruste
  Zion is the Lord's throne

Dit is syn woonplaetsein
  This is his resting place

Eeuwighey.
  For all eternity.

Did it seem to the Dutchmen, as it did to me, a terrible irony for the castle to be cast as the throne of Zion? Or was the church above the dungeon a reminder that sometimes, as Obama remarked at Cape Coast Castle, "we can stand by great evils even as we think that we are doing good"?

"This history is not told to open old wounds but to serve as education," the guide told us. "For you and I to come together to fight the slave trade. Together we stand. United we fall. The history is not also told to point a finger. No. It is basically told to bring us together." The guide said nothing about the expansion of African slavery in response to Atlantic trade. He offered no approaches to work through that history. He gave no information about the slave traffic going on in Ghana today. But with a great show of solemnity, he led us down a stone staircase through the transit dungeon and the room, dark as a cave, where slaves were once branded on the forehead, back, or arm with the stamp of the ship they would be forced to embark.

"Where did they think they were going to go?" whispered the retired wife from Brooklyn, removing her Panama hat. Moving slowly and groping the brick walls with our hands, we arrived at the Room of No Return with its exit to the sea, a narrow, provocative door. Originally, before the goods transported from the castle included human beings, this door was wider. It was made into a slit for the slaves, tight as a cattle shoot, to prevent them from stampeding or from seeing with clarity where they were going.

This, then, was the door. It struck me as vaginal. *Birth and Death, kindly pass to the next gate.* You passed through it and onto a ship for Suriname or Curaçao, or through similar doorways for Cuba or Jamaica, Savannah or New Orleans. You passed through it, lost everything, and became something else. You lost your language. You lost your parents. You were no longer Asante or Krobo, Ewe or Ga. You became black. You were a slave. Your children inherited your condition. You lost your children. You lost your gods, as you had known them. You slaved. You suffered, like Christ, the new God you learned of. You learned of the Hebrew slaves of old. In the field, you sang about Moses and Pharaoh. You built a church, different from your masters'. You prayed for freedom. You wondered about the Promised Land, where that place might be.

The sea has receded since those days. The pier where the dugout canoes were tied to collect, then carry, the slaves to the anchored ships is long gone, but the stones that propped up the pier are still there, like gravestones in the sand. The youngest of the children from Baltimore, no more than six and no doubt tempted by the peek of blue the doorway offered, dropped his plastic brontosaurus and tried to make a break for the beach.

"No you don't!" his father snapped, yanking the boy back by his collar and smacking him on the backside of his head.

Our guide held up his index finger to gather our attention. "Here was the point where the slaves broke down and cried," he said. As if on cue, the woman from Brooklyn broke down and cried. She reached into a Macy's bag, pulled out a beribboned funeral wreath of her own, and set it on the floor. Her husband later explained that the wreath was a gift from their church back home. "In Memory of Our Departed Ancestors. May We Keep the Torch Burning."

I thought about the eternal flames burning at the Holocaust memorials in Jerusalem and Washington, D.C., and felt the absence of such a gesture at this monument. I wasn't looking for anything as grand, or as grotesque, as the reenactment ceremonies staged here from time to time. But as a museum, the castle disappointed me. There was nothing written on the walls. There were no marks left by the captives. There were no maps to display the regions from which they'd been kidnapped, no paintings of how they'd lived, no glass cases to show their belongings. Nor were there any accounts in their words of the hell it was to be imprisoned here. What we know about them we know from the ledgers and journals of the merchants. The slaves themselves left no shadow.

The castle was cavernous, the lives it swallowed, digested, excreted too staggering to fathom. I once visited the Anne Frank House in Amsterdam with my mother. We gasped in the same instant before the pencil marks on the yellowed wallpaper where Mrs. Frank had measured Anne's growth. My mother had done the same for me and my brothers, and maybe all mothers do this for their growing children. When we confronted the topmost line, the point where Anne's life was cut down, we inhaled as if history had punched us in the gut. It was easier to measure the loss of one girl's life than the lives of six million. It was easier to cry when you could see that person's face and read her story. I wanted a moment like that. I wanted a yardstick. I wanted to know Burial 101's name.

"We think it was about sixty million slaves they shipped to the New World. Of that number, I am sorry to say, only twenty percent survived. But look at the bright side, my sisters and brothers. Now it is no longer called the Room of No Return because you have come back home! They left in chains but you came freely. Now it is more properly called the Room of Return," the guide said enthusiastically. "So!" He clapped and finished with a prayer: "May the ancestors rest in perfect peace, amen."

"Amen," we responded, crossing ourselves. The mother from Baltimore continued to cry. Her little boy cried too, but I knew from the way he rubbed the back of his head that it wasn't for the sake of the slaves. I wanted to cry but I could not. I couldn't buy the idea that we had closed some broken circle by returning. Our guide wore a bright red T-shirt that said COCA COLA, ST. GEORGE CASTLE. I do not know what the link was between Coke and the castle except that the tour felt as much an advertisement as the T-shirt. For sale was the notion that this was a reunion and that our visitation represented progress.

In the gift shop you could buy a postcard with a poem called "Living the Dream," which read:

Rosa sat so Martin could walk
Martin walked so Obama could run
Obama ran so our children could fly!

As if to suggest we'd crossed some racial finish line. Was this what black Americans wanted to buy? Was this really what they came to Ghana for? I was more interested in the book by David Rooney, also for sale in the gift shop, called *Kwame Nkrumah: Vision and Tragedy.* I purchased this book before lunching with the retired couple from Brooklyn in the restaurant attached to the castle.

"This fish is inedible," complained the wife, laying down her fork and batting away the flies with her hat. "Do they have to drown everything in palm oil?" Their trip to Ghana was a seventieth-birthday present for her husband. She'd also gifted him with a $350 DNA test through African Ancestry, a successful black-owned genealogy company that genetically linked him to the Hausa people of Nigeria.

"I told her not to spend all that money," said her husband. He wore cataract sunglasses and madras shorts.

"It was worth every penny," she insisted. "If we don't know our past, we can't understand our present."

"So why did you come here instead of going to Nigeria?" I asked.

"Nigerians are con artists," the wife said. "Don't you get those e-mails from Prince So-and-So asking you to deposit a thousand dollars in his bank account? I hate to think how many poor folks they sucker with that scheme."

"But how did it feel to figure out where your ancestors were from?" I asked the husband.

He shrugged and looked down at his Velcro sneakers. He seemed depressed, wiped out from the castle. "I guess it felt good to fill in a gap. But what do I know about the Hausa? We don't know them and they don't know us. All I know is that I always wanted to see Africa before I die. It was just easier to plan a trip to Ghana is all," he said.

They were lodging at a nearby hotel that catered to return-ees—One Afrika Guest House. The place was run by a former travel agent from the Bronx now called Seestah Imahkus Njinga, and her husband, a retired firefighter, renamed Nana Ababio. I'd been planning to stay there that night myself, but the tour of the castle had changed my mind. I didn't think I'd find what I was looking for at the One Afrika Guest House any more than the retiree from Brooklyn had found what he was looking for in his DNA sequence.

Instead, I called Elolo to come pick me up. I waited for his crappy car on the small bridge over the Benya River that connected the castle to Elmina town. Fishing canoes painted as bright as Kati's beads bobbed beneath me. The water slapped against the lettering on their hulls: JERUSALEM, DELIVER US, FATHER FORGIVE THEM, and the anomalous SEA NEVER DRY. The fishermen squatted barefoot and shirtless on the shore, untangling their wide blue nets with their backs to the sea, as indifferent to the castle as it was to them.

I opened my book about Kwame Nkrumah, hailed *Osagyefo*. Redeemer. Pillar of Fire. He was Saint George who vanquished the dragon of colonialism. He was the Moses who led his people to freedom. He was the hero who proclaimed Ghana's independence "meaningless unless it is linked up with the total liberation of the continent." His dreams for the fledgling republic were matched by his dreams for the freedom of black people everywhere. He envisioned a United States of Africa under a central government that he wrote "would become one of the greatest forces of good in the world."

Under Nkrumah, Ghana seemed at first to flourish. In the late 1950s, the prices of gold and cocoa soared on the world market. The capital mushroomed, the modernist arch at Independence Square sprouted up like a flower—its blossom was the black star and Africa's lost children watched it shine. Nkrumah built schools and roads, all the while preaching progress, self-reliance, development, and deliverance from poverty. He planned to execute these changes in one generation. The Akosombo Dam was the apotheosis of all those plans. An enormous hydroelectric facility, the dam would harness the Volta River and power the nation, flooding it with abundant light.

But for all of Nkrumah's ambition, his dreams took less than a generation to dissolve. The price of cocoa dropped precipitously. The extravagant building projects diminished national reserves. The aid from foreign nations decreased. Soon the economy was in ruins. In his pursuit of socialist policies, Nkrumah amassed a massive debt, yet the masses were as poor as before. They began to grumble about their president. Who was he to ban opposition parties? Who was he to declare himself president for life? Did he think he was God? The elite were distressed by his socialist aims. They disparaged him as dictatorial, despotic, immoderate, and dismissive of domestic affairs in his ardent desire to adopt and adapt the black world, whatever that was. Political turmoil brewed. In 1966, only a few months after Nkrumah switched on the power at Akosombo Dam, he was overpowered by a military coup. A few years later he died in exile.

Nkrumah's fall from grace was swift and punishing. His books were banned. His images were burned. Not even the special weave of kente cloth dedicated to him and his wife was spared. The cloth, called Fathia Deserves Nkrumah, became One Man Does Not Rule a Nation. The international airport was likewise renamed, not for Ghana's founding father but for army general Emmanuel Kotoka, one of the leaders of the coup that overthrew him. And when Nkrumah was cast out, so were most of the African Americans who'd supported him. Many of them returned to the States voluntarily. Some went elsewhere in Africa. The man who'd taken over Du Bois's *Encyclopedia Africana* project went to Zambia. Du Bois's widow, Shirley, once the head of Ghana television, moved to Egypt. Dentist Robert E. Lee and select others with technical skills were permitted to stay. Others were deported. It is said that while the African Americans cried at the news that Nkrumah had been overthrown, the Ghanaians were reveling in the streets and sawing off the bronze head of his statue in Independence Square.

I closed my book.

16

Points to Ponder When Considering Repatriating Home

I HAD A BAD feeling driving past the Obama billboards on the road back to Accra, a foreboding about treating a man like a Messiah. He was supposed to end racism, climate change, recession, and war. In our infatuation with our first black president, weren't we setting ourselves up for disappointment?

"What did you think of this Elmina?" Elolo asked me.

"Depressing," I admitted.

He nodded. "Don't mash up your face so. Didn't I warn you that is a serious place? I told you that you wouldn't like it. Wasn't I right?"

"You weren't wrong," I allowed. The castle was a serious place, impossible to like. I couldn't say Elolo was mistaken about its African American visitors, either. Myself included. We came departing from the wrong place, driven by personal pain and ignorant of the ravages of history on the African side. We came with blinders on. Yet I felt there was something crucial missing from Elolo's analysis of us. As we drove, a reggae mix played from tape deck of his car. A song by the reggae group Culture began:

When will this payday be?
For these retired slaves (Ya a listen me?)
My forefather worked down here
On this great plantation
True he didn't get no pay

For all their wasted days
Tell us now!
When will this payday be?

On its surface the song was about reparation. Maybe Elolo felt bound by its solid beat and cry for justice. Or maybe it spoke directly to the emptiness of his pockets. But the song wasn't just about money. It was about psychological redress, about acknowledging the hold that slave history still has on the present, about the collective struggle over black people's status, the bedeviling lacuna of the Middle Passage and the black diaspora's drive to fill that empty space. This was what drove people like me across the water to cry at the castle, to swab our cheeks and test our DNA, to seek the Right of Abode. This was a song about being disinherited.

I could have talked about that disinheritance with Elolo, but it wouldn't have mattered. Neither of us would be richer for it. Instead, I turned up the volume and we both sang along. He was surprised I knew the words. He'd taken me for Lebanese, but that didn't matter either. What mattered more was that for the remainder of the song, we had fun singing, and, for different reasons, singing it eased our pain.

ONE GOOD THING ABOUT MUSIC: WHEN IT HITS YOU, YOU FEEL NO PAIN. So read the sign outside Rita Marley's Studio 1 in the misty hills of Aburi behind the crowded city of Accra. Aburi reminded me of Kauai, Hawaii, where Victor had taken me to the wedding of a friend, and where the *Jurassic Park* movies were shot. The area was engulfed in a cloud that parted to reveal outlandish greenery: ferns, mangroves, red-berried pepper bushes, rubber trees, illupi trees, dragon trees, mangle-rooted baobabs, frangipani, bamboo, African silver beech, and silk-cotton trees with branches only at their very tops. I halfway expected a dinosaur to emerge from the jungle growth. Instead, there was this dinosaur-sized multimillion-dollar recording studio. A few months after my visit, it would be gutted by a mysterious fire in which some of Bob Marley's master tapes were reportedly destroyed. The police would describe its cause as a possible electrical fault, but common talk in the neighborhood would be that "they have smoked wee' so much that it has touched their own expensive building."

Inside the building I watched Rita Marley pull 360 cedis from the gold fanny pack around her waist and give it to her business manager to pay for several bags of weed. Behind the manager's desk hung the wedding portrait of Rita and Bob, a rudimentary painting of the African continent, and a certificate from the ceremony in which Rita was renamed Nana Akua Adobeah. After her chef served me some melon juice in the lobby, Rita Marley brought me into an antechamber to the recording studio, where we sat down to talk about her life in Africa. Unlike Robert E. Lee and Mary Ellen Ray, she was eager to discuss the subject. I suspected it was a welcome change from the topic of her ex-husband's megastardom. She was comfortable with my tape recorder, as you would expect of a celebrity.

"Don't call me Mrs. Marley. Call me Rita," she insisted.

I began by asking if living here matched her dream of what it would be to reach home.

"First, when you come, you want to lean back and enjoy the breeze and the sunshine," she said, settling into a thronelike chair upholstered in white leather beneath a charcoal drawing of Haile Selassie. Her outfit was a delightfully strange mishmash: flip-flops; gray culottes; a hot-pink shirt; a red, green, and gold scarf with black polka dots; and several necklaces, including a filigreed Star of David. "No, no, no. Africa is *work*. It's like you're starting your life over. It's not a fantasy. It's a reality. People might think that when you come to Africa it's a whole galaxy of stars, but the reality of coming into Africa as a home is tough. What makes it easier is like I say, we have been here before."

"What do you mean, you've been here before?" I asked.

"I mean you go back into your history. As a black woman and as a black child growing up, you ask where do you come from, right?"

"Right."

"'Cause there must be an identity for everyone in terms of your foundation, your base. And back in Trench Town I was always seeking to know, where did I come from? I'm an African because when I look at my skin, I see black. I tried to trace myself and find out yes, I'm a true African child and there's a place for me. You know there's a song that says, 'There's a place for us'? I think it's Diana Ross did it. That song, yeah. And I want to know where's my place."

"How did you trace yourself?"

"I went back to the book, the root of the Bible. And you find, in the book of Revelation, that Haile Selassie is the chapel. And research and research and research . . . Twelve Tribes brought that part of reading the Bible effort for their members. 'A chapter a day keeps the devil away.' And so we try to read a chapter a day, at the same time seeking an identity. Yes, and so Africa came up. We see the tribulations for Africans and they go back to slavery: mental slavery and the physical slavery. Like Bob said, every time I hear the crack of the whip, my blood runs cold. And it puts you back into that slavery period in Egypt where, yes, you were stripped, beaten, raped. So are you gonna take revenge or are you gonna go and take what's yours? And that's how I really came forward to Ghana to be able to grasp or take what's mine."

"How did you decide this land was yours to take?"

"Anywhere in Africa wherever the spirit leads us to be, we have the rights to go there and settle," she said forcefully. Elolo might have compared her to a British colonialist speaking of the Gold Coast, but I could hear a pioneer in a covered wagon speaking of the American West, or a right-wing Israeli speaking of Palestine. She seemed unaware of the irony of a "true African child" taking land from Africans, no matter what she had spent.

"Through the grace of God it was ordained for me to be here," she said.

"Are you speaking of Zion?"

"Yes, well, we know there is a Zion on earth. Most people think when you say heaven, you think about a place in the sky, but Zion is a reality, is not a fantasy. It is not something that you pray and just goes up in smoke and comes back in rain. No, no, no. Zion is a real place."

"But why did you choose Ghana?" I pushed.

"I didn't choose Ghana, darling. I was sent. It was a spiritual move. The spirit say, 'Do.' I don't fight against my spiritual feelings. If there's any doubt, I put it to God and He does the rest. I remember driving up to Aburi and saying, 'Oh my God, this place is where I want to be.' Coming from Accra where it's so hot . . . This is where I supposed to be."

I could see why Aburi, especially when compared with downtown Kingston or Accra, could seem like a piece of paradise, even more so when you could afford a manager, a chef, and an estate on forty acres of land. For her, it must also have been a retreat from celebrity, a place to be simply herself. "It's very peaceful up here in the hills," I acknowledged.

"Yes, I'm inclined to love hills. In Jamaica I have a home on Jack's Hill. Bob taught me that, to live on a mountaintop. Bob took me to St. Ann's after we got married and we lived on a hill. That's where his remains is right now, on a hilltop."

"I've been there," I told her, remembering the camel-hump hills of Saint Ann Parish. "I heard a rumor that you were considering moving his remains from Nine Mile here to Africa."

"That's true. That's Bob's dream. He said that in his interview. That he want to be in Ethiopia by his father. I think he deserves that dream to be fulfilled."

"Won't it be hard for Jamaica to let him go?"

"Jamaica don't own Bob. Bob is a global person. The amount of humiliation that they put us through coming up as young people . . . Rastas were defiled, abused, scorned. Since fame start now, everybody start say, 'Yay, yay, Bob Marley,' but it's not that he started out with true Jamaican love. Society always fight against him. It was even more rough for Bob as a half-caste."

"What do you mean? I thought it was better to be mulatto than black in Jamaica."

"No, no, no. You don't stomp on any permanent ground if you're between black and white. You don't have *no* grounds as a half-caste. You're rejected. It was a tribulation for him. You understand?"

"I think so. I'm a mulatto myself."

"I see that. At one time in our lives I remember Bob asked me to put black polish in his hair 'cause his hair was almost like yours. So he wanted it to be thick and look like an Afro. He said, 'Rita, put some polish in me hair!' He want to look as nigger as possible," she laughed. "At least he feel like, 'Yes, I'm a soul brother now.' And from that he go into Rastafari. But it wasn't easy. He had a lot of hurt. It gave him the ability to go beyond skin. He was able to reach out to all nations. The man was really one of the great psalmists. So it's not left to the Jamaicans where he should remain. They have no claim."

"The economy might suffer without his gravesite as a tourist attraction," I pointed out.

"Well, we don't have to tell them when we're moving him. They can still believe Bob's buried there." She winked in such a conspiratorial way, I wondered if she hadn't already transported him.

"You know I did a book about my life with Bob?" Rita asked.

"Yes, I've read it," I said. I told her that my favorite part of her memoir about being Bob Marley's wife and backup singer was in its opening prologue where she addresses a question she is constantly asked: What's it like to keep hearing Bob Marley's voice everywhere she goes? She writes, "If I hear his voice now, it's only confirming that he's always around, everywhere. Because you do really hear his voice wherever you go. All over the world. And one interesting thing about it, to me, is that most people only hear *him*. But I hear more, because I'm on almost all of the songs. So I also hear *my* voice, I also hear *me*."

"I like how you asserted yourself in that part," I said. She was in her husband's orbit, not his eclipse.

"Well, one of these days I really have to do a second book because half the story has never been told," Rita said.

"What would it be about?"

"Africa, darling! The journey to Africa. What Africa has taught me in terms of it's more than just saying, 'I'm African.' It makes a difference than just saying and dreaming it to walking into it and living in the village with the people, seeing where they get the dirty water, asking how can you prevent that? Seeing what's needed and providing what you can. We're opening a community center. I want to pass you by there if you have the time."

"I'd love to see it," I said.

Back in Kingston, Jamaica, I'd heard Rita Marley criticized for several things—attempting to pilfer Bob Marley's remains, renovating their house on Hope Road into a museum for her own gain, capitalizing on his name by suing everyone else who tried to use it, and establishing the Rita Marley Foundation, funded by his estate, as a tax shelter. I wanted to see what the foundation was doing for myself.

She had her driver take us past the remodeled Methodist Basic School, a recreational public park in progress, and a health care center she was establishing in the village of Konkonuru. I didn't see any villagers enjoying these facilities that afternoon, but the health center was near completion and indicated real commitment. It had a dining area, a fleet of wheelchairs, several examination tables, and a dispensary. Finally we stopped at Omega, Rita Marley's private estate, where another chef prepared us an early dinner of fish tea, seasoned rice, and breadfruit.

"A likkle taste of home," she said, raising her glass of Irish moss. "It's not like I'm drinking champagne on a private jet. You see the community I live in. It's very poor."

"Yes," I said, clinking my glass against hers, though in the entire afternoon we spent together, I hadn't seen the community at all. The seeds for the mangoes as well as the greens, melons, squash, citrus trees, and corn harvested on her land were all imported from

Jamaica. She preferred these varieties to the ones her staff could find here in Ghana.

"You can keep a seed in the dark for years and it will germinate in the right environment," said Empress Natika, a Rasta woman I met in the commercial district's art market next to Kwame Nkrumah Memorial Park. Born in Paris to a mother from Martinique and a father from Ethiopia, she'd lived in Ghana for seven years and ran a thatch-roofed Pan-African shop. She was a slight woman in a long denim skirt, a camouflage jacket, and a pink head-wrap. She looked tough and delicate at the same time. "If you are a spiritual person, then it will manifest. You cannot become what you are not," she reasoned. "You cannot become Rasta. You are born Rasta. It's not something you can import."

My question about her path to Ghana through Rastafari had incited an argument between the empress and another emigrant, a Jamaican Rasta of the Bobo Shanti house in a red Lion of Judah T-shirt and a white head-wrap, who was browsing through her bootleg DVDs. He accused her of not taking a firmer stance about her faith. But the more riled up he became, the more reposed was the empress's response.

"We as Rasta have to come out and preach truth to the people," he interjected with zeal. "Black supremacy defined oneness. One unity. Marcus Garvey organized our salvation here in Africa. Which one name we all gone shout? Selassie-I!"

Empress Natika shrugged. "Okay but the Muslims are saying the same thing about Muhammad."

"Islam not the true and final word," the Bobo dread argued.

"My bredren, I feel your freedom of speech, but salvation goes to every man. Not one people."

"When we come under one banner, we will feel free. You disagree, sister?"

"I agree with freedom," she said coolly.

"Good, because Obama has come to free black people. The man is a leader we can believe in."

"I'm not excited about Obama," she said. "He's just another guy in a suit sitting on the throne of Babylon."

"How can you talk so about the black president?" the Bobo dread demanded.

"We have over fifty black presidents in Africa and I haven't seen much good," she said. "You expect Barack Obama to part the waves and cross the Red Sea. I'm sorry. I'm not seeing it." That she couldn't care less what he thought of her opinion struck me as very French.

The Bobo dread looked at me and hooked his thumb at the empress. "She says she's not seeing it. Is she a prophet?"

"I do have a prophecy for you," the empress announced. "Today you will drink a glass of water."

The dread was affronted. "You no agree with the preachings of Bobo Shanti?"

"Me, I see even Rasta have to think beyond churchical order. Amazon forest people can be righteous without reading the Bible. When you study churches in world history, they are on the conservative side of the world. Bobo Shanti says salvation means women should stay indoors for twenty-one days in the month. But how can I stay indoors that long? How my pickneys gone chop? When you get children to feed you have to say, 'Wait. My revolution is small-small.' Me, I'm just trying to nice up the world. Teach what I can. Learn what I must. Why most of Rasta come to Ghana is to build churches. Nobody is building schools."

"Rita Marley is," I piped in. "I saw her school just yesterday."

"Rita Marley no got bumboclaat nothing to do with Africa!" said the Bobo dread. "Goat ought to know the size of its anus before it swallows the avocado seed." He sucked his teeth and left the shop in a huff.

"Did that man just tell me not to drink Rita Marley's Kool-Aid?" I asked the empress.

She nodded her head. "And meanwhile he is mixing a pitcher of his own."

"Why did *you* come to Ghana?" I asked.

"Paris is nice for tourists. Not for black people," she quipped.

"Why didn't you feel at home there?"

"It's home but it's not home. And they will never let you forget it. If you are black and try to rent an apartment they will tell you it's already rented or ask for your papers. And even when your papers show you are born in France, you can never be French."

She stopped to sing a snatch of the song playing from her stereo about burning down the cane field. "I learned Rasta from my mother. She dead but she still Rasta. Me, I don't know why, I knew I was coming to Ghana at age sixteen. At twenty-six I finally came. I've just been walking toward it. Sometimes following a vision can be dangerous. What if your vision was to kill George Bush?"

I laughed. "I had that vision once."

"You and ninety-nine percent of this earth, sistren."

"But it wasn't a dangerous vision that brought you here to Ghana, was it?" I pressed.

"It was a milk and honey vision. I don't see no honey and milk when I land at the airport. No milk coming from the tap. It's not like that sweet dream. On bad days really and truly it's not easy living here."

"Are you disillusioned?"

"Most repatriates are. They're bitter because Ghanaians think we have a bottomless pit of money. Ghanaians don't know about Europe or the United States. Most of us who make it here come with our last savings, not like her highness, Mrs. Rita Marley. But to my thinking, how can you come here and hate the people? You cannot call the forest that shelters you a jungle. Maybe they overcharge me, but even when I pay them *obruni* price, I see reflection of my black face on the currency. How often apart from slave times you can say black people part of economy? And on the subject of money, my sistren, what you going to buy from my store?"

I chose a self-published travel guide by Seestah Imakhus Njinga, the woman who ran the guesthouse in Elmina, called *Points to Ponder When Considering Repatriating Home to Mother Afrika: Ghana to Live or to Visit*, not because I was considering repatriating, but to support the empress in her endeavors.

After leaving her shop in the art market I walked to the Kwame Nkrumah Memorial Park next door. The park was an effort to restore Nkrumah's public image. It sat upon five and a half acres of the old polo grounds where Nkrumah declared Ghana independent of colonial rule. I bypassed his mausoleum to stand before the bronze statue that vandals had decapitated in 1966. Nkrumah was still headless, but the head, gone missing for over forty years, had recently resurfaced at the prodding of the government. It had not been rejoined with his shoulders but now sat like a giant soccer ball on a pedestal by his feet. Looking upon this absurdity, I was finally homesick. I recalled what the Banana Man said about ego standing in Zion's way. It was time to marry the temple of my body to the schoolroom of my mind.

Before leaving Ghana I returned to Kati Torda's bead shop to be fitted for waist beads. Of the émigrés I'd met in Ghana, Kati was by far the most content, perhaps because she expected the least of her adoptive home. She didn't need it to redress the wrongs of history or rejoice at her return. She didn't need it to accept her as an African, and this, ironically or not, made her seem more African than the Africans from the diaspora.

"What's your secret?" I asked her as she tied the strands of tiny sky-blue waist beads at the small of my back.

"No secrets," she smiled. "I'm not so complicated."

"I doubt that, Kati."

"None of us are all that complicated. We only seem so in the wrong company."

"But I mean, why are you so at home here?"

"I had to learn to let go of my logic," she said. "The logic I learned took me so far and served me so well, except not here. After I let go attempting to swim against the current, I took to Ghana like a fish to water. If you float, the water can carry you to fascinating places! But if you look for a story you already know, you will come away disappointed. I saw where Ghanaians didn't have stories like Romans and Greeks about gods, they had them about *beads*. I learned the mythology of beads, the sources and the mystery. 'These beads are found where the rainbow meets the sky.' Do you need a more beautiful story than that? Or, 'This bead is the excrement of the moon.' And then, 'These beads only a magician can wear because they attract lightning.'"

"Kati, you're a poet!" I said.

"No," she disagreed. To her, the beads were already poems. Kati's job, as she saw it, was just to string them together. She had learned to do this—just as she'd learned the fashion, the body language, the respect for elders, and the practice of giving gifts—by listening. She was exactly the kind of artist I wished to be.

"That reminds me," I said, paying for the beads around my waist and handfuls of necklaces to bring back home. "I need to get Mary Ellen a present." Rather than purchasing her something from Kati's shop, I chose to buy her a set of six drinking glasses so that she would more easily be able to serve the next black Tom, Dick, or Emily to come knocking on her door.

With these in hand, I showed up again at the Rays' gate.

"Where's Tut?" I asked when Mary Ellen opened it. The puppy wasn't there to chew at my shoelaces.

"He's been missing for three days," she said. "No point in posting any LOST DOG signs. By now somebody's probably fried him in palm oil for dinner."

I had to laugh. Once again, Mary Ellen's black humor reminded me of my aunt Alise. Back in Compton, when my father and I went to retrieve her after her fall, she'd flipped through an old photo album to show me the faces of the black family down South about whom I knew so little, the Nanans and the Parrains, the grandaunts and -uncles and cousins once and twice removed. This was why I'd joined my father to gather Alise. I wanted to connect with her, and with them, before she was gone. I sat next to her in the bed at the temporary convalescent home where she was healing from her broken hip. She named the family for me, one by one, then paused at a picture of my grandfather.

In the picture, the only image of him I'd ever seen, he stands between my aunt Alise at age thirteen, and my aunt Marlene, age twelve. Both girls are nearly as tall as he. He wears a fedora and highwater pants. It's a bright day and his eyes are closed against the sunlight or the flash of the camera. My father, who will take his name, is not yet born. Perhaps my grandmother, already heavily pregnant with him, is the photographer. Nobody in the picture knows it yet, but my grandfather is about to die in such an ugly way that my grandmother will take her daughters and her new-born son out of the South for good. His death was not discussed in our house, but it was the thing that divided us from Mississippi, which seemed a haunted but hallowed place, a home we weren't allowed to know.

"Check out the old man's mustache," joked Aunt Alise. "Doesn't he look like the black Hitler? And I'll tell you something else; he was almost as mean."

I'm not sure how my aunt read my confusion. How could she compare this man, whom I thought of as nearly holy, to Hitler? I must have looked something between bewildered and bemused.

"It's okay to laugh, honey," my aunt Alise said, shutting the photo album. "I knew him. He wasn't a saint. He was just a man."

I knew now the same could be said of Nkrumah. Obama. My father. My boyfriend. No person or place was here to redeem me. It came as a relief.

Shutting the gate, Mary Ellen asked, "Aren't you flying back home to your man today?"

"I am," I said. I must have looked as relieved as I felt.

"Don't tell me," Mary Ellen said. "After all this time in Africa, you miss black people."

I missed so many things, actually. Black people, Victor, my family, my friends, and even my country. The United States had an unexpected present and a mysterious future that I increasingly wanted to be a part of. Most of the pilgrims I'd met on my travels through Israel, Jamaica, Ethiopia, and Ghana seemed as focused on the past as on the present. Very rarely on the future. They were shackled by the old stories, as if there weren't any others to tell. I was ready to go back to America, my nation.

But not without my camera.

PART V:
BLACK BELT OF
THE AMERICAN SOUTH

THIS IS THE PLACE
YOU WERE DELIVERED

17

A Dollar and a Dream

I LEFT GHANA, RETURNED to New York, and got married. Victor and I had a joyous ceremony of twenty close family members at an Episcopal church in Washington Heights across the street from a bus station overrun by drug addicts. Together we bought a run-down one-bedroom apartment, joining our possessions, our hang-ups, our dreams. After moving in I forgot about my travels for a while. Maybe I hadn't found the Promised Land, but what I did have seemed pretty damned good. We settled into a comfortable life. It was because of this comfort, precisely because I'd stopped actively seeking, that I encountered the man who would lead me on my last pilgrimage. That man's name was Creflo Dollar.

It was Victor who introduced me to his program. I myself didn't usually stay up so late. Slouched on our thrift store loveseat in the middle of the night, we'd sleepily flip through the channels during commercial breaks of Victor's favorite, *Headbangers Ball*, or long after the curtain call of *Saturday Night Live*, and happen upon the stocky black televangelist prowling the pulpit. As Victor put it, the man knew how to fill a custom-made suit, and he wasn't above telling you how much the suit cost. In fact, Pastor Dollar considered his material wealth—the private jet, the Rolls-Royces, the mansion in Atlanta—points of pride as reflections of God's blessings upon his life. He was fond of mentioning that many of these possessions were gifted by members of his flock in gratitude for his deliverance of the prosperity gospel, a belief that God's devout followers will be successful in all endeavors, including financial matters, as an expression of His favor. How this success was meant to be achieved wasn't entirely clear, but it seemed to involve being born again into the faith and tithing considerable sums of money to Creflo Dollar Ministries.

His sermons often invoked the story of Exodus. "The Lord kept the children of Israel alive in the wilderness for forty years. He nourished them with the blessing of sweet manna from heaven. He wanted them to have plenty so they could be a blessing, just as He wants you to have plenty." This was the crux of the prosperity gospel—God did not intend for His chosen people to suffer, but rather to have plenty, to be full, to be spiritually *and* materially rich. The way Dollar used the myth of Exodus, which has sustained and unified black people through times of suffering since the days of slavery, was so far beyond crass that it had to be a farce. God's plan for us is to drive a Bentley? And we will attain it by giving 10 percent of our salaries to this huckster? *Really?*

Members are encouraged to tithe with automatic bank account withdrawals managed by World Changers Church. Fellow Atlanta ministers, who preach in the humble tradition of Reverend Martin Luther King Jr., rib Dollar for commercializing Christ. "Pass-a Dollar," they call him. "Cash-flow Dollar." But Victor encouraged me to consider the preacher's appeal.

"You've been trotting all over the globe searching for Zion. But if you want to know what Zion is for black America here and now, then you need to pay attention to this guy," he said.

"Why? What's his platform?" I asked, "'Obama wants change, we want dollars'?"

"Uh-uh. It's capitalism, baby. Plain and simple. The American dream."

I sputtered something about the integrity of the black church. I'd no doubt read it in one of my father's books about suffering and salvation. This was a topic I understood, not from having grown up in the black church myself, but through my Catholic upbringing and my father's intellectual lens. Christianity, as I knew it, was a religion of suffering. At the heart of the Christian tradition was the agony of Christ and the martyrs. Personal suffering bound the Christian to the suffering of the world. Faith and affliction were two sides of a coin whose worth nobody knew better than the slaves of old. According to my father, "The primary example of suffering Christianity in this country was the experience of African American slaves."

By shilling money as the thing that mattered most, men like Creflo Dollar, I complained to Victor, were cheapening our rich history of liberation theology, messing with the prophetic kind of faith that drove the Civil Rights Movement, our nation's proudest moment. My father taught a seminar on the religious history of that movement and these were themes he'd discussed with me for as long as I could remember. He'd grown up during that ennobling period. He was nearly the same age as Emmett Till would be if he hadn't been bludgeoned to death and dumped in a Mississippi river at age fourteen for talking too freely with a white woman. This was the backdrop against which my parents met at a Catholic university in Milwaukee in the 1960s. There my father helped organize a student movement that pushed for more minority faculty hires and student enrollment. Along with two roommates, he led a protest that shut down the university for two weeks.

Perhaps, like many children, I had a romance with the time of my parents' youth. Their heroes were Martin Luther King and Dorothy Day, whose *Catholic Worker* offered a moral critique of the country's drive for wealth and comfort. Wealth was a spiritual hazard that flew in the face of social justice. And didn't my hero, Bob Marley, say more or less the same thing? "A belly could be full yet hungry." A full stomach didn't ensure a full heart or a full life.

But Victor only laughed. "What's so funny?" I asked him.

"Darlin', I love you. I do. But you have the most convoluted way of trying to know your father."

"I'm not talking about my father," I insisted. "I'm talking about the problem of *Creflo Dollar*."

"Okay," Victor humored me. "Why should black people be holier than anyone else just because we've suffered? Why shouldn't we want the same comforts everybody wants, in the end? A mortgage, a car, a retirement plan?"

Victor was the son of an African immigrant and had an immigrant's sense of optimism about this land and its possibilities. His mother made us play the Mega Millions lottery because she believed we might actually win. I was the daughter of a black man who'd literally and figuratively lost his home. I'd inherited this sense of loss along with his sense of destiny. But in spite of our differences, it wasn't lost on me that Victor made his point around the time we'd signed our mortgage. We were not sufferers ourselves, not by a long shot. We were emissaries from the place the Rastas called Babylon Kingdom and we were free to travel anywhere in the world we desired. We were so liberated that we were practically dilettantes. Maybe it was time to let go of the old romance with suffering, to begin another narrative.

I began watching Creflo Dollar "Tell-a-Vision," at first as a skeptic and out of morbid curiosity. What had changed so drastically since the civil rights era that a major arm of the black church now saw Zion as a financial realm? What was liberation for? Was it simply to fit into the comfort and ease of consumer culture? I tried to put these questions to Dollar directly, but my attempts to reach him were as much in vain as the Rastas trying to communicate with the queen. I got as close as his public relations person, who brushed me off by saying he was a very busy man. Dollar was probably savvy to be guarded about granting interviews. His ministry was under investigation by a Senate committee for fraud.

Creflo Dollar's church attracts some forty thousand members, most of them poor and working-class blacks trying to pull themselves out of poverty and into the middle class. They're drawn by Dollar's lavish lifestyle, his optimism, and his instruction of the Bible as a manual for prosperity. We are in control of our destiny, he teaches. We are already in the Promised Land. This is our home. We built it. It is ours.

Soon enough, I, too, was mesmerized. More than that—I was hooked. Beneath the mustache, thick as a Band-Aid, the smile had a blinding wattage. The big teeth didn't look natural, and neither did his perfectly even hairline. His linebacker's shoulders were a holdover from his college days as a star football player. You don't build a ministry that takes in seventy million untaxed dollars a year from tens of thousands of members worldwide without charisma. Even after Victor fell asleep on the loveseat, I kept watching deep into the night, held by the flickering blue light of the ridiculously oversized flat-screen TV before us, trying to unravel Dollar's message.

As a preacher, his trick was the power of positive thinking. As a motivational speaker, his trick was the Bible. As a CEO, his trick was a wily concoction of both: self-help and Jesus Christ. It was a winning combination. Dollar's product almost couldn't lose, and his delivery was pitch-perfect. He was plainspoken, corporate, encouraging. He could sound like a Holy Roller and Oprah Winfrey in the same breath: "Get lack and insufficiency off your mind," he urged. "Get satisfied. The Lord shall increase you more and more. I believe that when you get increase on your mind, you're gonna receive increase in your life, and when you sow and give into the kingdom of God, it will trigger increase. Pray about sowing into this ministry and experience increase. It's time to reap your crop."

I was remarkably drawn to this snake oil salesman who used *increase* more often as a noun than a verb. A lot of what he said made sense. Just as he could sound like the Bible-thumping Pentecostal preacher Oral Roberts, whom he counted as a close friend, he could also sound like the black nationalist Malcolm X, who criticized the docility of the black church. Against my better judgment, I got sucked into a Black Entertainment Television wormhole—I followed Dollar's show religiously and then began watching other black televangelists too. These men were slick. There was Bishop Eddie Long, whose Georgia mega-church pulled around twenty-five thousand members, and T. D. Jakes, with about thirty thousand in Texas. One night Jakes recounted a visit to a Johannesburg museum where he encountered a proverb on the wall: "When the Dutch came, we owned the land and they had the Bible. When they left, they owned the land and we had the Bible." He asked his congregation one vital question: Why couldn't they have *both*?

"We should be able to hand our children more than our religious tradition," Jakes argued. "Our faith has been a blessing and a curse. It stabilized us in times of adversity. Where would we be without our faith when we had nothing else, when we were being beaten and raped and killed and murdered? What disturbs me about our faith as we were taught by our slave masters was to make us hope for heaven while we lived in hell on earth. There ought to be a way we can hand to our children more than our religious tradition. We can hand them a home, hope, a degree, and then use the faith to fuel our dreams rather than to anesthetize our disappointments."

I thought his words important enough to copy in my notebook. Creflo Dollar and Bishop Long preached the same hopeful message, in slightly different ways, but Dollar remained my favorite sermonizer. He was the best showman, which is probably why his World Changers Church had the longest reach, with offices in South Africa, Nigeria, Australia, and the United Kingdom. I visited its New York branch to see Creflo Dollar deliver the good word in person on Fat Tuesday, the night before the start of the Lenten season.

Down in Bay St. Louis, Mississippi, where my father was from, it was Mardi Gras. I didn't know if or how his people, who'd been displaced by Hurricane Katrina, were celebrating tonight, but I can tell you that the congregation assembled at World Changers Church, New York, was reveling. Not because tomorrow, Ash Wednesday, marked the start of forty days of deprivation and they wanted to let loose, but because they hoped tomorrow might be the dawn of their abundance and they wanted to give thanks. In fact, it was the second night of a financial empowerment seminar. Creflo Dollar had flown into New York from Atlanta on his Gulfstream III private jet to lead the service, as he does every Saturday, at a rented theater inside the Manhattan Center on Thirty-fourth Street. Across the street, at Madison Square Garden, Marcus Garvey had preached redemption to a crowd of twenty-five thousand, ninety years before. In terms of egotism, star quality, and the lure of black capital, Dollar seemed to have taken a page from Garvey's book.

This is the Gospel of Wealth:

Shiny buses from New Jersey stand in a line outside the theater when I arrive. With the efficiency and practiced cheer of an airline steward, an usher hands me a prepackaged communion wafer and a tiny foil-topped plastic cup of syrupy wine along with a powder-blue collection envelope before escorting me to an empty seat. The place is packed all the way to the topmost of four balconies and almost everybody is black. There is a buzz in the air. The woman next to me introduces herself as Gladys. She wears a nurse's uniform and tells me she's come directly from her work shift, just as she's done for a year of Saturdays, in order to get out of debt, praise the Lord. I watch her stuff a hundred-dollar bill into her collection envelope and lick the flap. I wonder how she's going to pay for groceries.

The lights dim and the navy-blue velvet curtains rise on the stage to reveal a thirty-member choir and two jumbo screens on which, after a chorus of hallelujahs, an image of a Wall Street sign and the American flag fades into the testimonial of an attractive, young, light-skinned woman with chandelier earrings and a burgundy weave. Her earrings twinkle as she confesses, "They shut down my credit on Black Friday but the next week, because I sowed in the faith, I experienced increase when God forced my boss's hand to give me a raise."

"Tell it!" shouts Gladys, waving her hand in the air.

The stage lights come up on Creflo Dollar, standing behind a Plexiglas podium in a pin-striped suit over a lemon-yellow shirt. He's in his late forties but has the chipmunk cheeks of a child. A hush spreads over the rented hall.

"Ain't nothing blessed about being poor," Dollar intones.

That's right!

"The poor man's poverty destroys him. Satan is the enemy trying to convince you that prosperity is a curse. Satan has frightened people into believing there's something inherently evil about money. He's spreading lies. He wants you to believe poverty is noble. Millions have been taken by his deception. I don't agree. Can I get an amen?"

Amen!

"Let's look at some urban legends. There's an urban legend that my real name isn't Creflo Dollar but Michael Smith. That there's ATMs in our church. That you have to show W2 forms to get into our church. So ridiculous. Satan's spreading lies. There's an urban legend that I'm stealing from my parishioners. Poor-minded, broke-minded church folk are contained in a prison of Satan's making to keep them that way, fearful of a preacher named Dollar who will take your money." He shakes his head, as if this pains him greatly. "When I came to you I came loaded already. You don't need a board to determine the preacher's salary. I'm proud to say I haven't taken a dime from this church. To run for public office would be a demotion. I work for the King of Kings."

Bless us, pastor!

"Jesus is abundant. The question you need to ask is, 'How do I as a believer gain access to his resources?' Can you tell I'm getting ready to operate on you? If you have a poverty spirit in you, I will drive it all the way to Queens! The most powerful spiritual force the devil has ever had to battle will be the church alive to God's purpose for prosperity. I am here to tell you, the farmer that plants a seed gets a harvest. My point is pretty clear: that you prosper."

The scriptural basis for the doctrine of seed faith, generally credited to Oral Roberts, is the parable of Jesus in Matthew 4. Just as the sower plants seeds that reap a thirty-, a sixty-, or a hundredfold return in the biblical story, the believer who gives an offering in church can expect a return on his or her investment. Dollar's innovation to the "seedtime and harvest" principle is that this act of devotion is a way to get out of debt. Before his lesson, a collection is taken up. I am accustomed to passing a basket, but at Dollar's church, they pass buckets. I am also more familiar with the verse in Matthew 19, where Jesus says it's harder for a rich man to enter

heaven than for a camel to pass through a needle's eye. It's star-
tling how quickly the buckets fill. I don't want to think this is just
vulgar materialism, or that Dollar is ripping them off, but instead
that the congregation is paying for sound practical financial advice.

Then again, I am a seeker. This makes me susceptible to gurus,
cults, and quacks.

When Dollar starts instructing us in the twelve steps to
recession-proof our lives, everybody pulls out a notebook and
joins me in taking notes. The first of the twelve steps is "I know
my God will supply my needs. Not the government and not the
state." I worry about a platform that encourages us not to expect
or demand anything of our elected officials, but the second step
accords with me more: "I refuse to fear when circumstances seem
to indicate failure."

Fear, Dollar tells us, is Satan's spirit holding us in an unsettled state
from which we might be delivered through God's true desire for
us to experience heaven on earth. He wants us to stop listening to
Satan whispering negative thoughts in our ear. He doesn't sound
so different from my yoga instructor when she tells us during our
meditation practice to block the distracting chatter of monkey
mind. It's a different vocabulary, but the effect is the same. I have
paid as much as twenty dollars a yoga class for the same lesson.

"I believe the spirit of God is gonna jump on you in public spaces
such that you can't hide it. You can't leave 'til the benediction's
given. Every head bowed, every eye closed. You ready, now?" He
softens his voice. "Trouble don't last always. God will prosper you."

At the end of the seminar, we pour out of the theater feeling
refreshed, renewed, rewarded. And although I'm more than a little
embarrassed to admit to my father how I've just spent the beginning of Lent, this is the revelation I share with him later that night
on the phone right before he drops the bomb that he has cancer.

I feel the prepackaged body and blood of Christ rise in my
throat. I swallow it back down. I have forgotten to eat dinner. My
stomach twists like a rag. My heart speeds. My heart. My muse.
My muse is dying, is going to die.

It's not aggressive, he assures me, it's slow growing and unlikely to be the thing that kills him in the end. Still, he's feeling dark and drained enough by the diagnosis to have decided not to go on a class trip he's planned for spring break with the co-teacher of his seminar on the Civil Rights Movement. He's made the same journey across the Black Belt before, so-called for the dark soil tilled by dark hands on the plantations. Birmingham, Selma, Montgomery, Atlanta. It won't be a loss for him personally to opt out. It may even be redundant for him to go again. On the other hand, he's not been down South since the flood. I know he's still depressed by Katrina, the cataclysm that has scattered his people all over the map. I believe both of these dilemmas, cancer and Katrina, are compounding to keep him off the bus.

Because I've just returned from Creflo Dollar's church, I feel a desire to experience what I imagine is a less materialistic version of faith. Something with the power to cure. Say the names of those cities to yourself—Birmingham, Selma, Montgomery—and try not to conjure the mythic struggle for civil rights, the opposite of the prosperity gospel. I knew what might wash the taste of Creflo's cheap communion wine from my mouth. The South. Immediately, I volunteered to go in my father's place.

The class trip coincided with Holy Week, the final days of the season of Lent. As a Catholic child I'd been instructed to give up a vice for Lent, such as thumb-sucking, back-talking, fingernail-biting, or eating candy. Almost always, these were sacrifices of the mouth. I knew the practice was supposed to bring me closer to Jesus, who spent forty days fasting in the desert, but that closeness seemed so abstract a reward. At the time, I would have preferred a sticker. Sometimes I got an Easter hat with a ribbon, which at least I could wear on my head. I hadn't given up anything for Lent in twenty years, but now I felt the pull of tradition. During my tour of the South, I committed to giving up the negative thoughts about my father's illness until we knew more. Under the influence of Dollar, I refused to fear.

In commemoration of the long-winded battle of civil rights, our tour would make several stops. It would conclude on Good Friday in Atlanta, the birth and resting place of Martin Luther King; Atlanta, which, according to the last census, had surpassed Harlem as America's black Mecca; Atlanta, home of Creflo Dollar's mega-church and the city to which some of our relatives had fled after the storm. After a week visiting the historic sites of civil rights, I planned to spend the morning of Easter Sunday in Atlanta under Dollar's dome. I would confront the man in his own house. The rest of the holiday I would spend with my cousins.

In the wake of the flood, and the infrastructure that failed them, I wondered how our people conceived of the Promised Land that Martin Luther King spoke of. Was it a lost dream or something to keep striving for? Had any of them prospered, as Dollar preached was their right? Where was home now? With these questions in mind, I kissed my husband good-bye, packed my camera, and boarded the bus.

18

Holy Week

THE TOUR BEGAN on a rainy Palm Sunday, in Birmingham. The rain was heavy and, in a Southern way, slow. It blurred everything outside the window into an expressionist painting. We rolled along the ghost town of Fourth Avenue, the former black business district, whose barbershops and beauty shops, mortuaries and saloons, motels and restaurants, were casualties of integration. I wondered whether the black people old enough to remember this heart of black civic life were nostalgic for it, though these were the businesses that served them because they wouldn't be served elsewhere. The shops were mostly closed now, in partial blight, though an old theater had been resurrected as a jazz museum, a barbershop was still cutting heads, and the black Masonic Temple was still in partial use.

My father had stopped in this city as a boy on the long drive down to Bay St. Louis from Michigan, where they ran after my grandfather was killed. He recalls his mother yanking him back by the collar from the wrong drinking fountain, reserved for whites, her eyes ablaze with a rage driven by fear. Though he was not beside me now, I felt his presence as I took in Birmingham through the bus windows. The rain was elegiac. The story of his father's murder ricocheted in my head.

There were twelve of us on the bus—my father's co-teacher, a teaching assistant, nine students, the bus driver, and me. I was a teacher but I wasn't these students' teacher. Listening to them prattle about final exams, senior theses, and their postgraduation plans, I realized I was too old to be the ingenue, old enough to be a wife and maybe, soon, a mother. Yet here I was, still on the road, still unfixed, still trying to enter Jerusalem, not teacher, not student, not mother, not black, not white—for now, not anything but my father's daughter. I attached myself to the driver, a thick-thighed, garrulous Vietnam veteran named Roscoe, with a Big Gulp in his cup holder. He pleased me by calling me sweetheart from the moment we met.

Roscoe parked the bus outside a photography studio. Our group filed in. A table draped with a black cloth in the reception area displayed before-and-after pictures of black families. Chris McNair could restore old photos; remove the wrinkles and blotches of time. He could colorize black-and-white images; turn gray cheeks pink and rosy. He could remove or add people from family portraits, erase the living, or bring back the dead. His daughter, Denise, was the youngest of the four Sunday school girls killed in the bombing of the Sixteenth Street Baptist Church in 1963. He'd turned one room of his business into a shrine to preserve her memory, but the whole place felt like a funeral home.

Denise McNair's roller skates, jump rope, paper dolls, and toy typewriter were displayed under glass, as were her red felt hat and poodle skirt. A box of tissues sat on top of a second, parallel glass case for people like me who are moved to tears by such details. This case displayed the things that touched the girl on the day of her death: a pair of black patent leather shoes and matching purse, a charm bracelet, a tiny two-inch-tall child's Bible, a blue floral handkerchief, and the jagged piece of concrete removed from her skull.

Denise was eleven years old when she was killed, her father told us, a seventh-grader at Center Street School. He spoke slowly when he said it, struggling with the words. He was in his eighties now, hunched like an old bear, his doughy face gathered up in pain and drooping on one side because he had recently suffered a stroke. Had his daughter lived, he slurred, she would be fifty-seven years old today. She wears a nightgown in the blown-up picture that presides over this shrine and is posed with her head tilting and her arms wrapped around a white doll with yellow hair. It's clear to me, though Denise appears to be communicating with us, that the conversation is actually with her father behind the lens.

The explosion that took Denise McNair's life was one of almost fifty unresolved, racially directed bombings lobbed by white segregationists as retribution for protests against Birmingham's discrimination laws. Between the late 1940s and the mid-1960s, that steady, violent hailstorm of hate earned the city its nickname, Bombingham. The Birmingham Knights was one of the Ku Klux Klan's biggest chapters, so it's not surprising that the city had a reputation as one of the most segregated in the South or that the Southern Christian Leadership Conference, under the direction of Martin Luther King Jr., chose it as the site of a major non-violent campaign. The SCLC organized a series of peaceful sit-ins, boycotts, and marches intended to provoke the mass arrests that would catch the media's attention and draw the nation's scrutiny with the camera's eye.

We'd all seen the footage. The clubs, cattle prods, and fire hoses turned against the youth in the Children's Crusade who took their parents' places when they were shoved in paddy wagons and carried to jail, the maws and snapping jaws of the police dogs. And, though King and the SCLC were criticized for putting children in harm's way, we knew what followed: the international outcry for justice, federal intervention, the crowning of King as the Moses of his people, and a push toward the Civil Rights Act of 1964.

But Denise McNair was still dead. The Sunday school lesson on the morning of the bombing was entitled, "The Love That Forgives."

"A lotta people ask me why I didn't leave after this happened," Mr. McNair told us after we gawked at his daughter's playthings. "Where the hell would I have gone? I couldn't change from black to white. I couldn't bring her back."

"Have you forgiven your daughter's murderers?" asked one of my father's students, tentatively.

"That's a naive question," slurred Mr. McNair. "It's been a few years since this happened, but the struggle isn't over just because we have a black man in the White House."

Then he started rambling about the water bill and the right to vote and how many bubbles were in a bar of soap and black folks being as bad as white, and how, really, you couldn't trust anybody. "You want to talk about forgiveness? We got plenty churches but it don't seem to matter a damn bit," he said with a bitter edge, adding that sometimes he thought God, if you wanted to call Him that, would destroy Alabama by wiping it clean with His hand. Hadn't He already wrecked the Gulf Coast with Hurricane Katrina and couldn't He work other storms? It sounded nearly like a curse, though Chris McNair couldn't have predicted that 140 twisters would slam this region on a single day two years from then, and at the time I didn't think him the cursing kind, just a man who'd been ravaged by a storm all his own.

After visiting his studio, we toured the Byzantine Sixteenth Street Baptist Church where, on the morning of September 15, 1963, Klansmen planted the bundle of dynamite that set off the blast that killed Denise. As a result of the explosion, the face of Christ was cleanly shattered out of the east wall's only surviving stained glass window. We looked upon the new stained glass window depicting a black Christ, donated by the sympathetic people of Wales; we attended a service in which the choir sang "We're Marching to Zion"; and we watched Preacher Price wipe the perspiration from his face with a white towel behind the lectern draped in purple cloth for Lent as he testified the old message that though we are all of us on our way to a storm, in the eye of a storm, or on our way out of a storm, the hardships in this life are the price of the reward in the next.

We're marching upward to Zion, the beautiful city of God! Beneath the lectern was a block of polished wood. It was engraved with Christ's words to his disciples on the night of the last supper: THIS DO IN REMEMBRANCE OF ME, only in the context of this church, even on Palm Sunday, the words seemed not to refer to Christ so much as to the four little girls who died.

In Denise's room of remembrance, its curator had seemed to
me a very gentle man who'd come out of a storm with a broken
mind. I said as much to Roscoe when we left the chapel to get
back on the bus.

Roscoe adjusted his veteran's cap and put the bus in gear. "Chris
McNair may well be broken, but he ain't never been gentle. The
man is a crook," he claimed, who had shamefully used his daughter's memory to win public office. After he was sworn in as Jefferson County commissioner, Roscoe revealed, McNair accepted
almost a million dollars in kickbacks for awarding contracts in a
sewer debacle but was discovered, arrested on charges of bribery
and conspiracy, convicted, and sentenced to five years in prison.
He was currently out on bond and had commissioned President
Obama to commute his sentence so that he might serve less time.

"Maybe he felt the city of Birmingham owed him something
for his suffering," I suggested.

"Nah," Roscoe disagreed, flicking on the windshield wipers.
"Don't let him fool you with that sad story, sweetheart. Don't
make him out like a saint. What happened to his baby girl shouldn't
never have happened. But he still just as selfish as the next man."

In the following days on the road there was time enough for me
to catch up with the class's assignment to read *Strength to Love*, the
volume of Martin Luther King's most famous homilies, published
in 1963. My father had told me once that King wasn't speaking
about a country when he talked about the Promised Land. But he
hadn't answered me when I asked what King meant. The answer
was so obvious to me now that I could hardly believe I hadn't
understood it before. He was talking about human relationships.

I thought about this in Selma, where, at the National Voting
Rights Museum, we met Ms. Joanne Bland, self-proclaimed journey
specialist. "You all know who *my* president is, right?" she asked us.
Nearly the same age Denise McNair would be had she lived, Ms.
Bland was a large woman with tired brown eyes, a deep, booming

voice, a military haircut, and an intimidating bosom. Her question was rhetorical, but to illustrate the answer she held up a copy of her self-published, spiral-bound booklet, "Stories of Struggle: Growing Up in the Segregated South," which she peddled to the tune of ten dollars. Ms. Bland was pictured on the booklet's cover, standing next to Barack Obama. "You all need to buy this," she pushed. The president's arm was gallantly and tenderly thrown around her round shoulder. His hair hadn't yet grayed from accusations that he wasn't really a U.S. citizen, among other national concerns.

"Obama talks about Selma in all his speeches 'cause he knows where he comes from," said Ms. Bland.

The picture was taken in 2007 when Obama came to Selma to give a speech from the pulpit of the historic Brown Chapel African Methodist Episcopal Church. In doing so, he claimed his lineage and indebtedness to the movement. A frequent strategy of his presidential campaign was to appeal to faith-based groups with a reminder that Moses never entered the Promised Land. Obama postured himself as Joshua, who succeeded Moses to lead the Israelites; who delivered the Israelites to Israel; who stood on the shoulders of Moses, just as Obama stood on the shoulders of Martin Luther King.

"Dr. King chose Selma as the battleground for voting rights and this was his headquarters," Ms. Bland said after leading us a few blocks to Brown Chapel AME. The ornate white edges and trim against the brick of the church's archways looked like the icing on a gingerbread house. Brown Chapel AME stood like an aspiration across from the bleak housing projects where Ms. Bland was raised in the fifties and sixties. "Duck if you hear gunshots," she joked. Then she pointed with disdain at the memorial erected outside the church. It featured a bronze bust of Martin Luther King atop a tall granite plinth.

"Does anyone see what's wrong with this thing?" she asked, indicating the words engraved in the stone.

From beneath our umbrellas we peeked wearily at the statue. It wasn't so different from the many commemorations we'd already seen on the tour. By this point, midway through our pilgrimage, the monuments had begun to blend in with one another, and our eyes were glazed. Visiting these sites made me remember the ritual of visiting the Stations of the Cross in the Catholic Church. At each station, we were asked to witness a moment of passion in the crucifixion of the man who suffered to save us. I tried to look with fresh eyes at King's form, but it was hard.

Before leaving Birmingham we'd photographed a sculpture of children being attacked by German shepherds and fire hoses pointed like canons. In Montgomery, we'd witnessed a reenactment of Rosa Parks's refusal to move to the back of the bus at the Rosa Parks Library and Museum. At the Civil Rights Memorial we fingered the names of the civil rights martyrs, most of whom were ordinary men and women, etched on a circular black granite table designed by Maya Lin. We'd explored the rooms of the white-clapboard house where Dr. King and his family lived when he served as pastor of Dexter Avenue Baptist Church. We learned that the church stands halfway between the state capitol, on the steps of which Jefferson Davis was inaugurated as president of the Confederacy, and an artesian fountain that marked an auction spot for the sale of slaves.

Standing in King's old pulpit, the church's current pastor, Reverend Thurman, told us, "There would not have been a movement without the church. There is no black community without the black church. It's at the center of who we are. Our values spring from our religiosity."

Clustered in front of a mural depicting Dr. King's life, we were surprised to encounter a youth group from Minnesota we'd met back at the Sixteenth Street Baptist Church in Birmingham. But perhaps we shouldn't have been surprised at all. This was an integral stop on the trip, an educational and spiritual journey that was also, let's face it, trauma tourism. Back on the bus, rolling along U.S. Highway 80, I wondered what it felt like for the congregations of Dexter Avenue Baptist and Sixteenth Street Baptist to have outsiders observing them during worship as though they were preserved in amber. Our bus was one of many, many buses. Between Montgomery and Selma we stopped at the National Historic Trail and wandered among mannequins posed like the marchers who spent five days walking fifty-four miles, eventually swelling to a crowd of twenty-five thousand along Highway 80 in the 1965 voting-rights march.

This was only the middle of our tour. It would end in Atlanta with a walk down the stretch of Auburn Avenue with the restored Victorian home where Martin Luther King Jr. was born, the Ebenezer Baptist Church he co-pastored with his father, and the marble tomb where he was enshrined behind an eternal flame. We hadn't even gotten to Atlanta yet, and already our senses were nearly deadened. It was hard to remember where we were, or even what day it was, let alone focus on the memorial in front of Brown AME; to register the words Ms. Bland wanted us to read; to spot the mistake she wanted us to catch.

"Wake up!" she barked like a drill sergeant. "What does that *say*, young people?" she asked, pointing with exasperation at the engraved words:

I HAD A DREAM.

"They put it in the past tense like they think the movement's over. That is a serious misquote. The man said, 'I have a dream.' Present tense. Just because the hands that picked the cotton can pick a president doesn't mean the struggle's done. I tell you, the people who commissioned this hot mess need to *fix* it."

This statue, like all of the memorials we visited on the tour, was designed to bring the Civil Rights Movement to life. I can tell you that none of those memorials succeeded in this task as well as Joanne Bland.

"I was there," she testified. "By the time I was eleven years old, I'd been to jail thirteen times. They'd stick forty or more of us children into a cell built for two. They fed us dry beans with rocks as punishment for demonstrating to get our parents the right to vote. They meant to break our spirit. You have to understand how many foot soldiers of the movement were children, and that the movement was a revolution. We were at war. There isn't a slab of marble big enough to fit the names of all the ordinary people who fought. Follow me."

Ms. Bland walked us from the chapel to the Edmund Pettus Bridge, which spans the Alabama River like a steel rainbow. The bridge was a lieu de mémoire, a site of memory, and she continued her story there with a nostalgic backward glance, as though still surprised to have been caught in the middle of that great drama, and even as though she missed it. "I was eleven when I crossed this bridge on Bloody Sunday in 1965. My big sister and I were part of the peaceful marches, but there were mounted state troopers in riot gear on the other side. The front line got pushed back. When I crested the bridge, I could see the police. I heard gunshots—what I thought were gunshots, since I had never heard gunshots before—but it was actually tear gas canisters. When tear gas gets in your lungs, you can't breathe, you can't see. We were surrounded. There was nowhere to go. They were beating people. What I remember the most is the screams.

"I don't know how long it lasted. It seemed like an eternity. If you could outrun those men on foot, you couldn't outrun the ones on horses. It was mayhem. They ran those horses up into the crowd and were knocking people down, horses rearing up, kicking people, hooves and billy clubs beating people. Blood everywhere.

"I saw this horse running full speed—I don't know why this woman didn't hear it. The clatter of his hooves on that bridge was something awful. She stepped right in front of it, and this horse ran right over her. The sound of her head hitting that pavement is the last thing I remember. I fainted," Ms. Bland said. "But forty-four years later, I can still hear that sound."

She regained consciousness with her sister leaning over her in the backseat of a hearse from the colored funeral home. "The hearse is being used as an ambulance," she explained. "When I came fully awake, I realized what I thought was my sister's tears falling on me was not her tears, it was her blood. She had been beaten. She had a wound on her head. Her whole face was covered with blood;

it was dripping into her blouse and soaking everything. And she was only fourteen."

To hear Ms. Bland tell it, Bloody Sunday felt like yesterday. Her account was violent and fresh. I knew we were the first of three tours she was to give that day. She would have to repeat this story again and again. I asked her if she found it traumatic to relive those combative years.

"It does make me kind of tired," she admitted, "but it's a cleansing kind of tired."

"He cleansed us with his blood," Reverend Warnock began quietly at Ebenezer Baptist Church in Atlanta on the final day of our tour. "He died for your soul."

It was Good Friday, the day of Christ's Passion, a dark holiday for remembering His crucifixion on Mount Calvary. But because this was the church Martin Luther King Jr. co-pastored, it was impossible not to think of his assassination at the Lorraine Motel in Memphis, Tennessee. Many feel he predicted his death in his famous final sermon, delivered the day before: "I just want to do God's will. And He's allowed me to go up to the mountain. And I've looked over. And I've seen the Promised Land. I may not get there with you. But I want you to know tonight, that we, as a people, will get to the Promised Land!"

There was no need for Reverend Warnock to draw an analogy between the two men, Christ and King, who died in service of our salvation. It hung there in the hallowed air of the sanctuary, partly because the reverend's intonation was a precise echo of Dr. King's—the same carefully placed caesura, the same vocal cascades and crescendos.

"Praise Jesus!" he called out.

Praise him! the congregation responded.

Reverend Warnock adjusted his wire-rimmed glasses with his long fingers and sped up the rhythm of his sermon, a long train beginning to pick up steam. "You ought to praise him because he's good. He's the answer to any problem we're facing today. I heard about people getting shot up, stabbed, the school system's failing, health care's a joke, the prisons are full of our men, the economy is hell, but I'm going to look to the hills. Lean on the God who delivered us through slavery. Lean on the God who delivered us in the fight for civil rights. He's the wheel in the middle of the wheel, the bread of life, the bright and morning star. Child of God, can I get a witness?"

Sweet Jesus died for my soul!

"This life is only a rehearsal. When we get over to the other side, we're going to have a good time. We'll never find enough contentment outside Jesus." The reverend grew stern. He pushed up the wide sleeves of his robes and growled, "Pockets of emptiness can't be filled with flesh or money. Only Jesus, our savior, can satisfy the sin-sick soul. They scourged him, made him to drink vinegar, placed a crown of thorns on his head, and nailed him to the cross today, but he's gonna rise day after tomorrow! He's gonna roll back the stone of his tomb and the weight on your shoulders. By and by, soon and very soon, Jesus gonna make everything all right. Somebody say, 'Amen!'"

Amen!

Again, my mind began to wander. I was so bored by the old message that the Promised Land was a pie in the sky that I could barely keep my eyes open. How many more days until I would sit at my cousin Tracy's table? Two, I counted. Just two more days 'til Easter.

"We all have an insatiable hunger it seems we can never satisfy. The best place to eat is not Popeyes! It's to dine at the Master's table for a spiritual banquet. Only what you do for Christ will last. Grace is God's riches at Christ's expense. He gave His only son to bless us. We are blessed by His blood. Blessed are the poor in spirit for theirs is the kingdom of heaven . . ."

Several members of the congregation joined the reverend as he recited the beatitudes: "Blessed are the meek: for they shall inherit the earth . . . Blessed are they which are persecuted for righteousness' sake: for theirs is the kingdom of heaven . . . For so persecuted they the prophets which were before you."

Across the street lay the American prophet. The inscription on Dr. King's white marble tomb reads FREE AT LAST! The water in the meditation pool beneath the tomb reflects the sky above and magnifies the pennies below. A sign asks that people not toss pennies in the pool. It is meant to be clear and smooth as heaven. But people have earthly wishes to make. They empty their pockets in the hopes of getting full. I too have made a wish in the water. We are distressed magical thinkers. We cannot help it.

While Jesus's suffering was the lynchpin of the sermon on Good Friday, it was strangely absent from the sermon I heard on Easter Sunday morning. In fact, inside Creflo Dollar's World Dome mega-church, there were no crosses or images of Jesus at all. In place of the crucifix there hung a large demi-globe on the axis of the American continent. It looked like a corporate logo but also reminded me of that gold sculpture in Tony Montana's foyer in the movie *Scarface*, skirted by the words THE WORLD IS YOURS. Flanking this globe were two ten-foot screens on which Creflo and his wife, Taffi, glowed in business attire. Stage lights gave the illusion of sunlight streaming through stained glass windows. Otherwise, the dome was planetarium-dark. Big as a sports arena, it sat on an eighty-acre campus that used to occupy a strip mall. In its massive parking lot I counted three SUVs with vanity plates in scriptural codes. The dome could seat eighty-five hundred worshippers and was near capacity when I arrived Easter morning.

Although Creflo Dollar was ordained as a Baptist minister, World Changers Church is nondenominational and takes all comers. Some members of the congregation were decked out in their finest hats and suits for the holiday and others were casually dressed in jeans and sneakers. I myself wore the sage-green silk drop-waist dress I'd worn onstage when I played Laura in a community theater production of *The Glass Menagerie*, and maybe because the dress had once been a costume, I felt like an actress playing a part. I took a seat ten rows from the stage between an old woman in a purple satin sequined turban with matching gloves, and a younger woman in a pink velour sweat suit and a gold name necklace that read PAULETTE. I asked both women what had brought them here.

"Pastor Dollar lifted me up out of the pit and I'm no longer pitiful," said the old woman in the turban. I smiled at her wordplay, which reminded me of the Rastafarians.

"He's not our parents' preacher," said Paulette with great relief. "He hates tradition."

These lines were spoken as if spoken or heard before. This was a grand production, and these women knew they were part of the show. Later, after careful editing, the service would be broadcast worldwide. A camera on a crane swept the crowd. It stopped to focus on a rabbity little man who suddenly appeared in a spotlight onstage. Like a carnival barker, he warmed up the crowd, spurring us to chant the words "WE WIN." Soon, the energy in the dome got to crackling and Creflo Dollar took the stage in his alligator shoes.

"Today is resurrection Sunday, a day when a man rose from the dead for you, giving you authority for abundant life," he began. *Praise Jesus!*

He sounded nothing like Martin Luther King Jr., but Dollar was an equally rousing performer. Our destiny, he seemed to say, wasn't about "saving the soul of the nation" in order to call it home, but rather to enjoy prospering in the home that we built. After the taxing examination of the Civil Rights Movement, it was an enlivening message to hear. I'd come with the idea of making him admit to his game by bumrushing him after the service with my tape recorder, or pretending to be saved just to gain access. But now that I was here, I could see that was preposterous. It would be impossible to get near him. He would never drop his mask. And besides that, it was more fun to play along. Kati Torda had said as much, back in Ghana. When you stopped swimming against the current, the water could take you to interesting places. She'd been speaking of the mythology of beads. This was just another myth.

"His blood was shed so you don't have to suffer. God knows what it takes to turn your life around. Your faith is about to bring you to your wealthy place."

"There won't be an excuse for anyone in here to suffer when he's done preaching," confided the old woman in the purple turban, patting me on the knee.

"It's important to go back to the word of God to see God's will," Dollar continued.

Tell it!

"The Bible says there was gold in the garden. There wasn't no recession! No need of a stimulus package. It was perfect. Then the serpent showed up. He slipped in and brought his creation. For some reason we credit God with creating poverty. Ain't nothing poor in heaven."

Talk about it, pastor!

"Oh, I'm-a talk about it 'til I talk the wig off your head."

Praise God!

"Deuteronomy 29:9 says, 'Keep therefore the words of this covenant that you may prosper in all that you do.'" The verse appeared on the screens above him and the people thumbed to it in their worn Bibles. "Repeat after me," he instructed. "I have covenant statements from God."

I have covenant statements from God.

"Stating that I will prosper in all that I do."

Stating that I will prosper in all that I do.

"Believe it. God will prosper you. You will lack for nothing. Satan can con believers into passively believing poverty is a gift from God. That Jesus was poor. Poverty is always and absolutely a curse. Our people aren't cursed. Poverty is a curse. Amen?"

Amen.

"We all know that tired old song." Dollar stooped his shoulders, clasped his hands, and, in mocking supplication, with his eyes rolled upward, sang, "Nobody knows the trouble I've seen ..." Then he straightened back up and adjusted his silk tie. "Shut up. Nobody got time for some old sorrow-preacher who don't know how to preach God's true word."

The crowd laughed uproariously at his bald disdain.

"Hope I ain't losing no members?" Dollar smiled with the confidence of a man who knew he was doing just the opposite. "Jesus wasn't poor. I'm telling you, the Catholics don't make no sense. A vow of poverty is a vow to be cursed! What fool would vow to be cursed when their own leader is the sharpest, most well-dressed man in the Catholic Church with custom-made gold slippers, a hat made out of rubies, and a bedroom on his 747? Pope want you to think you have to be a bum to be like Jesus. But you're not Catholic. You're born again. You're a through-the-book Christian."

Hallelujah!

"Your bail is paid. Step on out of jail. The door isn't even locked." Like Marcel Marceau, Dollar pantomimed twisting a doorknob, opening a door, and stepping through it to the other side. "Jesus is that open door. Poverty ain't nothing but a mind-set. You can't walk out of poverty until poverty walks out of you. Somebody shout, 'I ain't gotta be poor no more!'"

I ain't gotta be poor no more!

I been redeemed!

"The practical kind of prosperity that gets your bills paid is what Jesus promises. Southern Baptists hate this. They can't stand it. It's hard to grasp how much God really wants to bless us. Abraham was very rich in silver and gold. Solomon, Isaac, King David? Filthy-rich men. Won't somebody say 'I'm blessed'?"

I'm blessed.

"That's right. Name it and claim it. Now, God won't just pour a dump truck of cash over your eyes. Ed McMahon is not going to knock on your door with a bunch of balloons. I know you all want some sort of Scooby-Doo scheme. You just need to learn how to obey what God's telling you to do. Open yourself up to concepts and witty inventions. God told me to write a book. Then a big publisher came and paid me seven figures to write it for them."

In fact, Dollar has written several best-selling books. They were on sale in a gift shop off the lobby leading into the sanctuary: *Winning in Troubled Times: God's Solutions for Victory Over Life's Toughest Challenges*, and *No More Debt!: God's Strategy for Debt Cancellation*.

"Locate your passion," he encouraged us, "follow it, and it will lead you to your wealthy place."

A man behind me called out, "Blessing's working in me right now!" He raised his hands, fluttered them like moths around a lightbulb, rolled back his eyeballs, and started talking in tongues.

Dollar went on. "All of you have a covenant, a blood-bought right, to get wealth. From this point on, I do not call you average. I call you rich. Turn to your neighbor and say, 'I'm rich!'"

"I'm rich," Paulette told me, her eyes gleaming.

"I'm rich," trilled the old woman in the purple turban.

I was used to shaking hands and saying, "Peace be with you," at this point in the Catholic mass. I found it unsettling, but, not wanting to be rude, I greeted my neighbors as they had greeted me. "I'm rich," I demurred.

"Turn to your neighbor and say, 'I will never be broke another day in my life,'" Dollar commanded.

I will never be broke another day in my life! we repeated, enjoying the story that said we were winners.

"Somebody shout, 'God is a good God!'"

God is a good God!

"I want you to say this over and over. 'Paid for.'"

Paid for! the people shouted. With mounting excitement, they waved their blue offering envelopes in the air like traders at the stock market exchange.

"Every tongue confess, 'I will experience supernatural increase this week!'"

I will experience supernatural increase this week!

"You can expect many days of harvest in your life if you sow!" Dollar shouted, working himself up into a rhapsodic lather. "When you give, give with some hilariousness. Make a joyful noise. God loveth a cheerful giver. If the devil can't steal your joy, he can't steal your goods."

By this point, a third of the dome was talking in tongues. The spirit moved like an airborne virus and soon the dome was a buzzing hive.

"I smell something coming. You smell that?" Dollar called.

I smell the spirit!

"Don't you quit now, brothers and sisters. You're too close to your breakthrough. There is a heavenly supply running over. All you have to do is make your demand."

Thank you, Jesus!

"I don't know what NASDAQ is gonna do today!" Dollar continued. "I don't know what Dow Jones is gonna do today. But I know what we gonna do today!"

Praise God!

Dollar jumped backward. "Something just came alive in me. Something's getting ready to break loose!"

The ushers passed the buckets now with impeccable timing and the people stuffed those buckets until they overflowed. Others rushed to the stage with fistfuls of dollars like rowdy customers at a nudie bar. The security detail, a team of big men in black suits with sunglasses and earpieces, made a show of keeping them from climbing up onto the pulpit.

"No, no," Creflo ordered. "Let the lambs flock to the altar if they need to."

People clamored to toss money directly onto the stage. They threw stacks of bills at the preacher so that the cash rained down on him like confetti. He held out his hands and shut his eyes in a posture of ecstatic grace. I was reminded of an African concert I'd been to once at the Apollo, where Salif Keita, the Golden Voice of Mali, was tributed the same way. When his groove peaked at a fever pitch, the crowd fought to plaster tens and twenties to his sweaty brow. On the surface, this looked the same. The people were paying for entertainment. But I couldn't forget that today was Easter Sunday and that in Dollar's church, when people delivered an offering, they expected a return. What would happen if it never came?

"Every great deliverance took place at an altar," the preacher cried. "I believe deliverance is taking place in your finances. *This* is the place you received your deliverance!"

The room's wild energy increased until the altar was nearly carpeted with money. Disturbed by the show, I tried not to dismiss the crowd's yearning. Compared to Paulette and the old woman, I probably was rich already. It's easy to disregard someone else's desire when yours has been fulfilled.

"You have authority over this," Dollar shouted, as if trying to convince doubters like me that because the people had freely given, he wasn't robbing them blind. "Money is neither good nor bad on its own." He scooped up a handful of dollars and shook it like a paper tambourine. "Depends on who's holding it. Ladies and gentlemen, you obeyed God this morning. Congratulations!" He strutted over the money pile like a rooster. "I didn't tell you to do this. You did it on your own! Some folks would say, 'Look at that preacher taking those poor folks' money during a recession.' I didn't put up a sign saying make an offering. The same thing happened when I preached the Word in Ukraine. And I don't even speak Ukrainian!"

Praise God!

"You can't manufacture this! This is by the Holy Ghost. I feel His shadow upon me." A keyboard began rolling and Dollar, apparently moved by the spirit, began to wag his tongue. *"Baka rabado dekete lamondacom. Zebakese rokondo bakasta!"*

Tell it!

Creflo Dollar set his hands on his hips, threw back his head, and laughed in triumph. He said he was laughing in the face of Satan, but it was hard for me not to believe he was laughing at the audacity of his act. "Move over, devil!" he concluded his Easter sermon. "Today we have broken the back of lack!"

19

Survivors

I EXPECTED THE HOUSE my cousin Tracy Belle Joseph moved to after Hurricane Katrina to be broken and lacking. She'd left her home in Bay St. Louis reluctantly four years before, one of sixty-six thousand people displaced from the state of Mississippi. So when I showed up at the sprawling, salmon-pink, Italianate revival, stucco McMansion that matched her new address, I was surprised. It sat on a slope toward the end of a cul-de-sac in a planned community in Decatur, a suburb of Atlanta. The backyard had a gazebo and a fire pit. From the outside, Tracy seemed to be doing better here in Atlanta, with its wide horizons, than she had at home in Mississippi, the poorest state in the nation. But the inside of the house told a complicated story.

Above the fireplace hung a large, dewy studio portrait of Tracy's mother, Paula Raboteau Belle, my father's first cousin, who had died earlier that year. The slightly unfocused photo reminded me of the ones on display at Chris McNair's Birmingham studio, as if before it was shot, the camera's lens had been smeared with Vaseline. In the picture, Paula held a red rose. "Mama died before her time," Tracy told me.

Tracy had her mother's unblemished red-brown skin, a dimple in her chin, and a lion's mane of tightly woven spiral curls. She was a tall, thick, pretty woman, at peace with and proud of her domestic role as mother of two children, whom she homeschooled. She admitted to being unsure how she would make herself useful when her fourteen- and sixteen-year-old were grown. Maybe she'd train to become a doula, she said, to fill the empty nest. She thought she'd like to assist in the miracle of birth after witnessing so much destruction. Winking, she offered to come to New York and help my future baby into the world. Someday *soon*, she stressed. Or maybe she'd invent special holders for Georgia license plates belonging to drivers who moved here as a result of Katrina, a kind of frame imprinted with the name of the county they came from.

Transplants, Tracy called them. Or survivors. Tracy was a woman of faith. She was Catholic rather than Evangelical, but she used a tactic that would do Creflo Dollar's word faith proud. She strictly avoided the terms *victim* and *refugee*. "How can I be a refugee in my country?" she asked. "I'm a survivor." Many good things had resulted from her exodus, but she admitted that having Georgia license plates made her feel like an imposter. She couldn't stand how much time she spent cocooned in a car here in the big city. Back home, family and friends lived next door, down the street, around the corner, on the other side of the railroad tracks, where you could call out to your children from your porch at dusk and they would hear you, where jumbo shrimp could be had for four bucks a pound just across the bay in Pass Christian and where, in the summer, her kids could go to the same snowball stand beneath the giant oak tree at South Beach Boulevard and Washington Street that she'd gone to as a girl. Here in Atlanta, Tracy felt isolated. She wondered which of the other lonesome drivers on the interstate came from Hancock County, Mississippi, or from the counties in Louisiana and Alabama similarly savaged by Katrina. She would have liked to have been able to honk, as if to say, "I see you, I know where you come from. Keep on keeping on."

"Will you ever move back to the Bay?" I asked Tracy. I know the average Road Home grant paid just a third of what the homes were worth and that the cost of raising a new house was somewhere between twenty and fifty thousand dollars, money that might just as easily be used to start somewhere new, somewhere without so many ghosts. Tracy's family was never exactly at the bottom of the barrel, but Mississippi was a barrel they hadn't ever planned on leaving.

She sighed and told me that home was no longer home now that her mother was gone. "So many of my mama's generation died after Katrina. Maybe not directly, but from the physical and emotional toll. You know, some people blame the dirty flood water and others have conspiracy theories about the formaldehyde the government put in FEMA trailers. Who knows?"

"Katrina crud" was the Gulf Coast term for the toxic, bacteria-laden muck dumped from plants and refineries along the Baton Rouge–New Orleans Mississippi River corridor called Cancer Alley. After the storm surge, this polluted sludge coated many communities. That, as well as exposure to mold and other allergen, was also believed to cause respiratory problems called Katrina cough.

I asked Tracy what she blamed for her mother's death.

"Technically, Mama died of cancer, but if you ask me, she was done in by a broken heart," she replied. This was Tracy's first Easter Sunday without her mother. She seemed brokenhearted herself. But rather than dwell on the loss, she asked after my father. "How's Cousin Albert?"

"He has cancer too," I blurted. Quickly I feared it was an inappropriate admission. I didn't mean to overshadow her grief with my own worries, and maybe my father didn't want others to know he was sick.

Tracy's hand went straight to her chest. "Oh, honey," she said. "Oh, dear." She recommended a macrobiotic nutritional program that she believed extended her mother's life and told me my father would be in her daily prayers. Then she forced herself to brighten and invited me to the kitchen to greet the rest of the family.

I glanced over my shoulder at the portrait of Paula, my cousin once removed. The woman spent the end of her life in a FEMA trailer parked outside her flood-spoiled house. I'd never met her and wasn't sure my father had either, though she had the same signature halo of silver-white hair he and all the Raboteau cousins grew into with age. Some of them were gathered there at Tracy's house that Easter, including Aunt Rosemarie, in from the Bay. To everyone's great delight, she had brought a basketful of local candy from home. Rosemarie used to work at Casino Magic, but when it stopped operating after Katrina, she took a job with Habitat for Humanity, which had a lot of business to do constructing new homes. Next to Rosemarie sat Aunt Wanda, a chatterbox whose son, Frank—owing to the revenue from a chain of Applebees he owned in Louisiana—was able to hire a helicopter to save some of the family from the wreckage in the aftermath of the storm.

Tracy's sweet-faced son, Omari, was still catching up to his deep voice. He had the beginnings of dreadlocks and fed dog treats to the family's gangly Newfoundland puppy, Marley, while his big sister, Imani, all legs, pirouetted in and out of the kitchen. Imani pliéd when she spoke. She was a ballerina in training in the pre-professional program at Atlanta Ballet Company. The company was sympathetic to Katrina transplants and had rewarded her promise with a scholarship. Tracy told me it was one of the best of the mixed blessings resulting from Katrina. It looked like Imani was on track to becoming a professional ballerina.

"And if Imani wasn't a Katrina transplant?" I asked.

"You mean if she was just a regular black girl from Atlanta?" Tracy clarified while fixing me a plate.

I nodded.

"She'd be in Ballethnic. The black company. It isn't as good."

"So, things are still segregated here."

"'Fraid so. The ballet, the churches, the schools."

"Don't forget the strip clubs," joked Frank.

"Is it any different in New York?" asked Tracy's husband, Charles. But sarcastically, like he already knew the answer.

"Not so different," I acknowledged.

"Civil rights, my butt," Charles grumbled. "A black life in this country is still worth less than a white one. Plain and simple. Katrina shoved that in our face."

"Shut it, Charles," Tracy told him. "This isn't the time or the place."

Like the rest of the family assembled there that day, Charles talked in terms of before and after the hurricane, like BC and AD.

The storm was not just an abstraction for America's shame, but the great dividing line of their lives. Charles had retired from his post as a rocket engineer at NASA's Stennis Space Center two months before Katrina. "You can't get to space without going through the swamp first," he joked about his old job. I told him I believed Royal Woods, the man I knew as my grandfather, had worked there briefly as a janitor after leaving the Catholic priesthood, discouraged by the racism he found in the Church and so that he could marry my grandmother. He was the man who baptized my father at St. Rose de Lima, a black Catholic church, just a few months after Albert, my actual grandfather, was killed by a white man. Charles knew this story. Everyone at Easter dinner did. It was part of the family lore. Albert Raboteau the First is buried back there in St. Rose's churchyard, in a tomb I wasn't sure had weathered the storm.

"It's still there," Charles assured me. "The graves are still there."

The last time I'd seen Charles Joseph, he was playing electric bass in the band that backed the church choir at St. Rose de Lima. That was over ten years ago and he had aged considerably. Like me, Charles was an amateur photographer. He told me that his plan after retiring from NASA was to open a photography studio, but four years later he had still not done so. He admitted to being depressed, unfocused, unable to get it together enough even to teach photography to other children in the homeschooling community Imani and Omari belonged to, as he'd been invited to. Still, he was eager to show me the pictures he took on the day of the storm.

"Not at dinner," Tracy begged. "We're not victims, we're survivors. It's *Easter*." She had prepared a big pot of gumbo and rice, but over this bounty and against her wishes, Charles showed me the photographs anyway. He'd shot them at Aunt Dorothy's house, where the family sought shelter. They expected a thirty-five-foot surge and their own house on Citizen and Third was only two blocks from the beach. But even Aunt Dorothy's house in the neighboring town of Waveland was flooded by six and a half feet of water, as the dirty waterline in the ravaged dining room made clear. Home owner's insurance, for those who had it, would only cover damage above the waterline.

In the photos, after the water had receded, the house looked like a hoarder's home, a jumble of tables, chairs, and china. The refrigerator lay on its back. The dryer had moved to the wrong room. Tracy hovered behind us as we looked at these images. She seemed torn between wanting to move on from the hurricane and not being able to do so. Before we'd moved on from gumbo to bread pudding, she was telling the story to attend the pictures, alternating between past and present tense, as if Katrina was happening both back then and now, on Easter Sunday.

"That was the attic room where we waited out the storm. It was maybe a foot wider than a queen-sized bed and probably the length of about three and a half mattresses," she explained. "Not a whole lot of space. There were eight of us. Charles and I and the kids, that's four, my mom, that's five, Aunt Dorothy and her husband, Earl, and her sister-in-law, Miss Barbara, that's eight. And we're all big people except for my children. Charles was the slimmest adult there. And it was hot. It was extremely hot.

"Early that morning Aunt Dorothy came out of the bathroom and said, 'Tracy, come look.' The water in the toilet was coming back up. And I thought, oh, the streets are flooded and it's not going to go down. I went to the garage to get some water and ice in a cooler and put sodas in there so we'd have something cold. When I got back with the cooler, Aunt Dorothy was standing in her kitchen looking out the back window with a look of horror on her face and she says, 'Tracy, come see this.'

"I looked out the window at the water. Whoa. Water was just pouring into her backyard and it was kind of pooling, it was circling like a whirlpool. It was getting higher. I opened her back door and before I could blink my eyes her little patio was covered. I said, 'The water's getting ready to come in. We gotta get everybody up to the attic.'"

In fact, many people compared the wall of approaching water to a tsunami. Katrina, which made its final landfall near Bay St.

Louis at the mouth of the Pearl River with the highest storm surge in recorded U.S. history, came ashore during high tide. In under two hours she would smash the Gulf Coast to kindling, leaving hundreds along the coastline dead and over a hundred thousand homeless. Although New Orleans received the bulk of the media coverage, this region, which bore the brunt of the storm, would be a scene of near-total destruction, debris piled solid for miles, houses smashed, trees uprooted, tossed cars, dead animals, dead people, all of it covered with a layer of toxic muck, Katrina's ground zero. Two miles of the boulevard along the man-made beach, for whites only when my father was a boy, would be blasted to fragments of black asphalt, the streets rubbled, the fishing piers shredded, landmarks and bearings stripped away. The bridge that carried Highway 90, the coast road otherwise known as Jefferson Davis Highway, east to Pass Christian, then Gulfport, then Biloxi, collapsed on its pilings in sections, like a row of fallen dominoes. Nearly everything was ruined by the saltwater before the surging waves pulled back.

It was a natural catastrophe, but the one that followed was not. I thought of the many words for catastrophe I'd learned—Nakba, Maafa, Shoah—though this was not as large as they, and how Katrina, as a name, had lost its beauty when it blew the unwanted to the wind. At the castle in Elmina, I had wanted an account of one of the slaves, something like Anne Frank's diary, to put a face on that disaster. But there were none. Here was my cousin, to put a face on this one. When I asked for her permission to record the rest of the story, she said yes, of course, as if it was obvious all along that's what I was there to do. This was my role in the family, as sure as it was Imani's to dance. *What are you?* the airline security had asked me on my first trip to Jerusalem. I didn't know the easy answer then, but I knew it now. I was the scribe.

"Weren't you afraid?" I asked.

Tracy said she was too busy to be overtaken by fear. "Aunt Dorothy and Miss Barbara are telling me, 'You gotta get my medicine basket.' Aunt Dorothy was hysterical. She was cursing her husband, telling him to get this and do that, but he couldn't do it fast enough.

You couldn't keep up. My children and I were the only ones under sixty. So I'm the most able-bodied person in the house. It's on my shoulders to make sure we're safe. I'm trying to make sure I get their hypertension meds, their high-cholesterol meds. And then I'm thinking about the food. I don't know how long we're gonna be up there—and not just the food, but everything you need to eat food with—we need bread, we need plates, we need cups, we need napkins, forks, knives, we need everything we can get up there. And Charles is walking around with a *camera*."

Charles defended himself. "Somebody had to record it for posterity. You know what I'm talking about, little cuz," he said to me. I gave him a high five.

"Now, after it was all over with it was okay, and it's good to have a record," Tracy allowed, "but in the heat of the moment you need everybody to help out. And my husband is walking around with a *camera*. I'm telling you. I didn't even have time to be angry. You see how muddy that water is?" She pointed at a blurry picture of the rising water. Most of the pictures were blurry, maybe because Charles couldn't keep his hands steady while holding the camera, maybe because it was too dark to be shooting without a flash in spite of the fact that it was daytime, or maybe because he was moving too fast to keep up with the rising water to be able to properly focus the lens.

"That water wasn't just plain old rainwater. It was some of everything. It could make you sick," Tracy continued. "You could see through it but it was brown. The more water that came in, the browner it got. This is how quickly it came in—when the kids headed upstairs they were splashing in the water. It was covering their ankles. Fifteen, twenty minutes tops, then the water was over Charles's head. It was nine forty-five in the morning when Aunt Dorothy's clock stopped. I didn't have time to do much of anything. I told my kids, 'You all stay up there.'

"Imani was sick, she was throwing up 'cause she was scared. It was hot. Omari was hysterical. He would go to every adult asking, 'How are we gonna get out of here?!' He would just grab you and shake you. 'How are we gonna get out of here?!' He was so small, just ten then, and Imani was only twelve. I told them, 'We're gonna be okay.' Well, I had to say that. I can't tell my kids, 'We're gonna die,' even though I wasn't sure whether or not we were gonna be okay.

"My aunt is still screaming and cussing and fussing and Charles is snapping pictures. There was a ceiling fan in the attic with water dripping from its light fixture. Omari's frantic. Everybody's looking at me so I keep saying, 'We are going to be okay.' I said it and I thought, 'Oh my God, I didn't know my children were going to die today.' I thought about the date. August twenty-ninth. I didn't know this was the way I was gonna die. I just didn't know. It was getting darker and the water's coming up outside. And there's no way out.

"There's a window we can see out. The water just keeps rising and rising. I held my hands out like this to my kids. They grabbed my hands. They were ready to start praying. We prayed and prayed and prayed. I called out every promise that I could remember from the Bible and my kids fell in line right behind me. They said whatever I said. Soon everyone grabbed hands and we prayed. I couldn't stop. I *could* stop, but I was compelled to continue.

"We prayed for a long while. We prayed for everybody to be safe. For the structure we were in to withstand the storm. The house was groaning. I was thinking, 'I don't know if this room is going to hold,' because I'm telling you, there was some hefty weight up there. You can see from the pictures we're big people. I mean, the only people under a hundred pounds were my children and most everybody else was over two hundred. Miss Barbara, I tell you, she was closer to three. It was terrifying. I prayed for God to not forget us. I prayed for us to have a home to go back to. I prayed for all the family members that weren't with us to be safe. Until we were done, we prayed.

"And then we sat and we waited. It was so hot. I wouldn't let my children look out the window. At one point it looked like night. We were using flashlights. I remember Charles and Uncle Earl going to the top of the doorway looking down at the steps and talking really low. I remember I didn't want to look at my husband's face because I didn't want to know what was coming. When I was ready to handle the news, I went and saw the water still rising. We didn't see it going down.

"I asked Charles what we were gonna do. He said he didn't know. I said, 'What do you mean? We have to have some kind of plan.' He says, 'All I can see is we go out that window and climb up on the roof and hold on.' That was scary because that meant somebody was going to have to be out there to receive people.

"I'm thinking about my kids—I couldn't leave them in the house until last and I couldn't put them up there on the roof first. I'm thinking about my mom and I'm thinking about this big lady—Miss Barbara—I don't even know if she's gonna fit through the window. It was crazy. I didn't know if we were gonna make it. But I made a conscious decision to believe that we were. After we prayed, I knew God's not going to forget us."

"But how did you *know*?" I asked.

"Everyone else might forget us, but not God. He said whatever we asked in His son's name, it would be. And so, that's how I was able to calm down. We had practically nothing, but at the same time we had everything. We had each other. We had a five-gallon bucket for a toilet. We had a roof over our head protecting us. We had red beans and rice and my mama's bread pudding.

"We heard the house creaking like something was going to break, like it wasn't going to hold, but I knew by then that it would. The wind was whipping. We heard Aunt Dorothy's china hutch fall over and we heard the dishes. Whatever was loose in the house, all Aunt Dorothy's antiques, we heard those things falling. We wanted to open the window 'cause it was so hot, but we were afraid with that window going that it could tear the roof off. Eventually the wind stopped and eventually the water stopped rising. I was soon willing to look out the dormer window and see things floating outside. Things from the house, things from Aunt Dorothy's garage, a mantelpiece, some furniture. When Aunt Dorothy saw the damage she said, 'It's just stuff.' That was a relief because she has a reputation for being a person to fuss. The water was going down further and further. Finally I let my kids look out. We started seeing light. They knew we were going to be okay now.

"Next morning I changed my shoes and socks. I was ready to go see about my house and the rest of the family. My mom stayed with the kids. I knew we didn't have insurance—that's a whole other story. I knew there had to be corpses in some of the other houses and maybe they'd floated out to the street. I didn't want my children to see them. I expected roof damage and parts of buildings gone, but this was whole blocks gone, whole blocks of streets just gone. We walked from Aunt Dorothy's house to the highway. It was a mile and a half, maybe. We had to climb over fallen trees, limbs. Boats were in the trees. The railroad was out, the ties were gone, the car bridge was out. And it was eerie how quiet it was—no birds singing, no bugs buzzing, just quiet. It was a surreal landscape, piles of rubble, wood siding from houses with nails poking through. It looked more treacherous than these pictures show. It looked like an atomic bomb went off. You wouldn't think it was America. It looked like a Third World country.

"We'd lost our vehicles so we were stuck. We heard there were going to be buses coming along the highway picking up people and taking them to the hospital. That didn't happen. We heard there's a place up on the beach where you can go and get a signal to call out. Charles and I started trying to make calls, trying to let somebody know we were still there, we had survived and we needed somebody to come and get us out of there."

"She kept asking me, 'When are they coming?'" Charles interrupted. "I told her I sure as hell didn't know who 'they' was."

"I meant the people in the country that this didn't happen to," Tracy said pointedly. It was the closest she came to admitting anger at the nation, the government, for taking so long to respond and for so egregiously fumbling when it did. Everyone grew quiet around the kitchen table. Tracy was spent. I noticed she'd stopped telling the story of her brush with death at the point of her survival rather than with the details of the weeks that followed—the humiliating curfew imposed to discourage looters, the pitiful lack of aid, the news choppers circling overhead like a mockery of salvation, the hateful words of the congressman who said, "We finally cleaned up public housing in New Orleans. We couldn't do it, but God did." I wanted her to continue, to talk about the rest of the pictures and the ways the country had failed her, leading Frank to organize a rescue of his own. I pushed my cousin to keep going. But she was done. She refused to be trapped in a tragic story.

"You could learn all the bad parts from the TV and the newspapers," she said. "But what I want you to know about Katrina that you can't learn from the news is the reserves of goodness. It was a cashless society but all our needs were met. People came from all over, stayed in tents and cooked for us."

Charles disagreed, his voice trembling. "What are you talking about, woman? The military were only giving water and meals to one person when each person who could make it as far as a distribution point was representing their whole family. We could have starved to death. Some people did."

"No," Tracy insisted, her mouth a thin line. "God provided. Just look how well we're all doing now."

"What about the rest of the family?" I asked. My understanding then was that the family seat was destroyed along with the obliterated town, that there were barely any Raboteaux left in Bay St. Louis, and that when the few who remained died out, home would be nothing but an ever-receding memory.

"Oh no, no, no," Tracy corrected me, and I realized how little I knew that place in spite of how large it loomed in my imagination. "Plenty of our people are still there. Cousin Aida's celebrating her ninetieth birthday in July. We're having a big party. You should come," she encouraged. "You could bring your husband." But I would save Victor's first trip down there for a cooler season. I knew he couldn't hack Bay St. Louis in the summer. "You should bring your father," Tracy suggested next. "Oh, it would do his body good to go home."

20

Ishem

THE DAY AFTER Victor and I found out I was pregnant, my father and I flew down to New Orleans. It is a city we both love for its international flavor, its zydeco, its jazz, its Creole, its wrought-iron balconies, its ancient live oak trees dangling with Spanish moss and Mardi Gras beads, its ghosts, its stretch of the Mississippi River, its slow pooling of time, its shotgun shacks, its history living in the present, its pride, and, most of all, its proximity to Bay St. Louis, fifty miles west, where he was born but spirited away for his own safety. He only ever summered here. He didn't grow up in this region but continues to think of it as home.

Strangely, considering I can count the times I've traveled here on one hand, so do I. I am drawn to this place because my father is. It is our Africa, our Israel, the home that never was, the Zion that never will be, a dream place. It is also our Egypt, our Dixie, our black bottom, the land where we were beaten, the place we were delivered, a nightmare place. We cleave to it. My father's first teaching job was in New Orleans at Xavier, the black Catholic university, where he taught theology. I lived there too for a time, working the midnight shift at the Café Du Monde with the idea of becoming a writer. Had Victor not vetoed it because he "sweats too much to be a Southerner" and feared our house going under in some future flood, I should have liked to make our home in New Orleans, though it had inexorably changed. Before the flood it was a majority black city; afterward it was no longer so. Half of its hospitals were closed. Most of its public schools were damaged.

My father and I planned to stay there for a few days before heading to the Bay of St. Louis, where it empties into the Mississippi Sound, for Cousin Aida's birthday.

Even as I was happy to be going "home" with my dad after talking to so many strangers in strange lands, I worried he and I were in danger of flying back in time to land in a territory of woe. But what right did either of us have to despair when people like my cousin Tracy were living in a land of faithful optimism? Frankly, I preferred Tracy's vision to every other story I'd heard along the way.

On the airplane my father expressed excitement about his return. We didn't speak of it, but we both suspected it could be his last. He looked frail to me as he scrounged through his tote bag for the Chinese tea pills meant to help with the prostate cancer. The baby inside me was only the size of one of those pills. I felt now what I'd known from the beginning. Zion is within. I understood that I would forget this fact and, as with love, or faith, have to learn it again. I wanted to tell my father that I had gotten my wish, but it was too early to share the good news. When he fell asleep over his prayer book, I contemplated the anger I'd inherited, the terrible personal crime enacted in my father's hometown and the larger national crime that supported it. When he woke, I asked him a naive question. How did it make him feel that his home in the Deep South was wiped away? His answer was ambiguous. His anger was not. "It was never my home," he said. "It was the only home I ever knew."

There it was again. That paradox.

"Tell me again about our ancestors," I urged, needing to know how we were tied to the old place, what rooted us there still. The graves, Cousin Charles had told me, were still there. My father repeated the old story. He could go back as far as Mary Lloyd, his great-grandmother, a slave from New Orleans. Before her was an awful void. After Mary Lloyd came Edward Ishem, the son she named after his father, a German merchant marine who threatened to take the boy back with him to Europe. To save him from that fate and to keep him in her arms, Mary spirited her son to

Bay St. Louis, where he grew up and married a Creole woman called, deliciously, Philomena Laneaux. They gave birth to my grandmother, Mabel Sincere, and her favorite sister, Emily Ishem, for whom I am named.

Ishem.

I told my father about the trouble my middle name caused on my way to Israel ten years earlier when I was twenty-three. Because it sounded vaguely Arabic to the security personnel of El Al Airlines, because I was unable to trace its origins, because they would not believe I was an American citizen looking as I did, and, most of all, because of my bad attitude, they led me to the airport basement for a strip search, which, in turn, set me on the labyrinthine search for home that had me here again, at thirty-three, on a plane.

My father laughed. "That's ironic."

"What's ironic?" I asked.

"In addition to being a merchant marine, Ishem was a German Jew."

"Are you telling me we're part Jewish?"

"We're African American, Emily. We're part everything."

"Part Finnish?" I joked.

"Well, maybe not Finnish." He laughed again as the plane touched down.

To end any story, even one far simpler than this, is a magic trick. The Promised Land is never arrived at. A black president is not the end of race. One man does not rule a nation. No country is what it should be, just as no man is perfect. How should I finish this story, which is my story and a much larger story than mine?

If this were a comedy, I might end with my wedding march to Black Sabbath's "Iron Man" played on mandolin at the church around the corner from the building my husband Victor and I live in now, or with a scene of us, positively knackered, renovating our dump of an apartment by prying up old tiles with a crowbar and skim-coating the walls before hanging them with artwork from my travels—the barbershop sign from Accra, the banana-leaf collage from Shashemene, the Exodus painting from Jerusalem—or with the birth of our son (who will inherit us when we die) underwater in an inflated pool in the back room of the apartment, or Tamar's whooping "Mazel Tov!" on the phone soon after; I might end at Cousin Aida's birthday party, where the family that remained were no longer encamped in FEMA trailers but either back in their old houses, which—though still affected by mold and smelling of mildew—were nevertheless their homes, or living in newly built houses, and how at this reunion, in a circle of plastic lawn chairs beneath the carport, they fed my father and me, the prodigal son and his daughter, red beans and rice, fried chicken, macaroni and cheese, pound cake, and pralines while telling stories about the old people, including my grandfather, shot dead under Jim Crow at the age of forty-four by a white man who was never prosecuted, and about the young people—including the cousin who went AWOL in Iraq because he felt more like a slave than a marine, but also including Tracy's Imani, who was heading to dance for American Ballet Theatre in New York City because her jeté was weightless as a spear—and told these stories with the kind of grace that only comes from moving through floods and fire, and even, impossibly, with humor.

If this were a tragedy, I might end at my grandfather's graveside in our ancestor's plot at St. Rose de Lima, where my father and I placed the two small pink wildflowers we found growing outside the caved-in house of my grandmother's best friend, Nan Odette, on Easterbrook Street, a street now marked by concrete slabs and houses abandoned, boarded up, trashed by water, house, slab, house, slab, like a jawbone with half its teeth missing, the house of my father's godmother, Aunt "Zoom" Zenobia, vanished, my grandfather's gravestone overrun with weeds, wisteria, kudzu, the letters fading with time, the digits of the phone number to call for maintenance on the sign nailed to a nearby crape myrtle tree illegible, the myrtle dead, the fig trees, lime trees, pecan trees, and saw palmettos dead and gray as driftwood, Aunt Emily Ishem's house gone, my father enfeebled, aged, depressed by the decay and lost in the landscape of his old hometown, which was never really his, a picture of that saying that you can't go home again, to indicate that what he's looking for was lost in that place before he was even born.

If this were a photograph, I might end on the mural behind the altar at St. Rose de Lima, the battered black Church, which depicts a black Christ in the posture of the crucifixion yet somehow not dead yet, or rising already, his body intact, as if retouched, his eyes open beneath the crown of thorns, a live oak tree stretching verdant behind him, its leaves the darkest green, its branches embellished with the names of the parishioners, including ours, Ishem, Raboteau, too many names to count, name after name, branch after branch, reaching to the roof beams, to indicate the mystery of suffering and salvation.

But instead I will end on the road.

My father and I are in the rental car, driving from New Orleans toward the birthday party in Bay St. Louis through the swampland along U.S. Route 90. In the trunk is a painting on salvaged wood I have purchased from an artist in Jackson Square—the dark silhouette of an angel. Later it will go above my son's bassinet. Now the low-hanging sky is threatening and gray and pregnant with rain. The air is thick, as are the trees rolling past—mangrove, cypress, oak. I am trying to find the right words to forgive my father for his failings, and to thank him for his many gifts. We have passed the idle rollercoaster of the ruined adventure park, the space center, the red Xs on the doorways of eroding dwellings marking the numbers of the dead, the billboards for the casinos overtaking the wetlands with names that hold out the promise of fortune—the Silver Slipper, Hollywood, and Island View. His hand is on the wheel. My hand is on my belly. We don't yet know what we'll find at the homecoming. We'll be there soon. We're not there yet.

ACKNOWLEDGMENTS

I am grateful to many individuals and organizations for helping me produce this book. None of them are responsible for any inaccuracies it may contain or the views expressed by me.

My first debt is to my father, Albert Raboteau. His scholarship in the field of African American religious history was an inspiration and a launchpad for this work, which I consider an extension of his own. If I can claim to be a creative writer with a historian's impulse, it is because I was raised by a historian who knows how to plot a gripping story. Thank you, Dad, for writing *Slave Religion*, as well as for the bedtime stories you told us when we were small.

The Puffin Foundation, the Barbara Deming Memorial Fund, Harlem Arts Alliance, and the PSC CUNY Research Award Program provided necessary travel funding. Columbia University's Hertog Fellowship gifted me a diligent and thorough research assistant, Tenzin Dickyi, who lightened the load.

Tamar Cohen opened the gate to Zion and introduced me to Jerusalem. I continue to admire her social consciousness and fighting spirit. Rabbi Or Zohar and Feliza Bascara Zohar let me sleep on their couch in Tel Aviv and challenged my simple ideas about Zionism. Their daughter, Layla, taught me my favorite word in Hebrew: *flotz*. Thanks to the many Ethiopian Jews and African Hebrew Israelites who granted interviews in Israel, especially Daniel Admasu, Tezeta Germay, and Dr. Khazriel Ben Yehuda.

Master percussionist Larry McDonald of the band Dub is a Weapon deepened my appreciation of Jamaican popular music before I travelled there. The Reverend Mark Bozzuti-Jones of Trinity Church provoked me further with an excellent lecture on the spiritual message of Bob Marley. Dr. Carolyn Cooper gave me shelter in her beautiful home during my first week in Kingston.

At the University of the West Indies, Jalani Niaah made time to school me about the power dynamics of the British Commonwealth. Thanks to Aduke Thelwell, Herbie Miller, Colin Channer, Margaret Adams, Ucal Ebanks, Thomas Glave, the Rastas at the Twelve Tribes headquarters, and the many Jamaicans who let me pester them with impertinent questions.

Dr. Charles Rowell must be credited for his continuing showcase of literature and art from the far corners of the African diaspora, and for envisioning the *Callaloo* conference in Ethiopia. Dagmawi Woubshet was instrumental in orchestrating the conference and welcoming its participants. Andreas Ashete and Abiyi Ford made time during the busy proceedings to let me pick their brilliant minds. Nelly Rosario, Maaza Mengiste, and Elleni Centime Zeleke were excellent travelling companions and conversationalists. Nadia Nurhussein and Koritha Mitchell were enlightening co-panelists. Dr. Giulia Bonacci and Dr. Erin MacLeod were kind enough to share their previous studies of Jamaica Sefer in Shashemene. I appreciate the many Rasta settlers of Shashemene who counseled me during Haile Selassie's birthday weekend, especially Brother Leroy Bryan and Ras Hailu, the Banana Man. Special thanks to Genene Tasew for his important work with the Bridge Orphans, and to Abu for doing well in school. To the generous friends and family members who paid school fees of other children as a wedding gift to me, thank you for not getting me and the bridegroom a blender.

Catherine McKinley went above and beyond the normal bounds of friendship by inviting me on her family vacation in Accra. I value her empathetic, nuanced, and intrepid manners of traveling, seeing, and writing. She connected me to many fascinating women in Ghana at a time I needed the influence of strong women. They included Kati Torda, the late Mary Ellen Ray, and Vida Saforo, all of whom graciously opened their homes and hearts. Shamara Wyllie, Anne Adams, and Martina Odonkor extended even more hospitality. Margo Mack and Megan Cahill were upbeat travel-mates who made the trip fun. It was a delight to cross paths on that continent with my childhood friend Maya Mesola (née Smith) on a sojourn of her own, and to spend a memorable drinking night with her and a little person film star from Nigeria. Maya introduced me to Kofi Awoonor, who broadened my thinking about relations between Africans and African Americans.

Dr. Valerie Smith of Princeton University allowed me to join her seminar's Civil Rights Movement tour of the South and was the perfect guide. Ms. Joanne Bland and Mr. Charles McNair are treasures for testifying to those years in our nation's history. Chastity Whitaker and her dog, Liver, were my spirited cohorts in Atlanta. Tulane professor Felipe Smith shared demographic information about changes to New Orleans's infrastructure, housing, environment, politics, and labor rights post-Katrina. My little brother, Martin, was with my father and me on our last trip there. Though I couldn't work him into this narrative, I was so glad he came along. I would be remiss not to thank the transcendent city of New Orleans itself. To my dear cousin Tracy Joseph and all the Raboteaux in and out of Bay St. Louis, Mississippi, merci, and God bless.

For their useful feedback on various portions and/or drafts of this book and its proposal, I owe heartfelt thanks to Angie Cruz, Miranda Beverly-Whittemore, David Lobenstine, Nichelle Tramble, Carolyn Ferrell, Margo Jefferson, Retha Powers, Claire Lundberg, Nina Siegal, and the writing group in Amsterdam. Michael Vazquez, former editor of *Transition*, gave me the confidence to try my hand at nonfiction with the sage advice to keep it honest while telling it slant. My many walks in and around Harlem with Sharifa Rhodes Pitts, fellow seeker of black utopias, seem to occur outside of time. I hope for many more walks by her side, with strollers and without.

Amy Williams is a stellar agent. It's an honor to be her client; even more so to be her friend. Elisabeth Schmitz took a risk on a bizarre and amorphous book proposal and remained encouraging when my pregnancy delayed its production by exactly nine months. Both she and Jessica Monahan were expert editors at Grove/Atlantic.

Anne Horowitz and Muriel Jorgensen were careful copyeditors. Garnette Cadogan, hands down the best-read brother I've ever met, blessed this manuscript with scrupulous care.

Final praise-song goes to my husband, who makes my life as joyous as my work. For all our unfolding adventures, the best of which so far is our smiley son, Geronimo, I thank you, Victor LaValle.

BIBLIOGRAPHY

Afari, Yasus. *Overstanding Rastafari: "Jamaica's Gift to the World."* Jamaica: Senya-Cum, 2007.

Africa Unite: A Celebration of Bob Marley's 60th Birthday. Dir., prod. Stephanie Black. Louverture Films, Tuff Gong Pictures, 2008.

Appiah, Kwame Anthony. "What Was Africa to Them?" *The New York Review of Books* 27 Sept. 2007.

Arnold, Michael S. "Black Hebrews Hope Eurovision Attention Will Improve Their Plight." *Jerusalem Post* 28 May 1999: 6A.

Awoonor, Kofi. *The African Predicament: Collected Essays.* Accra, Ghana: Sub-Saharan Publishers, 2006.

Baker, Peter. "Obama Delivers Call for Change to a Rapt Africa." *The New York Times* 12 July 2009: A1.

Bardfield, Edward. "Judaism & Rastafarianism: A Study of the Falashas." *The Dreaded Library.* Spring 1998 http://debate.uvm.edu/dreadlibrary/ebardfield.html

Barrett, Leonard E., Sr. *The Rastafarians.* Boston: Beacon, 1997.

Baum, Dan. *Nine Lives: Death and Life in New Orleans.* New York: Spiegel and Grau, 2009.

Bekerie, Ayele. "The Case of Melaku E. Bayen & John Robinson." *Tadias Magazine* 18 Apr. 2007.

Bender, Thomas. "No Borders: Beyond the Nation-State." *The Chronicle of Higher Education* 7 Apr. 2006 http://chronicle.com/article/No-Borders-Beyond-the/34180

"The Black Hebrews." *Israel Ministry of Foreign Affairs* 1 June 1997 http://www.israel-mfa.gov.il/MFA/Facts+About+Israel/People/The+Black+Hebrews.htm

"Black Hebrews." *New York Daily News* 30 Nov 2004.

Bland, Jeanne Blackmon and Lynda Blackmon Lowery. *Stories of Struggle: Growing Up in the Segregated South.* 2007.

Bono. "Rebranding Africa." *The New York Times* 10 July 2009: 25.

Boyne, Ian. "Obama & America's Moment." *The Sunday Gleaner* 8 June 2008: G1.

Brackman, Harold. "Jews, African Americans, and Israel: The Ties That Bind." *Simon Wiesenthal Center/Museum of Tolerance.* Jan.–Feb. 2010.

Brooke, James. "Du Bois Still a Great Hero to Ghanaians." *The New York Times* 10 May 1987.

Campbell, James T. *Middle Passages: African American Journeys to Africa, 1787–2005.* New York: Penguin, 2006.

Carruthers, Iva E., Frederick D. Haynes III, and Jeremiah A. Wright Jr. *Blow the Trumpet in Zion: Global Vision and Action for the 21st-Century Black Church.* Minneapolis: Fortress Press, 2005.

Chan, Sewell. "Coffin's Emblem Defies Certainty." *The New York Times* 27 Jan. 2010: C1.

Chevannes, Barry. *Rastafari: Roots and Ideology.* Syracuse: Syracuse University Press, 1994.

"Colonization." *Mr. Lincoln and Freedom, a Project of the Lincoln Institute* 14 Dec. 2010 http://www.mrlincolnandfreedom.org/inside.asp?ID=34&subjectID=3

Cone, James H. *Black Theology & Black Power.* 1969. Reprint. New York: Orbis Books, 1997.

Cooke, Mel. "'Glave' Matters in Treasure Beach." *The Sunday Gleaner* 8 June 2008.

Cooper, Carolyn. *Sound Clash: Jamaican Dancehall Culture at Large.* New York: Palgrave Macmillan, 2004.

Davis, Barry. "Ras Jazz." *The Jerusalem Post* 10 Aug. 2006.

Dawes, Kwame. *Natural Mysticism: Towards a New Reggae Aesthetic in Caribbean Writing.* 1999. Reprint. Leeds, UK: Peepal Tree Press, 2008.

Dyson, Michael Eric. *Debating Race with Michael Eric Dyson.* New York: Basic Civitas, 2007.

Edmonds, Ennis Barrington. *Rastafari: From Outcasts to Culture Bearers.* New York: Oxford University Press, 2003.

Elliman, Wendy. "Integrating Ethiopian-Born Youth into Israel." *Israel Magazine-on-Web, Israel Ministry of Foreign Affairs* June 1999 http://

www.mfa.gov.il/MFA/Israel%20beyond%20the%20conflict/
Integrating%20Ethiopian-Born%20Youth%20into%20Israel

Enav, Peter. "Israel Recognizes Residency Status of 'Black Hebrews' Community." *Chicago Tribune* 28 July 2003.

Esensten, Andrew. "Three Decades After Exodus from America, First Black Hebrew Becomes Israeli Citizen." *Haaretz* 23 Mar. 2009.

Eshun, Ekow. *Black Gold of the Sun: Searching for Home in Africa and Beyond.* New York: Vintage, 2007.

"Ethiopian Jews Struggle in Israel." BBC 9 Aug. 2006.

Gaines, Kevin K. *American Africans in Ghana: Black Expatriates and the Civil Rights Era.* Chapel Hill: University of North Carolina Press, 2006.

Gebrekidan, Fikru Negash. *Bond Without Blood: A History of Ethiopian and New World Black Relations, 1896–1991.* Trenton, N.J. and Asmara, Eritrea: African World Press, 2005.

Gettleman, Jeffrey. "Welcome Back, Son. Now Don't Forget Us." *The New York Times* 12 July 2009: WK3.

Gilroy, Paul. *The Black Atlantic: Modernity and Double Consciousness.* Cambridge: Harvard University Press, 1993.

Goffe, Leslie. "Stars in their Eyes." *BBC Focus on Africa.*

Goldin, Megan. "Whatever Happened to The Lost Tribes of Israel?" *The Ross Institute Internet Archives for the Study of Destructive Cults, Controversial Groups and Movements.* 21 Aug. 2000. 30 June 2006 http://www.rickross.com/reference/black_hebrews/black_hebrews14.html

Goldman, Vivien. *The Book of Exodus: The Making & Meaning of Bob Marley & The Wailers' Album of the Century.* New York: Three Rivers, 2006.

Goodstein, Laurie. "Believers Invest in the Gospel of Getting Rich." *The New York Times* 16 Aug. 2009: A1.

Grant, Colin. *The Natural Mystics: Marley, Tosh, and Wailer.* New York: Norton, 2011.

Grant, Colin. *Negro with a Hat: The Rise and Fall of Marcus Garvey.* New York: Oxford University Press, 2008.

HaGadol, Prince Gavriel and Odehyah B. Israel. *The Impregnable People: An Exodus of African Americans Back to Africa*. Washington, D.C.: Communicators Press, 1993.

Hansen, Thorkild. *Coast of Slaves*. 2002. Reprint. Accra, Ghana: Sub-Saharan Publishers, 2009.

Harrison, Milmon F. *Righteous Riches: The Word of Faith Movement in Contemporary African American Religion*. New York: Oxford University Press, 2005.

Hartman, Saidiya. *Lose Your Mother: A Journey Along the Atlantic Slave Route*. New York: Farrar, Straus and Giroux, 2007.

Isaac, Ephraim. "The Question of Jewish Identity and Ethiopian Jewish Origins." *Midstream* September/October 2005.

"Israel Rejects Black Hebrews as Jews." *Scripps Howard News Service* 20 Nov. 2002.

Jackson, John L. Jr. "All Yah's Children: Emigrationism, Afrocentrism, and the Place of Israel in Africa." *Civilisations* 58-1 (2009): 93-112.

Kapuscinski, Ryszard. *The Emperor: Downfall of an Autocrat*. 1978. Reprint. New York: Vintage, 1989.

King, Martin Luther Jr. *Strength to Love*. 1977. Reprint. Philadelphia: Fortress Press, 1981.

Lacey, Marc. "Ethiopian Jews Want to Enter Promised Land." *The Seoul Times* 9 Aug. 2006.

Landing, James E. *Black Judaism: Story of an American Movement*. Durham: Carolina Academic Press, 2002.

Lawrence, Curtis. "Ex-Chicago Sect OKd to Live in Israel." *Associated Press* 29 July 2003.

Lawrence, Curtis. "Finding a Home in the Promised Land." *Chicago Sun Times* 21 Aug. 2003.

Levy, Rabbi Sholomo B. "Rabbi Arnold Josiah Ford: A Moses to His People." African American National Biography. Eds. Henry Louis Gates Jr. and Evelyn Brooks Higginbotham. New York: Oxford University Press, 2008.

Lewis, James, ed. *Odd Gods: New Religions & the Cult Controversy*. Amherst, N.Y.: Prometheus Books, 2001.

Lewis, William F. *Soul Rebels: The Rastafari.* Long Grove, Illinois: Waveland, 1993.

Ludden, Jennifer. "Black American Couple Finds Home in Ghana." *Las Vegas Sun* 8 Aug. 1997.

Maguire, Ken. "Ghana Re-Evaluates Nkrumah." *GlobalPost* 21 Oct. 2009.

Marley, Rita and Hettie Jones. *No Woman No Cry: My Life with Bob Marley.* New York: Hyperion, 2004.

Miller, Randall M., ed. *"Dear Master:" Letters of a Slave Family.* Athens, Georgia: University of Georgia Press, 1990.

Murrell, Nathaniel Samuel, William David Spencer, and Adrian Anthony McFarlane, eds. *Chanting Down Babylon: The Rastafari Reader.* Philadelphia: Temple University Press, 1998.

Mwakikagile, Godfrey. *Relations Between Africans and African Americans: Misconceptions, Myths and Realities.* Dar es Salaam and Pretoria: New Africa, 2007.

Nesvisky, Matthew. "Culture Shock: Thousands of Ethiopian Jews Are Now in Israel. How Are They Doing?" *Present Tense* 14.1 (1986): 12–19.

Nossiter, Adam. "Obama's Ghana Visit Highlights Scarce Stability in Africa." *The New York Times* 11 July 2009: 6.

Obeng, Samuel, comp. *Selected Speeches of Kwame Nkrumah.* Vol 1. 1979. Reprint. Accra, Ghana: Afram, 1997.

Palti, Michal. "Whitney Does Dimona." *Haaretz Daily* 29 May 2003.

Perbi, Akosua Adoma. *A History of Indigenous Slavery in Ghana: From the 15th to the 19th Century.* 2004. Reprint. Accra, Ghana: Sub-Saharan Publishers, 2007.

"The Present Situation of Ethiopian Jews in Israel." *The Jewish Virtual Library* 9 Aug. 2006 http://www.jewishvirtuallibrary.org/jsource/Judaism/ejdesc.html

Raboteau, Albert J. *A Fire in the Bones: Reflections on African-American Religious History.* Boston: Beacon Press, 1995.

Raboteau, Albert J. *A Sorrowful Joy.* Mahwah, New Jersey: Paulist Press, 2002.

Raboteau, Albert J. *Slave Religion: The "Invisible Institution" in the Antebellum South.* New York: Oxford University Press, 1980.

"Rastafari Movement: Interview with Giulia Bonacci." *Religioscope* 26 Aug. 2002 http://www.religioscope.com/articles/2002/016_rasta.htm

Redkey, Edwin S. Black *Exodus: Black Nationalist and Back-to-Africa Movements, 1890–1910.* New Haven and London: Yale University Press, 1969.

Resnikc, Laura. "Music Earns Black Hebrews Some Acceptance." *Associated Press* 5 Apr. 2006.

Richards, Sandra L. "What Is to Be Remembered? Tourism to Ghana's Slave Castle-Dungeons." *Theatre Journal* 57 (2005): 617–637.

Ross, Rick. "The 'Lost Tribe' from Chicago?" *The Ross Institute Internet Archives for the Study of Destructive Cults, Controversial Groups and Movements.* 16 Nov. 2002. 30 June 2006 http://www.rickross.com/reference/black_hebrews/black_hebrews14.html

Ryle, John. "Burying the Emperor." *Granta* 73 (2001): 107.

Salamon, Hagar. "Blackness in Transition: Decoding the Racial Constructs Through Stories of Ethiopian Jews." *Journal of Folklore Research* 40.2 (2003): 3–32.

Sanneh, Kelefa. "Pray and Grow Rich: Dr. Creflo Dollar's Ministry of Money." *The New Yorker* 11 Oct. 2004: 48.

Savage, Barbara Dianne. *Your Spirits Walk Beside Us: The Politics of Black Religion.* Cambridge: Belknap, Harvard University Press, 2008.

Savishinsky, Neil J. "Rastafari in the Promised Land: The Spread of a Jamaican Socioreligious Movement Among the Youth of West Africa." *African Studies Review* 37.3 (Dec 1994): 19–50.

Secretan, Thierry. *Going into Darkness: Fantastic Coffins from Africa.* New York: Thames and Hudson, 1995.

"The Shadowy Kingdom of Yah Turns 30." *Reuters* 1999.

Shaftel, David. "The Black Eagle of Harlem." *Air & Space Magazine* 1 Jan. 2009.

Shuman, Ellis. "Black Hebrews to Receive Permanent Home in Negev Agricultural Villa." *Israel Insider* 26 Nov. 2002.

Simms, Rupe. "'I am a Non-Denominational Christian and a Marxist Socialist': A Gramscian Analysis of the Convention People's Party and Kwame Nkrumah's Use of Religion." *Sociology of Religion* 46.4 (2003): 463–477.

Spector, Stephen. *Operation Solomon: The Daring Rescue of the Ethiopian Jews.* New York: Oxford University Press, 2005.

Steinberg, Jessica. "Land of Milk, Honey a Lost Dream for Ethiopian Jews." *Jewish Telegraphic Agency* 18 July 2006.

Thomas, Mark G., Tudor Parfitt, Deborah A. Weiss, Karl Skorecki, James F. Wilson, Madgel le Roux, Neil Bradman, and David B. Goldstein. "Y Chromosomes Traveling South: The Cohen-Modal Haplotype and the Origins of the Lemba—The 'Black Jews' of Southern Africa." *American Journal of Human Genetics* 66 (2000): 674–686

Thompkins, Toby. "The Obama Effect: Ghana Reacts to the President's First Visit." *Ebony* Oct. 2009: 77.

Walker, Alice. "Journey to Nine Miles." *Living by the Word.* New York: Houghton Mifflin, 1989.

Walton, Jonathan L. *Watch This! The Ethics and Aesthetics of Black Televangelism.* New York and London: New York University Press, 2009.

Walzer, Michael. *Exodus and Revolution.* USA: Basic Books, 1985.

White, Carmen W. "Living in Zion: Rastafarian Repatriates in Ghana, West Africa." *Journal of Black Studies* 37.5 (May 2007): 677–709.

Wilkerson, Isabel. *The Warmth of Other Suns: The Epic Story of America's Great Migration.* New York: Vintage, 2010.

Williams, Prince Elijah. Kuelker, Michael, ed. *Book of Memory: A Rastafari Testimony.* CaribSound, 2005.

Williams, Juan. *Eyes on the Prize: America's Civil Rights Years 1954–1965.* 1987. Reprint. New York: Penguin, 2002.

Wilson, Frantz. "Testimony of Frantz Wilson in Support of House Joint Resolution 22." *The Religious Movements Homepage Project at the University of Virginia Library* 5 March 1998 http://religiousmovements.lib.virginia.edu/cultsect/mdtaskforce/wilson_hearings.htm

Wright, Richard. *Black Power: A Record of Reactions in a Land of Pathos.* New York: Harper & Brothers, 1954.

Zornberg, Avivah Gottlieb. *The Particulars of Rapture: Reflections on Exodus.* New York: Image/Doubleday, 2001.